PIONEERING SPIRITS

A TOUR OF SCOTLAND'S 21ST CENTURY WHISKY DISTILLERIES

DAVID STIRK

First published in the United Kingdom in 2024

Copyright © 2024 by David Stirk

Cover Design by Valentina

Interior Design by David Stirk

All photos supplied by David Stirk other than those on pages 72, 141 & 142

Published by Stirk Consultancy Co Ltd

ISBN: 978-1-3999-9490-3

For my Mother

Thank you for instilling in me a pioneering spirit and the confidence to believe others may like to come along for the ride

CONTENTS

Foreword

Roy Duff
Creator of Aqvavitae and founder of Dramface
Glasgow, August 2024

There are a lot of whisky books.

Yet, just as we can learn something from everyone we meet, I also believe that, despite the sheer number of whisky-specific books available today, we can learn something completely new from every single one we pick up.

Let me offer a recent example: "Independent Scotch - The History of Independent Bottlers" by David Stirk. It taught me heaps of new facts, figures and fascinations about the drink I love. Yet it went a little further still; unique in its mission, it offered me an entirely new perspective.

This was, of course, David's personal perspective based on his varied - and significant - roles within whisky's remarkable growth and transformation over recent decades. I tore through it at a great rate, and then I read it all over again. I recommend it heartily; it fortified my understanding of so many things in whisky and, from my own perspective as an enthusiast, so much of it felt like a privileged peek behind the curtains. In that sense, it's not dissimilar to this book. Which is terrific. But there are other similarities.

This project is different in its scope, certainly, but it makes perfect sense that an idea such as this should follow on from Independent Scotch. While that release was a comprehensive guide to the industry's independent bottlers, this is a condensed, almost travelogue-style spotlight on independent distillers. Interestingly, these two things are not very far removed at all. Indeed, a word that flows throughout these pages ties the two together quite nicely, and that word is independent.

Scotch whisky is an industry which is wonderfully inter-connected. Some, like me, may go as far as to suggest there's a symbiosis. Competition exists, like any healthy industry, but there also exists mutual respect and a constant, collaborative eye on the general state of things: peers looking out for peers. Whether you're a large corporation responsible for supplying the planet with blends or a smaller concern making the best you can with what you have, it operates very much on that age-old but under-leveraged belief that a rising tide lifts all vessels. In this context, 'independent' does not, therefore, necessarily mean isolationist. However, we've perhaps seen something of an unintentional division in recent times, and a few very obvious dynamics betray what that is.

I share these thoughts without the intention to rant or draw controversy, although David would hardly stand in the way of me doing either! But today, as a consumer, enthusiast and layman, I sense a significant crevasse opening between the established, loved and globally distributed whisky brands, often owned by much larger concerns, and the huge swell of exciting and innovative independent distillers, blenders and bottlers. I also sense, relatively speaking, this is a new thing.

Although Scotch whisky has witnessed its patterns of boom and bust over the years, it's my belief that this is the first time we've seen the growth of an entire new layer flourishing from within the Scotch landscape. I refer specifically, of course, to the boom of the independent distiller/brand owner. But why is it happening today?

In the past, almost every new malt distillery - up to and including Isle of Arran's Lochranza in 1995 - would have been built around the bulk-supply model of making spirit for blending purposes. We've had Springbank doing its own thing since the 1980s, but the idea of building a distillery with its focus on creating a single malt for its own sake, to sell as a high-quality, flavour-first liquid under its own branding, is so 21st century. Spurred on by the global interest from enthusiastic flavour-chasers after premium malt whisky experiences, what we've witnessed since the turn of the century is nothing short of a true renaissance. It's driven by passion, passionate makers, and impassioned consumers.

However, despite huge investment, excitement and a general sense of zeitgeist, I feel challenges are inevitable on the road ahead for new distillers, especially the more nascent. The number we witness today is such that it's impossible for any everyday enthusiast to keep reasonable track of things, let alone a casual whisky sipper. Of course, it's not actually necessary for anyone to keep up to date with everything all of the time; even this book does not attempt to do so, and it's just as well.

While the names and brands grow, the whisky supply chains wrestle with capacity and retailers struggle with shelf space as eager bottle-chasers constantly re-evaluate the elasticity of their whisky wallets. Because, for the invested consumers, whisky botherers and enthusiasts, these are exciting times and every whisky excursion, these days, turns up something new. The choice we have today is unprecedented and more choice on offer in the near future plays into our curious nature, but we are a fickle and choosy bunch. It's not

Pokémon, and 'gotta catch 'em all' is rarely the goal.

So, just how much choice could we have? Well, if this book were to attempt to catalogue all the operational and work-in-progress distilleries planned for Scotland since the year 2000, the number would make the project almost unthinkable, at least as a single volume. Should these projects all receive funding and the necessary permissions to go ahead, we would be cataloguing a distillery count approaching 80 before the decade is out. A number not too far short of the entire operational malt distillery list back when Lochranza was founded.

This is a staggering amount, but to try to keep things in perspective, we need to also consider scale. As I write, there are around 140 operational malt distilleries in Scotland, and many of the incumbent, established distilleries have seen massive capacity expansion in recent years. There are already two capable of producing greater than 20 million litres of alcohol per annum each: Glenlivet and Glenfiddich. Macallan, the third largest, will soon be joined by Miltonduff with capacities of around 15 million litres each. These are, currently, the largest among a count of around 100 'old-guard' established producers, both incumbents and revived.

In terms of capacity, however, it would take dozens of our new independent malt distilleries to reach such a production number. They are a fraction of that scale. With only a few outliers, most of them produce between 50,000 and 500,000 litres per annum. The vast majority of these are in existence to establish themselves specifically as single malt whisky brands. The retail shelves - and associated complexities of serving so many brands - continue to swell with each inaugural release or new core range edition, not to mention the plethora of small-batch, limited releases and single casks - bearing not the name of an independent bottler; but the livery of an independent distillery. Quite different from our established old guard, they are here to bolster choice; transient variety over staple consistency and, hopefully, quality over quantity.

In general, the new wave of amber nectar which excites us as enthusiasts today, comes directly from smaller, more focused, independent projects with a mind toward provenance and flavour; where and how it's made matters much more than how much of it is made. It's almost as if the geeks got fed up asking for the stuff, they just took the inevitable initiative to make it themselves.

There is some truth to that, but it's case by case. In so many scenarios, the increase in demand for good Scotch whisky globally has meant a production shortfall, which meant a contraction in available stocks for independent bottlers, which forced many of them to move into independent distilling; to either brand as a single malt, trade, or both. Yet their customer base remains largely the same: enthusiasts, invested whisky appreciators, geeks, botherers and aficionados.

So, to return to this 'divide', today the blurry line between large-scale producers and independent distilleries becomes more defined with each new release. While the brands we've known for years chase price-sensitive, lucrative volumes at one end, with halo bottlings of über-expensive luxury and aspirational lifestyle or 'collectible' releases at the other, newer distilleries eschew both the pursuit of pure production efficiencies as well as superfluous gilding and tempting bling. They have moved into the middle-ground; the vacuum left by bigger brands as they weaned themselves away from their once-upon-a-time growth from enthusiasts and those 'in the know'. These new producers sense that, should they succeed in producing a good quality, flavourful spirit, they may command a more premium price attracting those chasing a genuinely flavourful, higher quality - and fully natural - experience.

There are already a lot of these around.

I must confess, personally, I am maniacal in my pursuit of chasing flavour and little excites me more than the anticipation of new single malt Scotch whisky; new liquid pouring from a new bottle from a new producer. We've been spoiled, these times we live through have never been witnessed before. Upon the shelves closest to my desk sit more than 30 of them. That's thirty different single malts that didn't exist when I first fell in love with whisky in 2005. It's almost like we need to take a breather; to take stock. Perhaps we could have someone document things or take a tour, do an Aeneas MacDonald or - dare I suggest - an Alfred Barnard? Perhaps before the first quarter of the twenty-first century is out? Who is there to take on such a thing?

Well, of course, there's David Stirk.

Now, I know he'll forgive me for quickly saying that this is not MacDonald's "Whisky", and most definitely not Barnard's "Whisky Distilleries of the United Kingdom", not yet, but it is similar in spirit. It is a much-needed snapshot, a look under the hood of some of the most impactful pioneers that have appeared so far this century. But this is obvious. Other things in the pages ahead, however, are less so.

Because what we have in David Stirk is not only someone predisposed to such an idea - possessing the experience, enthusiasm, curiosity, time and means to meet the task - he is the epitome of a true independent voice in Scotch whisky. I feel genuinely grateful that he exists to undertake these considerable projects. Direct and inquisitive, yet critical in thought, we need someone who'll ask the questions, understand the implications and just lay it out as it is. However, in each of his releases, he betrays something more.

What unfolds in the chapters ahead of you is yet another example of David as not only a true Whiskyphile, but also a clear Caledonophile;[1] a lover of Scotland.

---

1 - If we're going to mix Latin and Greek, why can't we mix Gaelic and Greek? I prefer 'Albaphile', but it's not a word. Neither is 'Whiskyphile', yet.

In his anecdotes and descriptions, you'll find a respectful warmth and a quiet admiration toward the place he has made his home, coincidentally during the years that witnessed all of these new distilleries being born. When he first arrived in Scotland, Glengyle was still just dilapidated buildings, Kilchoman was an impertinent twinkle and Daftmill was 'only' a farm. As an Englishman, as he levelled up in distillery access and whisky culture, he downgraded in annual days of sunshine. Yet he stayed. Scotland is his home and he seems to like it - and its whisky - very much.

Despite this book being necessarily selective, it's typically full of all of those little nuggets of insight and pearls of wisdom we discover when we take the time to speak to people. And when we can't speak to the people at the front end of this flourishing whisky scene, we're fortunate to have people in place, like David, to do so on our behalf.

As we pick up a bottle and raise a glass, we can vicariously enjoy whisky-themed jaunts around this tiny country and read about their individual, earnest efforts and get a true feeling for what makes them tick. The trials of the new independents; the tribulations of the 21st century's Pioneering Spirits.

As I close out the last few pages, I'm not left thinking there are too many whisky books; I'm actually left hoping there's a sequel.

Introduction

"Scotland's f*****g beautiful. There's no one there."
Joe Rogan

Contrary to what the man behind the world's most popular podcast thinks, quite a few people are in Scotland. Around five and a half million call this country home – slightly more than the Republic of Ireland, well over two million more than Wales and a similar number to nearby Norway – a country four times larger. Scotland's favourite neighbour is, of course, England,[1] and a comparison of the two countries does go some way in backing up Mr Rogan's colourful statement. England is larger, despite how maps make it appear, 50,000 square miles to Scotland's 30,000. England is home to just over 57 million people, ten times that of Scotland, and when you consider that 4.3 million of Scotland's inhabitants live in what is called the Central Belt, it is not surprising that there are large swathes of Scotland that feel like no one is f****** there.

But numbers do not always make a great story, and neither often does barren wilderness. Thankfully, a great number of pioneers took it upon themselves to take what Scotland's nature provides and make something from it. And not just a little something either, a drink that, in its complexity and nuance, can be found on the shelves of every decent, and some not-so-decent, bar, hotel, dive and speak-easy around the world.

What Scotland may lack in population or industrial might, it makes up for in the quality of its products. Be you in Vancouver, Buenos Aires, Cape Town, Wellington, Osaka or Reykjavik, ask for a 'Scotch' in a bar, and you'll get a glass of whisky distilled, matured and dispatched from the small[2] nation of Scotland. Not content either, with making some of the world's biggest and best-known whisky brands, a new movement - one towards small batch, niche products and a more locally-made attitude - has roared into the mix and taken the Scotch whisky world to new levels. It is now common that when you ask for a Scotch, the bartender may pause and ask 'Which one?" And that, my friends, is the beginning of a long and epic journey of discovery.

Much will be laboured over in the course of this mini adventure – and I shall

---

1 - Given the number of words, energy, and backhanded compliments unleashed in their direction, I can only assume the English are the favourites.

2 - It's not tiny – small will do.

certainly make it a personal adventure; these are my impressions, conclusions, exploration and admiration of a part of the whisky industry and, more pertinently, part of the culture and psyche, that is permeating through this great land. This book will only be concerned with those distilleries north of the border. Another time, perhaps one day, in another book, you can explore the distilleries in the south, southwest, and west. Beyond the waters surrounding the United Kingdom, there are several lifetimes' worth of work exploring all that is considered whisky.[1] The concentration on Scottish distilleries is not due to some snobbery or tradition or with any notion of 'pity the poor-imitations'. Much has changed over the past two to three decades in the whisky world, and arguably, one of the most significant and most satisfying revisions has been that whisky, great whisky, can be made anywhere.

The self-imposed limitation to visiting and exploring the first twenty-five of the 21st century distilleries operating only in Scotland is due to several factors. First and foremost, the whisky story is more closely intertwined with Scotland than any other country. Whilst Ireland most likely made it first, it was Scotch whisky that was carried to the four corners of the world. And it is certainly from Scotch, at least I believe it to be, that the explosion of interest in whisky has arisen worldwide. "Ha! You Scots would think such a thing!" I hear somebody cry. Well, in this case, you're mistaken. Firstly, I can lay no claim to being a Scot, nor do I believe that there is such a thing as the best whisky, nor a country that can claim to make the best.

What Scotland does have, is a prolonged, developed and far-reaching industry. One that, whilst at times, believed itself to be the guardians or gatekeepers of what should and should not be considered whisky, has been the bedrock of the wider whisky industry. And to take that further, to avoid any unnecessary bias or blinkered attitude, when you boil it down to single malt whisky – which is about 90% of where this journey will take me – then Scotland, Scotch, its traditions, history, industry and passed on practices, really are the engine at the front of a long and varied train.

The isles of Orkney and Shetland aside, this journey will take me to Scotland's four corners. Had I waited another five to ten years, I could have added the outlying northerly islands to this list as there are plans and actions in place to build new distilleries on both islands. Indeed, in another five to ten years, I, or someone else, could write a second book with at least another 25 distilleries releasing their first whiskies between then and now. Keeping up with the planned, announced, part-built, built, and yet-to-be-released distilleries has become impossible. So, I haven't tried to keep up. Instead, I have concentrated on those that meet my 'Pioneering Spirit' criteria, which has proven enough. The first quarter of a century into the 21st century has given me ample material to dissect the new breed of distillery and the pioneering spirits behind them.

---

1 - Or whiskey.

I begin many of my journeys from my home village of Thornhill, which rests in the middle of Scotland's border county of Dumfries & Galloway. I have had the pleasure of living in this little bubble of parochial heaven for the past dozen years, give or take. I have managed to squeeze, or encroach my passion, on some of the locals and have a small whisky club that meets every six weeks or so – it's not regimented and often has to fit into the farming schedule. I bring this up for a couple of reasons; firstly, it's nice for you to know my starting point for each journey, and secondly, my club members are excellent levelling agents. I enjoy honesty and frankness, and with not a single self-proclaimed expert in my small club, the ability to cut through marketing spiel, self-propelled grandness, public relation bumph and hyperbole is more than refreshing. To a member, and I feel I can speak for them here, they all subscribe to a simple philosophy regarding drinking whisky: Do I like it? Can I afford it?

I have tried, wherever possible, to ensure this book is not dated. While every distillery has released whisky, to judge them now in 2024 seems pointless. Most of the distilleries featured are still maturing[1] and to record their current releases for posterity is akin to judging the character of an adult on what they were like as a toddler. With just a few exceptions, none of the whiskies I tried or could buy will still be available in a year or less. Also, who cares what I think about the whisky, really? The book's point is not to show off the whiskies I have tried or to pretend I am some guru when it comes to tasting and appreciating them. Instead, this is a push, an amuse-bouche for the reader to seek out the whiskies and visit those distilleries open to the public for themselves. You can then make up your own mind about the whisky and create your own personal tasting notes and memories – it's much more fun this way.

I have broken up my tour monologue with individual distillery write-ups and occasional tangents on aspects of life in Scotland or whisky-related topics. Feel free to ignore the first chapter if the industry's history does not interest you or you are an expert on the subject. Pop the cork on a bottle, pour a dram, and once you are comfortable, let's head off into one of Scotland's corners and see what all the fuss is about.

[Author's note: Most of the photos within this book are my own. I am easily one of the worst photographers ever to hold an iPhone (my preferred method) and had intended to source professional and stunning photos. However, what this trip has taught me, and I hope you will agree, is that even someone as photographically challenged as I am can capture some of the majestic scenery in and around the distilleries. I am reminded of the book "Raw Spirit" by the late author Iain Banks, which has no pictures. Since my writing will never be as successful as Mr Banks, perhaps my slap-hazard photography will do instead.]

---

1 - Read that as 'getting better with age'.

Exhibit 'A' of my 'point and shoot' photography – Lochaline at dusk

The spread across Scotland of the 25 distilleries that I visit

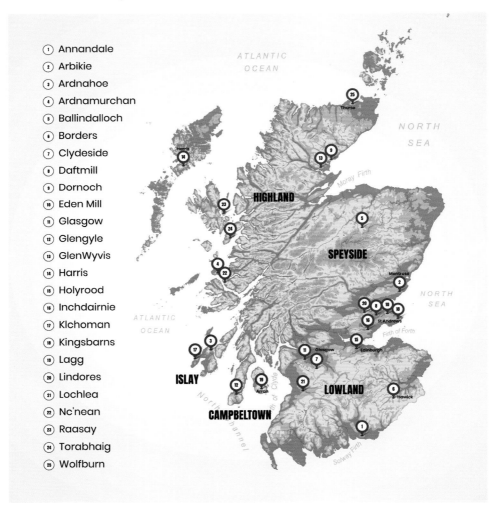

1. Annandale
2. Arbikie
3. Ardnahoe
4. Ardnamurchan
5. Ballindalloch
6. Borders
7. Clydeside
8. Daftmill
9. Dornoch
10. Eden Mill
11. Glasgow
12. Glengyle
13. GlenWyvis
14. Harris
15. Holyrood
16. Inchdairnie
17. Kichoman
18. Kingsbarns
19. Lagg
20. Lindores
21. Lochlea
22. Nc'nean
23. Raasay
24. Torabhaig
25. Wolfburn

CHAPTER 1

A LITTLE ON THE PAST...

"A niche product for a specific consumer rather
than a mass product seeking mass consumption."

As Carl Sagan once stated, "You have to know the past to understand the present". Thankfully, we needn't travel too far back to get to where we pick up the story (several books delve deep into the long history, should you be interested). The Scotch whisky industry is over 400 years old, so let's whizz through several centuries to the 20th century. Much of the early part of the century was overshadowed by the Pattison crash of 1898. Again, there are better accounts of this incredible collapse, but essentially, two brothers created a torrent of activity in the industry with ever-growing orders for spirit. The 1880s were already a boom time for distillers and distillation - no fewer than 43 distilleries were built and opened between 1881 and 1898[1] as orders continued and credit lines were extended. This all came to a fateful end in 1898 when the creditors realised the Pattison's were massively over-extended, and the Scotch whisky industry experienced its worst crash.

From the fallout, several larger firms merged, creating The Distillers Company Ltd (DCL). Under the careful management of William Ross, its first Chairman, DCL set out to consolidate the market and control the losses. This new organisation was the genesis of the company we know today as Diageo – the largest of the Scotch whisky distilling companies. With the turn of the century, there was little appetite to build or even revive lost distilleries. The two Great Wars saw rationing brought in, which reduced the amount of grain available to existing distilleries, and this meant that little more than a distillery a decade was built between 1901 and 2000. For the first independent distillery to be built since the 1890s, we need to march forward one hundred years with the construction of the Speyside Distillery

---

1 -Many of those built are still in production today; Bruichladdich, Bunnahabhain, Scapa, Glenfiddich, Craigella-
chie, Strathmill, Balvenie, Longmorn, Knockdhu, Aultmore, Dufftown, Aberfeldy, Glendullan, Glen Moray, Glen-
tauchers, Speyburn, Tamdhu, Tomatin, Ardmore, Benriach, Benromach, Dalwhinnie, Glen Elgin and Knockando.

in 1990. It wasn't until a new distillery on Arran was built in 1995 that an air of possibility began to permeate through a sceptical and slightly dormant industry.

Even as the Lochranza Distillery on Arran was being planned and funding sought, many in the industry felt that the man behind it, Harold Currie (who had previously been Managing Director of Chivas Brothers), would fail. Currie equally felt that his survival would rely on being able to sell a significant amount of Lochranza's distillate to blending companies. The 1980s saw a large shift, especially in the biggest markets (the USA in particular), away from what was considered 'brown' spirits and towards white spirits,[1] which are easily mixed and often cheaper to produce. This caused the closure of no less than twenty distilleries and even the green shoots of recovery in the late 1980s were insufficient to poke the larger companies into the costly and capital-consuming construction of new distilleries or re-commissioning silent ones.

Harold Currie had enough drive and possessed enormous courage, vision, and passion to see the potential in a new distillery. The industry was dominated by companies who were fixated on the idea that only blended Scotch whisky would continue its dominance. Despite his misgivings about how much Arran distillate he would have to sell to make the business viable, Currie had enough faith in the turning tide of consumers wanting to drink single malt Scotch whisky. Many felt that no distillery could be built and rely purely on sales of its 'self-malt' as it was once called. In fact, until the building of Glengyle in March 2004, no distillery had ever been built with the sole intention of releasing everything made as a single malt. The idea now that you would build a distillery and not rely on its single malt as the breadwinner is a business model limited to companies such as Pernod Ricard or Diageo (among a few others).

It must also be stressed that the launch of Speyside and Arran whisky in the late 1990s was not quite the success story we have witnessed in the 21st century. The 1990s were a decade of change in drinking habits, but it was a slow burner. Whilst festivals, magazines, books, writers, and speakers were in the ascendency, it took a little while for this to percolate through. The last embers of those departments clinging onto their beloved bulk blends and established 'number-of-cases' driven markets were not giving in to the malt whisky drinker without a few last desperate swings. The oddity, certainly looking back now, is not that malt whisky won and blended whisky skulked off to find space on only the lowest shelves, but that blended Scotch whisky never went away. Malt whisky has grown from around 2-3% of total Scotch whisky consumption in the 1980s to around 12% of the total today. The real growth has not been in the quantity of liquid sold but in the value of that liquid.

It is the growth in the return on investment that has been the primary driving force for the explosion in the construction of malt whisky distilleries. Specific markets

---

1 - Vodka became the most significant competitor.

moved from being blended whisky only, or certainly predominantly blended, to taking an ever-increasing amount of single malt whisky. This is best demonstrated by the US market, which once accounted for 60% of all Scotch whisky sales (France is the largest importer by volume). The USA is still the most important market as the largest importer of single malt Scotch whisky.[1] Consumption, in terms of litres of alcohol, has been relatively stagnant for decades while value has grown exponentially. That is not a result of consumers buying more expensive blends; it is solely due to the explosion of malt whisky. This trend can be seen throughout many of what were considered 'established' markets and those where historically blends struggled due to import tariffs or practices that caused consumers to be turned away from the product. This included Germany, The Netherlands, Italy and Taiwan. Other markets often picked up the slack of the dwindling blend sales, which continues today.[2]

Much of the groundwork of bringing drinkers into a fuller understanding of single malt whisky was done by the independent bottlers, a side industry (perhaps unique to Scotch whisky) of businesses and individuals that were able to buy stocks of mature or maturing whisky and bottle under their own label (often including the distillery name and other information such as cask type, or the number of bottles and so on). Independent bottlings demonstrated a distillery's character in a new or revelatory light. Often, distilleries that could only be seen from a roadside or those long demolished were solely available to taste from these small bottling companies. The passion, dedication and ambassadorial role of these businesses brought single malt whisky to a new drinker - one seeking information, sensory exploration and a greater understanding of what Scotch whisky was and could be. Suddenly, terms such as 'Non Chill-filtering", "Cask Strength", "Natural Colour" and "Single Cask" were commonplace. A new breed of whisky drinker emerged, perhaps more conscientious of what had been done or not done to the drink as much as the brand or marketing of the drink itself.

This tour will tell its own story, but I will wager that not one distillery I visit will ever admit to using something like caramel colouring or chill-filtering when bottling their whisky. The strengths of bottled whisky will usually be higher than the 40 or 43% standard[3] the industry commonly uses. These 21st century whiskies will be made by fanatics, for fanatics and in a way that pleases the fanatic. A new style of open-door marketing with no laboratories, no white coats, small batch production, single casks, and plenty of cask experimentation. This new breed of distiller is an extension of the independent bottler who wanted to show the alchemy and palette of the Scotch whisky world. They are a new group of passionate whisky makers making a niche product for a specific consumer.

---

1 - Resulting in it being the most profitable market.

2 - These are emerging markets such as Latin America and Africa.

3 - Scotch whisky must be bottled at a minimum of 40% alcohol by volume (abv).

The Production Process

Just like when I was a child waiting for the next edition of The Beano, I can get overly excited when a new intriguing whisky hits the shelves. But I should point out that my 'geekiness' about whisky, for want of a better word, stops there. Although I have made whisky, from the malting floor to the bottling room, the production of it – the technical aspects that produce the vagaries, nuances and differences - are not what grabs my interest. I am very much the person who, throughout the section of the tour that covers production, is thinking, 'Cool story, but what does your whisky taste like?' Also, and perhaps more importantly, any in-depth discussion here will ruin the revelations waiting for you on every tour. But for those of you who maybe can't tour or, like me, tune out a little, here is a very simplified version of how whisky is made.

For starters, you will need a cereal. Pretty much any will do, depending upon how you want it to taste – and don't be confused by those countries distilling potatoes, rice, sugar cane or toenail clippings - that is not the Scotch whisky way.[1] The cereal contains carbohydrates and starch, which are unlocked when certain enzymes within the cereals are triggered by steeping in water. This process is known as 'malting'. Once dried, to ensure the grain does not use up its stored energy, the now malted cereal can be boiled ('mashing'), which converts those starches into sugar. With some yeast added, these sugars ferment into alcohol, and at this point, we've got a crude beer (known as 'wash') at around 7% in alcohol by volume (abv).

The rest of the process is even more straightforward; by boiling (distilling) it once, we can remove some of that alcohol from the wash, resulting in a liquid of around 21% abv. By distilling it a second time (and taking the 'middle cut'), the spirit rises to around 68% abv. The new distillate is then put into oak casks for a minimum of three years,[2] and hey presto: we have Whisky!

Boiled right down, it really is that simple. Had it been a much more complex process, I am not sure those quickly erected (and even quicker to dismantle) illicit distillers scattered around Scotland's glens, caves, and woodlands would have progressed very far. What creates the differences are the materials used and practices utilised in each step. What is the strain of barley; where did the barley come from; how was the barley dried in the malting process; what sort of liquid (worts) from the mashing process is obtained; the yeast(s) used; the fermentation time and what size of the middle cut is taken from the Spirit still, all have an effect.

---

1 - Barley is the predominant choice for pot still distilleries.

2 - By law for Scotch whisky.

You can go into more detail regarding materials used to make the washbacks (where fermentation takes place), how the stills are fired, the shape of the stills, the tilt of the 'Lyne Arm' (the arm off the top of the still that allows the alcohol to run off); how the hot alcohol is cooled and how fast the distillate comes off the stills (and there are more variables than I have listed here). All of that is before we begin to discuss micro-climate, water source (minerality, hardness and softness), seasonal differences and, of course, all of the oak varieties and the cask's previous contents.

If you are lucky enough to tour a few distilleries you will notice each distillery is slightly different in its approach, but essentially, by law, they all have to follow my overly simplified outline above. The real beauty of this wonderful process is that no two distilleries taste the same, and nor can a distillery ever be repeated. This is a blessing and a curse, but in reality, it is much more of a blessing than a curse. Had the industry been able to simply replicate a distillery and its product, then this book would likely be one chapter long and quite dull.

My interest is piqued by distilleries with significant differences or new techniques. For example, Inchdairnie, The Borders & Arbikie make a rye whisky – something that has not been done for as long as anyone can remember; Annandale is built on the site of an older distillery, and attempts have been made to replicate the flavour (without anyone alive being able to recall what the original whisky tasted like); Dornoch and others are experimenting with yeasts, fermentation times and different oak varieties and so on. But in truth, as intriguing as all these points of difference are, my only genuine interest is in the finished product. 'What does it taste like?' And in truth, I'm not going to tell you. I'll leave that up to you to discover...

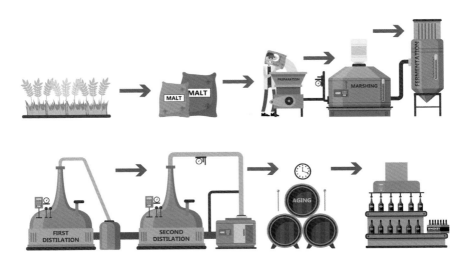

CHAPTER 2

THE BEATING HEART
OF AN EMPIRE

"A city that insists on keeping a cone on the head of one of its most prominent statues tells you all you need to know about its inhabitants."

I may have visited Glasgow more times than any other city. It is hard to calculate. Having lived in Southern California, where any drive from Los Angeles, no matter which direction, will take you through countless cities, barely registering one from the next, before reaching mountains, woodland, the sea or much of northern Mexico. Those cities aside, as hardly counted as 'visited', Glasgow is my most visited city. There are only nine cities you can visit in Scotland. None farther north than Inverness or farther west than Glasgow. Just over a week ago, I was up (as living in Dumfries & Galloway, a trip to Glasgow is always 'up') presenting whiskies to the Glasgow Whisky Club.

The club meets twice monthly at the Bon Accord in the western part of Glasgow, situated on North Street – which, as you would expect, faces south should you be walking the other way. The 'Bon', as it is more commonly referred to, is as famous as whisky bars can get and is a fitting venue for a club to meet. Good bars, I believe, are simply an insight – an over-the-wall peek - into the living room or happy place of its owner. I recall one bar in the small town of Leek, northeast of Stoke, that was very much the owner's living room. Called the 'Earl Grey' a step inside was as likely to find the owner sitting with a TV dinner watching 'Coronation Street' as it was to find no one about at all. It was a heavenly escape and so is the 'Bon'.

Paul McDonagh was one of those publicans who deeply cared about the ambience of his pub. Not in a 'let's refit every six months to satisfy current demand for uncomfortable pine chairs and chintzy faux-plants' attempt at creating an atmosphere. Instead, the Bon's tone reflected Paul's personality. Sadly, Paul was taken from us just as his well-deserved retirement began. A reminder to us that there is little justice in this often cruel world. The most fitting legacy to the whisky world's loss is not even that the Bon has continued unchanged, but that his family, and very much Thomas, his son, has picked up pretty much exactly where Paul left us.[1] If you are ever in Scotland's great city and need a restorative half, or dram, or chat, or all three, head to the Bon – there's almost always someone about looking for a blether.

Regardless of it being a Monday, my night at the Bon presenting whiskies continued until the last orders bell was well and truly rung. Despite having some seriously well-read, well-travelled and 'experienced' members (and industry insiders), the Glasgow Whisky Club is always a welcoming group. The chat migrated from current affairs to lost bottlings, retired industry legends and recent distillery trips. There was also much discussion about the whiskies that had suddenly appeared, like rabbits magically being pulled out of a hat, and were slowly rotating around the group - propelled by their own magnificence.

It occurred to me, at that moment, how often I take this sort of arrangement for granted. I am reminded of my first attempts at creating a whisky club (and if you're reading this and not part of one, go join one; you can thank me later). People and places are not important here, but it was definitely in England, and I remember that some pubs outright ignored me (don't waste your time asking any pub that is part of a chain – you might as well ask a supermarket if they would be willing to stock the honey from your garden). Other pubs stated there would be a corkage fee – or in other words; we would have to pay them to stock the whisky or be forced to purchase measures for the club which would be served by the bar - a futile exercise in killing any joy the evening might have offered. With no such aggravation at the Bon, this evening demonstrates what whisky and well-run bars do best.

Just over a week later, I'm loading my car and heading back to Glasgow, but this time to visit the eponymously named distillery. It's a typically misty and damp start to the day. Spring is around the corner, and there are signs that the green pastures I live amongst are stirring into life. The incredible-to-drive but dismally named A702 road cuts through from the A76 (this is the Dumfries to Kilmarnock road), shaving several satisfying minutes from the journey and also providing a John Constable-like scene for the drive to the M74 motorway. The winding road, referred to locally as the Dalveen Pass, is banked, heading north, by hills to the left and a valley to the right. Away in the distance I can see an old radar station that was recently sold. I imagine a Bond-style villain building a secret layer that is no doubt staffed by bionic sheep – the only animal seen for miles. This part of Scotland is full of Anglo-Saxon-inspired names such as Durisdeer, Wanlockhead, Leadhills, the quite Tolkien-esque, Elvanfoot and every visitor's favourite; Ecclefechan.

---

1 - Thomas has two whisky clubs that meet at the Bon each month.

This is known as Sassenach country. Contrary to its continual misuse, the term Sassenach does not mean someone from England. It refers to anyone considered Saxon or Saxon-speaking and only pertains to those within Britain, which would mean anyone not speaking Gaelic. In 1771, Tobias Smollett wrote in his book 'The Expedition of Humphry Clinker', "The Highlanders have no other term for the people of the low country, but Sassenaugh, or Saxons." I'll talk about the Highland/Lowland line later in the book, but the term Sassenach incorporates a big chunk of what is Scotland and around 90% of the country's population. If ever used as a derogatory term, ensure you remind the ill-informed 'Teuchter'[1] that the very language they used to demean you qualifies them to be Sassenach.

Along the A702, I pass what I am reliably informed is the source of the River Clyde. It is hard for me to imagine that this series of continual S-shaped bends and banks is where the Clyde begins its life. The most challenging thing for my brain to fathom is that this river starts south of the city – water doesn't care about my sense of up and down; it just heads to the lowest point. It is also the first time I realise that the rain I watch fall, more often than not, around my village is the very beginnings of the mighty Clyde.

A Virgin train speeds past as I go over a small stone bridge large enough for just one car. The picture I have of the train, hills, river, trees, and fields full of heavily pregnant sheep and the odd lamb would make a fantastic painting. Sadly, I am no painter, and there is no way my camera phone, with my abilities, could capture any of this. I pause briefly to take it all in before joining the M74 motorway, which will take me to the heart of Glasgow.

People Make Glasgow, or so the slogan goes. The weather plays a vital part, too. I'm not sure pleasant weather makes the happiest people. For instance, if you ask anyone in Scotland, besides someone from Edinburgh, which of Scotland's major city's inhabitants are cheerier, Glasgow will come out above the capital. Yet Edinburgh enjoys considerably more days of sunshine and about half the rainfall; with such a difference in treatment from the weather gods, one would expect Glaswegians to be grumpy, sour and melancholy. Yet that is often the stereotype given to the citizens across the M8.[2] The wettest I've ever been was in Glasgow and was from a completely unexpected downpour one day after a meeting. Suited, booted, and umbrella-less, it was a ten-minute run back to the car. It's funny how you feel 'wetter' the more clothes you have on. The episode did not blot the city's copybook for me – looking back, it was rather funny.

I've been visiting Glasgow since I was a child in the 1980s, and the transformation from that decade is remarkable. Yet it maintains a reputation around the rest of the UK as a 'hard' city – somewhere you might get head-butted for fun. Certainly, those in the UK who have never visited consider it a place to keep the voice down and talk to a minimum. Most

---

1 - Pronounced 'chook-tuh'.

2 - Don't shoot the messenger here; I have an affinity for both cities. Also, these are mass-sweeping generalisations. Writers love them...

of the UK fails to realise that the 'hard' element generally only cares about one thing: the defeat of the 'other' Glasgow football team.[1] It is a strange part of life within certain parts of the UK in that there are often only two teams you are supposed to support, and you are invariably asked which one you follow. I learned early on to state I'm a rugby fan – this always dissipates the discussion and avoids awkward follow-up questions.

Around twenty years ago, I walked up Buchanan Street with Euan Mitchell, now Managing Director of Arran Distillery. We discussed the city's incredible transformation and how safe it had become when we happened upon two chaps embroiled in a feisty discussion about something neither I nor the native, Euan, could decipher. After a few moments, and blood now dripping off each other's skulls, they vacated the side street, half-hugging, half-holding each other up. It was all just a bit of fun, no doubt wholly resolved by a pint, or eleven, in Waxy O'Connors. Euan and I decided we could have a pint without requiring a beating, so we headed in the opposite direction.

In truth, I've never felt unsafe in Glasgow. Sure, I've had my share of toothless wonders persistently asking me for things such as money, cigarettes, booze and even 'if I want some'. I have always done my best to avoid eye contact and have never been intrigued enough to ask what 'some' is. Glasgow is no more dangerous than Manchester or Leeds or Bristol. If you go looking for 'some', you'll likely find it. Like 99.9% of those who visit and enjoy the city, its sights and offerings, you're pretty much guaranteed not to get 'some' if you don't want any.

From such an industrial background, one of shipbuilding, engineering, architecture, trade and invention, the city is now a hub of education, IT and financial services. Glasgow is also Scotland's main retail hub and despite the council's best attempts in reducing cars, remains the central destination for anyone seeking retail therapy. This results in a juxtaposition of odd bedfellows walking, perusing and residing in the city centre. Just the short walk through Glasgow's main shopping districts paints a colourful and diverse picture of the city. Starting from the east on Osbourne Street and passing by the Enoch Centre, you will encounter a ripe and less elaborate group of shufflers. Once you get to Buchanan Street, with its designer franchises and Argyll Arcade, housing most of the jewellery and watch retailers, the clientele appears taller, better dressed and certainly more pleasing with their fragrance. At the top of Buchanan Street, the tour turns left onto the famous or infamous Sauchiehall Street. Once again, the demographic changes with a more international feel from overseas students and the recent proliferation of specialist barbers and beauty therapists. In just a ten-minute walk, one can gain a hugely insightful parade of the array, assortment and aroma of Glasgow's myriad of inhabitants and visitors.

Glasgow, originally known as Glaschu, and if you're not a native, resist calling it Glasgae, was once the second city of the British Empire. It is one of the great cities of the UK and up there worldwide. Like most great cities, however, it will be good when it is finished as cranes and demolition crews take down yet another old decrepit warehouse flanking the Clyde's northern bank. This was once the epicentre and beating heart of the whisky world. Row upon row of bonded warehouses where all of the great names would blend, store and bottle their whiskies. Once ready, the Clyde would provide shipping either to the rest of the UK or heading to the US and, through the tentacles of the empire, the rest of the world. Whilst the odd grand office or warehouse siding remains, much of this history is lost. Inner city blending and bottling was moved to more convenient, upgraded and cost-effective sites such as Hillington, Paisley and Leven. Now, barely an office of the larger whisky companies can be found in the city centre.

The World's Most Important Whisky City

In Scotch whisky's infancy, the two main markets of Scotland, just as they are today, were Glasgow and Edinburgh. Edinburgh, although blessed with castles, palaces and ancient markets, was always playing second fiddle to the larger, mightier and West-coast situated Glasgow. Thus, when whisky began to find its way south of the border and beyond, it was Glasgow that became the focal point for much of the bottling and shipping. Both cities housed large distilleries but Glasgow's Dundashill, Yoker and Gorbals Distilleries dwarfed the output of Edinburgh's.

Huge banks of warehouses were built on the north side of the Clyde, and from there, bottled goods were shipped to all corners of the globe. During World War II, Roosevelt's Lend-Lease Deal allowed ships, having been emptied of food, fuel and munitions from the USA, to be stocked with whisky for their return journey. Thus, the American G.I. was able to bring bottles of Scotch back across the Atlantic or further afield to the Great East beyond. The world's largest market got a taste for Scotland's national drink, and it is mostly through Glasgow and the River Clyde that Scotch whisky, and Britain's exchequer owes a debt of thanks.

Glasgow was also tragically the location of the last great warehouse fire – and one that would have a lasting impact on the city and its business, and on warehouse safety in general. A warehouse owned by Arbuckle, Smith and Company somehow went up in flames on the 28th of March, 1960. Inside the warehouse were around 21,000 casks of whisky, and as the heat intensified, it caused numerous 'boiling liquid expanding vapour explosions'. This caused the front and rear walls of the building to collapse, killing several firemen. The fire took 450 officers an entire week to extinguish and claimed the lives of 19 in total. This fire and a subsequent outbreak on James Watt Street in a repurposed ex-whisky warehouse changed the laws regarding warehouse construction and placement within urban areas.

The last of the great Glasgow whisky warehouses closed in the late 1980s. Many of the offices closed, and bottling halls were built out of town in much cheaper and more convenient locations. When Port Dundas Distillery was closed in 2011, Strathclyde Distillery became the city's last remnant of a once-thriving whisky industry. The Glasgow Distillery and Clydeside Distillery have put Scotland's great city back on the whisky map where it belongs.

The issues of building or repurposing within inner cities are perhaps why Glasgow Distillery was constructed from an old storage warehouse on the opposite side of the motorway from Diageo's sprawling bottling plant, Shieldhall. This part of Glasgow is more known for its Braehead Shopping Centre and the row upon row of bathroom, bedroom, kitchen, tile and flooring showrooms. It is also home to one of Scotland's three Ikea stores, and I must admit that I took more than a little delight to not notice a single Askersund, Ödmjuk, Billy or Björksta within the Glasgow or Clydeside distilleries. By nobody's standards, would this area be considered glamorous; in fact, the words that spring to mind lean more towards oily, perfunctory, industrial and uninviting. An architecturally-designed landscape; if the architect had been smuggled out of East Berlin and then told not to add any colour. A tourist destination this is not.

And yet, something must be going on in this concentrated, swilling mass of warehouses, taps, tiles and tyre-tracks. Arnold Clark, the UK's largest car dealership, has built their rather swanky head offices here (and by the looks of the size of the car park, they must be giving away free cars to every staff member and their extended families). Porsche and Audi have dealerships on opposite sides of the main roundabout, which takes you on and off the motorway. Land Rover Jaguar are also here – possibly so that the AA Road Assistance or RAC repair vans don't have far to travel on a daily basis. Harley Davidson is a few doors down – which must cause havoc for all customers when realising their journey home will require a moderate turn back onto the Motorway (moderate, but beyond the ability of most Harley Davidson motorbikes). Perhaps most surprising was the addition of a Ferrari showroom that I'm sure was not there the last time I was here. I'm tempted to get a bag of take-out Burger King[1] and slowly eat it whilst walking around the six-figure cars to see how quickly someone plucks up the courage to kindly ask me to go to a garage with cars I can afford.

Sebastian Bunford-Jones (and I'm sure, like me, he prefers his full name until you feel you are friends, and then a shortened version) is waiting for me at the gates of Glasgow Distillery. Only recently, with the purchase of the neighbouring warehouse and yard, could the distillery boast its own entrance. Two things to bring up at this point: firstly, Glasgow Distillery is not open to the public – so don't turn up looking for a tour. If, and this is a big

---

1 - Also nearby.

'if', you are a very small group of real fans (and stress this when contacting them, 'die-hard fans'), and assuming they are not in the middle of something really important (like the Friday afternoon dregs session) you 'might' be allowed a brief tour. Secondly, as double-barrelled surnames are uncommon in Scotland, I must remember to ask Sebastian about his.

I'm not going to lie about Glasgow Distillery being in any way picturesque. Had this been a painting brought home by a child to their mother, it would mysteriously never make the fridge door where the other art pieces are suspended by holiday magnets. It won't make the cover of glossy lifestyle magazines and certainly won't be painted on cask ends and sold at festivals worldwide. However, last time I checked, there was no correlation between the quality of whisky made at a distillery and any aesthetic values one could give to the building. There are far more beautiful distilleries that can only dream of getting the exposure that Glasgow Distillery is currently receiving. Glasgow is that kid in the class who might not easily find romance, but everyone likes, a lot.

I turn into the courtyard and am immediately directed next to the solitary warehouse. "If a truck appears, you may have to move," Seb[1] informs me as we shake hands. "The new warehouse has allowed us to begin storage on-site for the first time. It's really impacted how we operate. When we're getting ready to bottle the next small batch or a rum bottling, we can bring in some of the casks and discuss whether they are ready, if they need water and what the whole team thinks of them."

Alex Foulis, Head Brewer, and Libby Barmby, Sales Manager, join Seb and I in the warehouse. Alex produces a bung hammer and extracts a sample from a Tokaji cask. "Tokaji is one of our favourite casks for further maturation," Alex explains. "We feel it adds a whole new level of funkiness to the spirit." The whisky is light but with sweet pickles and honeyed fruit flavours. This cask, I'm informed, is not quite ready but may see the inside of a bottle later in the year or the following year. It surprises me as I am usually not a fan of Tokaji finishes – one to look out for.

---

1 - Trusting we are on such terms now to allow the shortened version.

Glasgow Distillery

www.glasgowdistillery.com
Small groups can be catered for by appointment only

A career in the drinks industry, one spent planning, developing and strategising for other people's products, set Michael Hayward and Liam Hughes on a path to create their own brand. A new single malt whisky was always going to be the mission, and Glasgow was a natural choice for the pair: "It is a city with a rich heritage of entrepreneurialism, spirits production and whisky – however, there hadn't been a new independent single malt Scotch whisky distillery in the city for a long time. As Scotland's biggest city, bringing single malt back to Glasgow seemed like a no-brainer." Michael informs me.

The original 'Glasgow Distillery' was founded in 1770 and closed in 1902 – the current bottled series is called 1770 as a nod to the city's past. Despite Glasgow being the most important city in the world for Scotch whisky, Glasgow Distillery, completed in 2015, was the first malt whisky distilled in 40 years[1] and the first independent distillery in the city for over 100 years. "The city reflects the qualities of myself and Liam in

---

1 - The last was Kinclaith Distillery in operation from 1958 to 1975. It was housed within the Strathclyde Distillery (which is still in production).

many ways: industrious and down-to-earth; a city full of great stories and storytellers; and importantly, full of character. We wanted to create a fresh and interesting distillery that didn't feel pressure to conform to tropes or industry rhetoric whilst still respecting heritage and history. Glasgow ticked all the boxes in that regard."

Unlike some of the other new distilleries in this book, Michael and Liam were working within a specific budget, meaning big, glamorous sites with potential for expansive visitor centres were not primary in their planning.

"Our current site was a combination of accessibility and necessity. It's a site that sits on the city's industrial outskirts, so it is readily accessible, next to the M8 and close to Glasgow airport and a wealth of suppliers. It was also part of a wider bonded site, which enabled us to get up and running as fast as possible. We didn't start with a wealth of capital or investment compared to many of the new distillery projects that have followed, so setting up shop and working on creating great spirits quickly was important. That ethos is still very much part of how we operate; we're a lean and agile team that invests our money into our raw materials, production, and people, focusing on creating the best products possible."

To all that have tried the Glasgow whiskies, certainly in the last few years, the emphasis on having a range of quality products has paid dividends. "We have never been focused on creating a style of single malt based on our location, and conversely, we have never had an agenda at play by trying to do something different from what is typically 'expected' from a Lowland distillery.

"From the beginning, we have focused on flavour - we knew we wanted to create a range of styles so that the flavour spectrum within the final output would be broad and we could make a wide variety of releases. Our motto has been 'Why create one style of spirit when we can create multiple', exponentially widening the range of whiskies we could create."

The distillery produces three core styles of whisky: triple distilled, peated and unpeated. "We're trying to showcase that one distillery can make delicate and elegant whiskies as well as robust, oily and waxy – and everything in between. We do a fair amount of cask experimentation across our three core styles, which is really interesting – understanding how each of our core three styles stands up to different types of maturation and getting to really know each of the three spirits in turn. A great part of the job is watching the whisky's development and seeing how spirit and wood combinations develop over time."

Glasgow Distillery proves that a determined group of investors can make dreams a reality. "Building the distillery from scratch has been one of the most challenging experiences of my life," Michael tells me. "But also, one of the most rewarding. It fills me with immense pride when I see how far we have come in a relatively short period."

Although, as described, Glasgow Distillery was not built to welcome tourists, Michael has not ruled out the possibility of a visitor's centre in the future. "Whisky is a long-term business, and for us, we are just concentrating on creating the best products we can to develop that reputation for creating great quality products, and the rest will follow in time, I am sure."

What is sure is that the team at Glasgow are making products that are attention-grabbing to new and old whisky drinkers. And they are also one of the most engaging new distilleries in the market. Decisions are clearly made with the customer in mind – releases are full of flavour, proudly backed, and with a lack of cynicism or self-propelled hype. With their array of distillates and cask finishes, there is a Glasgow Distillery bottling for every whisky drinker.

Glasgow Distillery's Annie Still

Next to the warehouse is the compact area that houses the distillery and offices. Despite being a small setup, Glasgow Distillery now boasts two sets of stills. There is just enough space between the stills and the office for resident cooper Hugh McMurray, known as Shug, to hammer away at some fresh ex-Bourbon barrels. "These all have cracked staves, so I'm just repairing them, and we'll fill them today." He lifts a discarded stave, and sure enough, a significant crack or tear can be seen across it. "I take them apart and then fix them using one of the spare good staves."

"Just like that," I suggest, winking at him. Shug grins back at me knowingly. It is not that simple, but with his experience, it is not a problem. Shug gestures to a pile of what looks like dried bits of tar. "It always makes me laugh when people get hung up on the filtering part of bottling whisky. When you look at all the stuff that can come out of a cask, people worry about tiny bits getting into the bottle."

Shug relates to me a story of when he worked for Diageo at their cooperage. Two of the young warehouse workers were setting casks out into the sun to allow the heat to leach alcohol out of the wood. A small amount of water would be added to help the process, and then, they would endeavour to drink the contents using a small tube. This is referred to as 'cask-bunging' although, at the time, Shug and his colleagues referred to it as 'extracting the giggle-juice'. On one memorable occasion, Shug explains that the two lads happened on a bountiful cask, and much merriment ensued. A day or so later, after the cask had been dismantled, it was discovered that a rat had somehow found its way into the cask and subsequently died. I was laughing too hard at Shug's recounting of the story to ask about the condition of the two fellow workers – but I am sure lessons were learned.

Seb's tour is informative but not stuffy as he possesses a casual yet assured demeanour. He is an ebullient, amiable ambassador who clearly loves his work. "We approach every bottling with input from just about every team member," he tells me. "We have found that several voices allow for a better-finished product. Rather than having one palate dictate what we consider Glasgow whisky to be, the team effort results in much broader feedback, and we feel this is a better representation of our buying public."

We both share a belief that this team approach to blending marks a shift in the whisky industry. Historically, the Scotch whisky industry had promoted the idea of a 'Chief Blender' – someone with almost superhuman powers of sensory perception. Recipes of blends were closely guarded secrets and blenders would be treated as if only they had the ability to put together something extraordinary. The new wave distillery and brand owners are offering a new take on blending as being something more organic and democratic. Slowly, the industry is ditching this idea of a 'Chief Blender' and much of the pomposity that goes with it.

Glasgow Distillery are a refreshing and welcome addition to the Scotch whisky landscape. Personally, I'm very taken with their peated malt. "Peat in Glasgow?" I hear you ask. And you'd be right to ask, as the peat has nothing to do with the city. This is not uncommon – other than a few distilleries (such as some on Islay), the peat is not local. What I find in the Glasgow Peated whisky is a thick and oily quality that fits so well with the industrial history of the city and the distillery's location.

My time with Seb is up, and I return onto the M8, the motorway stretching across Scotland's central belt heading east. There is now a convenient link to the M74, which will take me south. I once lived in Cambuslang (nicknamed Casablanca for its glamour and style...), situated just outside Glasgow, and at the time, worked in the West End of the city. My journey to work was around nine miles, which, before the completion of the M74 link, would take around 40 minutes. This journey can now be done in less than 15. Naturally, the volume of traffic has since increased, and this motorway link can sometimes cause long jams. None of this is very interesting, but chances are if you travel around Scotland, you'll join one of these large tar-topped arteries. As I negotiate the multi-lane discipline of Scotland's main motorway, I realise that I forgot to ask Seb about his double-barrelled surname. It shall have to remain a mystery a while longer.

How <u>NOT</u> to be Taught How to Drink Whisky

"Whisky is a serious drink...
although its drinking should never be taken seriously."

There is an educational video watchable on the great Interweb that attempts to help you in your journey into appreciating whisky. In truth, there are several, but I will focus on just one as the actions of the host, Richard Paterson, have gone viral. In this video, Richard advises pouring a small amount of whisky into a glass, giving it a swirl and then tossing it away. This, he reassures us, will ensure your glass is now free of any contaminating elements, and one can thoroughly enjoy the whisky on its own merits.[1]

It is great theatre. Richard also tells you to pop your finger into the water jug, ensuring the water is not warm (as this abhorration has previously ruined his dram three times!). Then, one must bring the whisky to the nose, getting your full snout in several times before allowing the liquid anywhere near the mouth. This, and other slightly stodgy and over-the-top videos, are a bit yesterday – a touch preachy and archaic. The 'dos' and 'do nots' of whisky drinking that dominated the last century are now replaced with the 'however' and 'whatever' for the current drinker.

'How do I drink whisky'? However you like.

'What do I add or not add to my whisky? Whatever you prefer.

I rarely mix my whisky with anything other than a dash of water or occasionally an ice cube - especially when high-strength. That is my preference, but there shouldn't be any 'musts' when it comes to your enjoyment of a whisky. And for the love of all things clean and sanitary, please do not pop your finger, or anything else for that matter, in the water jug.

The truth is that there is no right or wrong way to enjoy this drink. There is no expertise for enjoyment either. I am continually informed by friends and new acquaintances 'I am not an expert on whisky' to which I always reply, "Do you like this whisky?" There are only two possible answers, and it doesn't matter which one is offered. Assuming you have an opinion, my reply is: "You are an expert on what you like, and that is enough." I'm not sure how any greater expertise will add to either liking a whisky or not liking it. Occasions,

---

1 - There is a good chance that you may be thrown out of an establishment, or home, for performing this act. The video does not go on to explain how to best to clean up the discarded whisky.

memories, moments, events and people will add to the enjoyment. For instance, 'when I smell this whisky, I am immediately transported to [insert place]' or 'this whisky reminds me of [insert person]'. This can add very much to the pleasure or displeasure of a dram.

A few things to consider. Firstly, whisky is best not 'necked' straight out of a bottle. Not just because it is socially frowned upon but because the whisky (and almost certainly the drinker) needs some air. Other than that, whatever receptacle you prefer is perfectly fine. Some folk really dig drinking whisky out of a coffee mug. This also allows a dram during an online meeting or in a social environment when everyone else uses their mug for something hot. Perhaps the meeting at 17:00 on a Friday with the HR department can be tolerated if there's a dash of a decent whisky in the mug instead of tea? Do not be conned into believing that expensive glasses are the be-all and end-all of the glassware discussion. A large wine glass will often work best – just mind the size of the measure.

Whisky straight-up or mixed is up to you. "Smoky Cokie" is a real thing, and I'm pretty sure I don't need to spell out the ingredients. I am not a huge fan of cocktails, possibly because the best ones take a little preparation, and I often can't be bothered, but also because many are too sweet.[1] But whisky cocktails are big at the moment, and the better whiskies sometimes have a bigger hit of flavour to add to the mix. Whilst this is not a 'must' I would always recommend trying any whisky neat first. Give it a chance, and let it take you from there. Perhaps it is too strong and needs some water, perhaps just a few drops, perhaps a tonic or soda or ice. The world is very much your oyster – it's your fun, after all.

This brings me nicely to tasting notes. A dog can learn more about another dog by smelling its rear than anyone can learn about a whisky by reading the tasting notes on the bottle. Regardless of whether any scientists, journalists, companies, institutions or anyone else believe there are 'proper' descriptors to whisky, I say nuts to the lot of them. When I first discovered whisky, I revelled in the fact that, unlike wine, one could simply state whatever came to mind, and others would either nod in agreement or struggle to agree. Tasting notes on bottles and websites now range from just a few commonly used descriptors to small dissertations. If I truly want to squeeze dry every ounce of pleasure from a whisky, it is by trying to pin down every single nuance and note from the exact herb to which brand of paint the nose prickle reminds me of.

It is certainly not helpful in describing things that are too personal when writing notes for something public – say for an online review, a label or a book. Coming up with something like 'Grandma's knickers on a hot summer's day' is likely to gain a snigger but not overly helpful to anyone trying to pin down a specific smell in the whisky. And frankly, anyone agreeing with that tasting note is likely to raise a few awkward questions.

You will notice whilst reading through this little adventure that I barely mention

---

1 - Which is slightly odd considering I love a Negroni.

the product at all. This is a conscious decision as, firstly, many of the expressions I taste will no longer be available by the time this book is in print, and secondly, my observations are just that, mine. I have never felt comfortable in trying to persuade anyone that they will like something because I do. There are certain common tasting notes (or 'congeners' as they are referred to) such as vanilla, oak, caramel, berries, cloves, pine, coconut, bananas and so on. The thing is, reeling off congeners is not really a skill – don't believe for a second that there are people out there with 'super noses' – some sort of genetic ability to smell things the rest of us can't[1] and can therefore appreciate whisky in a way that is superior. And even if that were the case, it doesn't change or affect your appreciation of the whisky.

Much of this identification of flavours is down to practice and confidence. I have been in enough tasting environments where the shy and retiring, not wanting to give any opinion often from fear of saying something wrong, only go on to then highlight a note that everyone else immediately agrees with. This sharing of smells and tastes is fun and can be revealing, but again, I'm not sure it sways you one way or the other as to how much you like the whisky. I've had bad whiskies about which I could write pages of taste descriptors. It's still bad, in my opinion. Again, there is no right or wrong regarding tasting notes – it is entirely personal. If you smell Saharan sands, flip-flops, or wet dogs, that is all part and parcel of your life and memories. Revel in it and enjoy whatever you get out of it – and view with suspicion anyone who dares to disagree.

Whilst the Glasgow Distillery is tucked into the corner of a sprawling industrial estate built with functionality and a fair nod to frugality, its nearest distilling neighbour, Clydeside Distillery, is a beacon of Glasgow's past and future. As I drive up to the converted hydraulic pumping station, I realise that whilst I have passed it numerous times, I did not join the dots that this was the Clydeside Distillery. I have this idea in my head that so many of these new distilleries are tiny shacks where small amounts of spirit are made and squirrelled away in small warehouses. Some are, of course, but Clydeside is anything but. In truth, it was a long and challenging build for Tim and son Andrew Morrison.

---

1 - Some people have a stronger sense of smell (noticeable for strong odours such as onions or sulphur), just like some people suffer from anosmia or 'nose blindness'.

Clydeside Distillery

www.theclydeside.com
Open to the public

"Distilling gets into your blood." Clydeside's Managing Director Andrew Morrison tells me. Not many can claim to have had their name associated with distilling in the way the Morrison family have. When I started my interest in whisky, Bowmore Distillery was still referred to as the Morrison-Bowmore Distillery. The distillery was acquired by Andrew's great-grandfather, Stanley P Morrison, in 1963. The purchase was a spur-of-the-moment action by Stanley, apparently a common occurrence for the dynamic businessman. Morrison-Bowmore Distillers would later acquire Glen Garioch Distillery near Aberdeen and Auchentoshan Distillery in Clydebank.

When the Morrison-Bowmore company was sold in 1994 to Suntory, Stanley's two sons, Brian and Tim, went their separate ways, each starting new independent bottling companies; Brian began Morrison-Mackay,[1] and Tim started A D Rattray. But

---

1 - Now known as Morrison Scotch Whisky Distillers, owners of Aberagie Distillery in Perthshire (which as of the Summer of 2024, has yet to release whisky).

bottling whisky was never going to be enough. "With no control over supply, we could only watch as demand increased and stocks dwindled." Andrew continues. "It became a straightforward decision for us: either get into production or see no growth in the business."

Initially, Tim and Andrew looked to acquire an existing distillery, but when a deal that had taken much effort, expense and time fell through, they turned their attention to building one from scratch. Several sites were considered until an old Victorian pumphouse, which controlled a swing bridge, became available at the old Queens Dock. What made the site even more fitting was discovering that a not-too-distant relative, John Morrison, had been instrumental in raising the building's water source, Loch Katrine, and instrumental in the building of Queen's Dock. For the Morrison's the family links reinforced their desire to begin distilling in the city of Glasgow and at this exact site.

As the tour explains, the building was a shell and in a state of disrepair. Due to being a listed building, the Morrisons could not change the layout but could add a modern extension that housed much of the distillery. The mix of new and old is a perfect testament to the site and its position between the exhibition centre, the Hydro music venue and the Riverside Museum. In 2017 the first distillate ran - Tim Morrison and his family were distillers again.

Every effort has been made to remind and pay homage to Glasgow's industrial past and the distillery's historical roots. The distillery has been built to resemble the innards of an ocean-going ship - industrial and engineered. The bottle and branding replicate the local architectural design and hark back to boat designs and colours. Even the Mash Tun has been painted to resemble a ship's hull. Having previously been part of the Lowland region when owners of the Auchentoshan Distillery (just a short drive up Great Western Road), the Morrison family was keen to add to the area. "I can't remember a single moment when someone specifically requested a Scottish Lowland malt whisky," Andrew states. "A Highland malt, for sure. A Speyside malt, no doubt. An Islay whisky, hundreds of times. A Campbeltown malt, regularly. But a Lowland malt? Never to me, nor to anyone else I was around."

I suggest that The Clydeside is strutting a new style of whisky - and one very few drinkers will have ever tried before - a malt whisky from Glasgow. Andrew agrees but is more than happy with being considered a Lowland malt and reinvigorating the category. "The lack of enthusiasm for Lowland whiskies comes down to lack of understanding," Andrew continues. "For years, I thought of the Lowlands as the home of triple-distilled whiskies, only later learning that process applied only to Auchentoshan and the former Rosebank. Both Bladnoch and Glenkinchie [the only other two working Lowland malt whisky distilleries at the time] were possibly lighter in style but double pot-stilled just like most other Scottish malt whiskies."

What the Morrisons have achieved is nothing short of remarkable. In an area of the city that was once the industrial hub of an Empire that spanned the globe, The Clydeside Distillery is the first chapter of a renaissance that will last long into the future. The distillery is part of a full and immersive visitor experience and already boasts around 100,000 visitors a year. As one of the most accessible distilleries in Scotland, it may soon likely claim to be the most visited in the country.

Clydeside stillhouse

Whilst I arrived just as the distillery opened, I was not the first at the gates. Nor did it take long for the car park to fill. I am met by Alistair McDonald, Clydeside's Distillery Manager, and as we ascend the steps to the still house, a busload of tourists (from their accents, I guess mostly American) enter the distillery. The gift shop quickly becomes a crowded affair. This is clearly a common occurrence, and all of the steps taken to accommodate large numbers of tourists are paying off. The closures due to Covid were a huge concern at the time, but that now seems a distant memory.

Alistair is an Ileach (someone born on the Isle of Islay) who followed a passion for engineering into the whisky world. This led him to a job working at the Bowmore Distillery and eventually a move to Auchentoshan. "I worked with the Morrisons and then continued with Beam Suntory after they purchased the company. I thought that was me until this project came up, and when offered a chance to work with the Morrisons again and to create a new and unique whisky, I had to take the chance." Quite so, I reckon. Standing in the still house with the view over the Clyde, Alistair must not have taken too long to decide.

The Clydeside Distillery will quickly become the burgeoning first step for many new converted whisky enthusiasts. Soon, hordes of tourists will associate whisky with the city of Glasgow from their visits to the Clydeside Distillery. Whilst this will be their gateway to further adventures within the Scotch whisky industry, I can't help but feel how suitable it is that this distillery will become the beacon, the first step, for so many. It is also fitting that Tim Morrison and his son Andrew and their team be the first impression of this incredible industry. I can't think of any better first foot forward.

The view towards the Maritime Museum from Clydeside Distillery

Scotch Whisky Regions

"Reductio ad absurdum?"

There are few things we like better as a species than to categorise things. We'll subdivide just about anything and split hairs whenever possible. Take musical genres as an example. Every new band or artist is instantly labelled as Pop, Rock, Prog, Metal or Hip-Hop and so on. When you get someone like David Bowie, who straddles several genres, we split their work up into smaller groups such as Hair-Metal, Prog-Rock, or Gangster Rap. Sometimes, though the categorisation is to allow a straightforward one-model-fits-all approach to describe things – this can result in times when certain things that ought not to be compared or lumped together are.

And so it was, and nobody knows exactly when, that the entire Scotch whisky industry was split into five categories: Highlands & Islands, Lowlands, Speyside, Islay & Campbeltown. This categorisation began with the division between the Lowlands and Highlands, created by the Wash Act in 1784. This act was introduced to restrict the amount of alcohol produced in the Scottish Highlands, making its way to England (particularly London) in large quantities.[1] The act reduced duty on alcohol and instead tied it to the size of pot stills and the amount of wash that could be distilled in a day. The larger Lowland distillers were thus granted an advantage, and a significant division within the industry was formed.

Over time, and simply as a way for blenders to categorise, more regions were forged into existence. To add to the Lowland and Highland whiskies, the great seam of distilleries placed within sight of the River Spey[2] became known as Speyside whisky. Islay and Campbeltown were highlighted for their unique style and close conglomeration of distilleries. The rest, including all of the other islands, was lumped in with the Highlands. Little consideration was given to this simplified division of Scotland, perhaps until Campbeltown was threatened with anonymity due to being reduced to only two distilleries (whereas the Lowlands had three).

1 - It should be noted that we are not discussing what we identify as 'whisky' here – this would have been spirit that was often rectified into Gin or flavoured with local herbs and sweeteners.

2 - Legend has it that in order to be labelled as a 'Speyside' distillery you had to be able to stand on your land and urinate into the Spey (not necessarily directly, it just had to find its way there). This would be quite the feat for anyone working at Benromach...

Now, with as many as 40 new and planned distilleries in various parts of Scotland,[1] the idea that all can be simplified into five regions seems, at best, simplistic and, for many, confusing. Regionality was a way of broad-brushing a 'style' of whisky. The word 'style' would suffix whisky whenever someone wanted to describe a whisky; 'this is typical Lowland-style whisky. Light and fruity.' I can guarantee you will hear 'light and fruity' repeated in every corner of Scotland where they make whisky (although not every distillery). The idea that any of this represents a regional style is plain nonsense.

Some of the newer distilleries, such as The Clydeside and Kilchoman, have revelled in being part of a region. Meanwhile, others, such as Raasay and Inchdairnie, have found the regionalisation confusing, limiting and, coupled with the regulations set by the Scotch Whisky Association in 2011, controlling, complex and, in many ways, erroneous. Perhaps Fife is the best example to discuss. Before the 2011 Scotch Whisky Act, no distillery in the Fife area was offering a product to the customer. Now, there are five, with a few more being planned. As the Lowland line engulfs all of them, they are lumped in with the Bladnoch and Lochlea distilleries on the other side of the country.

Is the answer to split Scotland up into numerous smaller regions? Possibly. If regionality is so essential, then why not? But I would lean toward dismissing them entirely. They have no relevance anymore, and all the distilleries should be allowed to name their product with any non-conflicting regionality. I suggest non-conflicting to prevent a second distillery on Raasay from wanting to call itself 'Raasay Scotch whisky' In this instance, it would have to suffice with Hebridean or Island – whichever is preferred. The whisky industry already enjoys the nomenclature 'Scotch', a terrific badge of honour to rival any French wine-growing region or any other classification you wish to argue.

This question around 'Regions' stems from a desire that I, and many others, have for distillers, branders, marketers and salespeople to forego the lazy categorisation and let their product stand on its own legs. Gone are the days when association with an area was an arbiter of quality, taste or desirability. The proliferation of the new distilleries and their championing of the locale and its people should warrant enough uniqueness without being lumped into a centuries-old system of sub-categorisation.

The idea that Glengoyne Distillery and Wolfburn Distillery, just a mere 270 miles apart, are a similar style because of a nearly straight line through the middle of Scotland is bordering on being risible. I suggest you approach all of these whiskies, in fact, all Scotch, with an open mind and a willingness to understand why it tastes the way it does because of where it is situated and the people behind it, rather than any archaic categorisation.

---

1 - There are over 140 distilleries currently operating, with around 40 in either planning or in the first few years of their maturation. To keep up with the list, visit www.scotch-whisky.org.uk

The Clydeside whisky, at least to me, is robust and not delicate. It is not triple distilled like its near neighbour, Auchentoshan, a process that is usually associated with making a lighter spirit. The Clydesisde team are also advocates of allowing the distillate to do the talking, and whilst we can read from this that their best is yet to come, it does mean that anyone following the distillery will be able to watch how the whisky changes over time. The philosophy at Clydeside is to minimise releases as stock and ages build up. "We bottle purely for the intrigued and what interests us." Andrew insists. "We have no desire in seeing our bottles turning up on auction sites or being 'investable'; what we bottle now is to show the development of the whisky. And we are very proud of what we can offer."

My time is up in Glasgow. Well, for this trip, at least. Scotland's largest city, the country's industrial hub, historical powerhouse and beating heart, can only boast the two malt whisky distilleries. Well, for now at least – and it is worth remembering that this is two more distilleries than it could boast before 2015. The Glasgow Distillery and The Clydeside Distillery offer very different pictures of the city and, more importantly, the city's whisky. But both are industrial, born out of entrepreneurialism, a love for the city and its people and a desire to create something that shouts Glasgow from the rooftops. Michael Hayward and the Morrisons have put Glasgow on the whisky map - and no city anywhere in the world deserved that more.

CHAPTER 3

THE ISLES OF SKYE & RAASAY

"The hospitality of this remote region is like that of the golden age. We have found ourselves treated at every house as if we came to confer a benefit."
Samuel Johnson writing about Skye in 1775

As I type, Storm Kathleen is battering the north-west coast of Scotland. Thankfully, the storm's full force is mostly being vented over the Atlantic, but it has affected my travel plans. For the sake of a true-to-life trip around Scotland, having the weather dictate part of my journey is to be expected and apt. The storm meant a ferry journey to Harris could not go ahead. I'm frustrated and relieved in equal measures – had the ferry not been cancelled, I would now be sailing from Uig to Tarbert across the strait known as 'The Minch',[1] probably losing my breakfast and a stomach lining from the choppy waters. Instead, I shall drive to Torabhaig Distillery before heading to the Isle of Raasay Distillery.

Such is the layout, remoteness, and general decay, not forgetting the historical systematic removal of public transport within Scotland; I have not entertained any mode of transport other than driving to the Isle of Skye. From my house in the Lowlands, it is a drive of just five and a half hours (and remembering my American roots, this is a mere 'one side of California diagonally to the other' kind of road trip). It will be on memorable roads with scenery galore and the odd interesting stop at places like Tyndrum, Glencoe and Fort William. Had I been forced to take public transport... well, I shudder at the thought. Without my car, the journey to Torabhaig Distillery would take more than eleven hours and require no less than nine changes of transport. In fact, were I to set off right now, it would take public transport just under 24 hours to get me there. Alternatively, if I chose to go by bicycle, I could arrive around five hours earlier than the numerous buses and trains. Granted, I would likely need to collapse upon arrival and require some resuscitation – but then I would be at a distillery; I'm pretty sure they would have something restorative to hand...

---

1 - Or is it 'The Little Minch'?

Coat, wellies and waterproofs, or shorts, t-shirts and sunscreen? Yes

"There are two seasons in Scotland: June and Winter."
Sir Billy Connolly

There is a running joke for all those who receive tourists in Scotland. The more far-flung you live, the better the joke is; a tourist will spend a few days in one part of Scotland and enjoy glorious weather, blossoming flowers, fields ripe for harvest, calm waters, blue skies and a pleasant atmosphere. Filled with a near overwhelming and new-found love for the area they are visiting, they say, "I would love to live here". To which, more often than not, the nearest local will state, "Aye, when it's like this, I feel the same. You want to spend a six-month winter here when the rain is so heavy that the animals are either lining up two by two or trying to climb a tree."

'There's no such thing as bad weather, just the wrong clothes."
Sir Billy, again.

Unless one is prepared to brave the elements in a rubber suit and face mask, I'd like to argue Connolly's point a little. However, this would be a lesson in futility, as I am positive Sir Billy would jump at the chance to promenade in a rubber suit and face mask. We, the British (and Irish), are weather-obsessed – and I must add that we are obsessed with all weather. Should someone we know travel anywhere, even to the nearest city or large town, our first question is always, 'What's the weather like?' If on proper overseas holidays, this obsession becomes borderline fanatical. Questions such as 'How hot is it?'; 'How hot does it feel?'; 'Is it a dry heat or a sticky one?'; 'Is there much cloud cover?' Pity knowing anyone having travelled to the south of Spain that gets as much as an hour of rain – this is a story for retelling the rest of the year.

I'll give you an example of how obsessed we are with weather. For my 40th birthday, my wife and I drove from Los Angeles to Las Vegas in a black Corvette Stingray. We stayed at the impressive Bellagio Hotel and watched its fountain displays. We visited almost every attraction imaginable: shows, shopping, dinner and drinks. We witnessed an actual American police car chase right through the Boulevard. We looked on, horrified, as the slot machine zombies poured quarter after quarter into uncharitable machines. And yet, from all that we partook of, participated in and witnessed, the only story we ever tell is how, for about ten minutes, the Las Vegas Strip received the lightest dusting of snow. Granted, that is in a desert, so it is mildly interesting, but even so, the weather is an obsession. Other nations are obsessed differently. For instance, in Los Angeles, the weather reports could spend half an hour discussing temperature differences of just a few degrees from the sea to the valley to the mountains - as if these minor separations would require a change of attire or plans. Californians are obsessed with temperature but need more weather to be obsessed with it. Parts of Britain, and especially in the Highlands and Islands of Scotland, can experience more weather in a day than Southern California does in a year.

My first visit to the small village of Dufftown in the Speyside area of the Highlands taught me how suddenly the weather can change. Having walked in glorious sunshine from the crossroads down Fife Street to walk around Mortlach Distillery, I returned in a blizzard of snow. Everyone in the UK can relate to a similar story – and will do so at the drop of a hat. Any talk of Brits being reserved, bashful, not forthcoming and stiff-upper-lipped goes out the window if the topic of conversation is weather. And if anyone dares say 'Good day' when it is clearly inclement, someone will always reply 'Is it?'

The weather has played a large part in making Scotland the home of whisky. Few drinks fit their climate better. I often joke that the discovery of Uisge Beatha, the precursor to whisky, had two enthralling side-effects to those who first discovered how to make it; first, the drinking of it made them feel warm – a rare treat in the mountains and glens of Scotland. And secondly, the more they drank, the more attractive the opposite sex became - another rare treat for the rugged folk. Had Scotland enjoyed prolonged summers of sunshine, heat and perspiration, I'm sure we would have ended up with some watery beer, probably carbonated and suffixed with words like 'light' and 'low' (hardly in keeping with the hardy image of Claymore-wielding clans).

I am slightly embarrassed to admit that this will be my first time on the Isle of Skye. Despite living, working and travelling throughout Scotland for almost twenty years, Scotland's largest Island has just slipped through my net. I was supposed to visit over two decades ago as part of a 'Classic Malts Cruise' - packaged, sponsored and paid for by Diageo. Unfortunately, when sailing into Lagavulin Bay and having just listened to the captain of the boat regale us with tales of shipwrecks in the area, we hit a rock, and the boat instantly ground to a halt. I went head-first down a hatch from the upper deck to the lower one, bypassing the stairs. A mild concussion was enough to send me home, and alas, the sailing from Islay to Skye and what would have been a wonderful tour of Talisker Distillery was missed.

As it turns out, Storm Kathleen has not just changed my itinerary but also my route. Whilst my setting off at six in the morning means I am too early to peruse the shelves of the whisky shop at The Green Welly Stop in Tyndrum, I have enough time to buy tickets for the

Mallaig to Armadale ferry. Had I been heading straight to Harris as originally planned, this ferry journey would not have been on my itinerary. The route takes me up the west coast of Loch Lomond and reminds me of the size and length of this body of water. A tenth of my trip to the Mallaig ferry will be tracing the shores of Loch Lomond from its widest point (five miles across on the south side) to its narrowest point twenty-two miles later, where the River Falloch near Ardlui feeds it.

Loch Lomond is not the longest loch in Scotland (Loch Awe is a couple of miles longer) and comes second to Loch Ness for volume (and for those interested in these facts, Loch Morar, which I shall pass later, is the deepest). The road up Lomond's west coast, and very much the main artery for the western Highlands and Islands, is the northern section of the A82 – the same road that heading south will take me to Campbeltown. It is pretty clear that this road, for many miles, was built too near the loch and far too narrow. Trucks slow to a crawl to pass each other, and in some places, traffic has to stop to allow one side to clear. This is not such a problem heading out in April, but I dread to think how slow the going is in tourist season.

Once past Tyndrum, the landscape changes dramatically as lochs, trees, and greenery give way to bracken, heather, boulders and steep rising hills that fill the horizon. A barrenness overwhelms the view. Everything is granite, solid and relatively untouched. At times, it appears the road, cut off from view in the distance, must magically take you through one of the mountains before reappearing on the other side. But the road is so cunningly laid that no matter where it takes you, the hills always remain on either side of it. Had Peter Jackson, the director of Lord of the Rings and The Hobbit, not been so adamant about filming in his native New Zealand, I am confident this is the world or topography that Tolkien envisioned. At any point, I expect to see a city carved into the rock face of one of the mountains or cave miners heading in a line to an entrance only known to them and only visible in moonlight. The peat bogs, lochs, rock faces and valleys, all with a distinct lack of human interference, would have made a perfect backdrop for small Hobbits, Orcs, Dwarves, Goblins and even Tom Bombadil.

Passing Glencoe and heading up the east shore of Loch Eil, the town of Fort William removes any thoughts of Middle-earth. As the wild landscape is replaced with the familiar sights of supermarkets, housing schemes, offices and shopping arcades, I am reminded that people, not fantastical characters, live in this part of Scotland (more's the pity). I decided not to stop and continued to the Glenfinnan Viaduct. This is now uber-famous and sure to become a World Heritage Site. It owes much, and let's be frank, about 99% of its current fame to an appearance in the Harry Potter movies. Oddly, there are two car parks, one of which is a National Trust and an adjacent one run by a charity. Both were extremely busy, and neither offered the best views (which would have been from above or on a train passing over it). A group of young adults pour out from a recently arrived coach. They are rounded up by a teacher who is not much older than the students (and who is wearing a tweed jacket with leather elbow patches and purple moleskin-like trousers, clearly in an attempt to emphasise the couple years of seniority). "Hands up those of you that have seen the Harry Potter movies?" he asks. Not a single hand goes up, and from the back, a desultory voice yells out, "Harry Potter sucks!" I laughed, a little too loudly perhaps, as 30 pairs of eyes turned towards me and, in unison, rolled. A clear indication that it was time for me to go.

The Mallaig to Armadale ferry is a pleasant affair and takes just over half an hour. The day's weather is demonstrating the calm after the storm, so I sit outside on the deck and in the sun, watching as Skye comes into view. As I disembark the ferry, Skye is mostly hidden by hills, but the coastal road is a rewarding drive and before I know it I'm pulling into Torabhaig Distillery. I am immediately struck by how utterly perfect the distillery looks – at least to me. An old farm steading has been completely re-purposed, but in the most sympathetic way, with a modern extension (complete with Pagoda roof) all above the bay with its magnificent views out towards the mainland. It would be harsh to call any of the new distilleries 'out of place', but Torabhaig not only feels 'in place' but also in keeping with expectations of a 'distillery'. The distillery is situated on the Sleat Peninsula, known as the Garden of Skye. Sleat is an old Norse word for smooth or even, and the peninsula got the name despite not being particularly flat but due to how rugged and mountainous the rest of the island appears.

I am met by Anne O'lone, the Visitor Centre Manager. "The building is listed, so whilst we were allowed to repair and repurpose it, we cannot change the layout of what was already here." Anne informs me. The buildings were bought from the estate of the late Sir Iain Noble. It is worth a little tangent here to delve into Sir Iain's life, as his story is one of passion more than heritage, family or any birthright. Born in Germany, his father was a British diplomat, and his mother was the daughter of a Norwegian diplomat. The Noble family's original links were in Dunbartonshire and Argyllshire, not Skye. Yet, having created and sold Noble Grossart, a merchant bank, Sir Iain used the proceeds to buy 20,000 acres across the Sleat Peninsula.

What made Sir Iain different was his love of the Gaelic language. He was not a native Gaelic speaker, so he had to learn and use his position to promote the language in a way that brought him much interest and some notoriety. He famously rallied against English-speaking immigration into Gaelic-speaking communities. This did not go down well, even with the Scottish Countryside Alliance, who denounced it as "sounding like something out of Nazi Germany in the 1930s." That he was precisely an English-speaking immigrant was evidence of a definite lack of self-awareness. However trite these views were, Noble's contribution to the island and the Gaelic language is irrefutable. "It had always been Sir Iain's intent to turn this site into a distillery," Anne tells me. "We were able to turn that dream into a reality." His contribution has not gone unnoticed as the Wash Still has been named 'Sir Iain' and the Spirit Still 'Lady Noble' – a fitting tribute.

Torabhaig Distillery

www.torabhaig.com
Open to visitors

The most surprising fact about Torabhaig Distillery is that it is only the second licensed distillery on the Isle of Skye. Ever. How has this incredible island bypassed the periods of expansion, and why has no one ever thought to cash in on the popularity of Talisker, Skye's solitary distillery, for nearly 200 years? The argument of remoteness is possibly relevant, but it is much easier to get to Skye than either the Islands of Islay or Orkney. Nor could it be argued that the area lacks tourism.

Building on from the initial work of Sir Iain Noble, the team behind the Torabhaig Distillery identified an old farmstead from whence the name derives, and once the water sources of the Allt Breacach and Allt Gleann were secured, the painstaking work of restoration began. With restrictions on what could be done to the existing building, the distilling plant was designed to fit mostly into the longer section of the steading. The roof had to be specially designed so that future work and replacement stills could be installed without any disturbance to the restoration work that was completed.

At the corner of the walkway from the car park leading into the distillery's courtyard is a view of a ruined castle called Caisteal Chamuis. An analysis of the remains determined that the stone had been taken from the late 15th century castle to build the steading, which was then converted into Torabhaig Distillery. From a fort to a farm and now a distillery – although it was clearly not that simple. Planning permission was received in 2002, but work did not start until 2014, and what was expected to take two years turned into just under four.

"When I joined in 2017, the distillery had already begun distilling, but there were not yet any provisions for visitors. I was a Visitor Centre Manager without a visitor centre." Anne laughs. "Everything you see now, from the reception, the shop, the tour and our café, has been added since I joined." From what was a derelict crumbling building, the birth of Torabhaig has provided twenty locals work, and more importantly, a conscious decision was made to promote locally. Rather than sweep up Brewing and Distilling graduates or advertise nationwide, the distillery has trained locals to become distillery operatives. Torabhaig is very much a local company for local people – on an island with just over 10,000 inhabitants, these jobs are a welcome addition.

Torabhaig Distillery has been able to limit its releases in a way most other start-ups can only envy. Being owned by Swedish Billionaire Frederik Paulsen Jr, the distillery has been allowed to release a minimal number of whiskies onto the market. "We have not sold a single cask of Torabhaig whisky to anyone else." Stewart Dick, Torabhaig's Brand Ambassador, tells me. "I realise it is a privileged position, but it has allowed us to control everything we do completely, including the release of every drop of Torabhaig. It also allows us, should we wish to collaborate or bottle for anyone in the future, to be 100% confident in any release."

The team behind the distillery are also responsible for the independent bottling firm Mossburn Distillers, whose first bottlings coincided with the launch of Torabhaig Distillery. In addition, the company runs a small grain distillery in Tweedbank, Galashiels. Named The Reivers Distillery, it allows the company to experiment with different grains and production methods - it is believed a Rye whisky will be released in the future. Torabhaig is the centre-piece for this new firm and has been as keenly anticipated, especially for those dreaming of a second distillery on Skye, as just about any other distillery.

However hard Sir Iain worked to get Gaelic back as a spoken and recognised language, what becomes quite clear to me is how many non-Scottish 'locals' there are. Perhaps, and I'm just casually throwing this out there, what Skye, the Highlands and the Hebrides needed was not necessarily a harking back, or re-emphasis of old traditions but rather a greater integration, more enterprise and a sense of place. The owners of Torabhaig are not from Skye but realised that Skye is an ideal place for a distillery. As a further fitting example, my tour guide, Carol, was originally from St Helen's in England and is no less capable of offering an expert tour than any Gaelic speaker or Skye-born resident.

As Stewart Dick is present at the same time and also not a native of Skye (nor a Gaelic speaker), it allows me to quiz him about pronunciation. "As I understand it," Stewart reasons, "pronunciation is very localised. Gaelic is often a language passed down from one generation to the next and can be completely different from one village to another." A recently released Torabhaig whisky is a good example: 'Cnoc Na Moine'.[1] Some parts of Scotland would treat the first 'C' as silent, therefore 'nock'. According to the Torabhaig team, it is to be pronounced almost like 'Croc'. "I think most locals appreciate any effort to try and pronounce Gaelic names, but don't be too put out if these pronunciations change every time you try," Stewart says, shrugging. This becomes quite apparent when Anne and Stewart ask me where I am staying. My attempts at saying Sligachan are laughable, but my best guess from hearing it pronounced several times is to start with 'Slee' and then trail off before attempting any remaining syllables.

Clutching my bottle of Cnoc Na Moine Torabhaig whisky and a branded coffee mug,[2] I head to 'Slee...' and the eponymously named hotel. As I prepared for this trip, I was struck by how busy Skye was. Initially, I had tried to book a hotel room in Portree, the central hub for the island, but found it booked solid. It is a lesson for anyone planning their visit to book well in advance. Sligachan takes its name from the loch to the north, visible from the hotel. My room is more than comfortable, and my only slight complaint was that Stewart had advised me the hotel boasted an impressive whisky bar. This must be in another locked part of the hotel, as the bar selection was average. However, it's a small complaint, and I'm quite happy with the local beer.

Coffee mugs (a pathetic, first-world rant)... Can I politely ask distilleries (and tourist attractions) to cease selling those dreadful tin cups as a poor excuse for a tea or coffee mug? Only a few people in the world will ever use them. I get it; they are lightweight, therefore portable and can take a beating in a rucksack and still be usable, but all who wild camp, hike and the like, have at least one already. For the rest of us (and that is more than 99% of everyone) we like ceramic mugs that are made to keep a drink hot. I have about fifty different distillery mugs (I'm a mug for a mug) but now refuse to buy these horrible tin ones as simply never use them. It reminds me of visiting a fairly local Highland distillery gift shop and seeing everything from keychains to tea towels, socks, tissues and cufflinks, all branded with the distillery's logo (and the winner for having the most branded gear has to go to Bushmills in Northern Ireland – they also have the best coffee mugs). I enquired about branded coffee mugs. "Coffee mugs?" was the reply, "Huh, that's a new one. Why would anyone want our logo on a coffee mug?" Shot down in flames, I left empty-handed, questioning my life choices.

In the morning, I notice a sizeable statue within walking distance. Approaching the bronze from the rear, it is quite a statement piece as two gentlemen, one perched and

---

1 - Simply translated this means 'The Hill of Peat'.

2 - It's ceramic but perhaps a touch 'petite' for my liking.

one standing, are gazing directly at the peak west of the loch.[1] There are footpaths laid out in several directions. Taking one, I head out, and it is not long before the only sound I can hear is that of rushing water from a nearby burn – its movement reverberating off the surrounding hills, making it considerably more menacing than it really is. Skye and much of the western Highlands appear like a centuries-old battleground where giants once fought each other. The hills and mountains look like cover, hastily built from surrounding lands. The giants forcing the earth into something to hide behind as boulders or shields, as more earth wrenched from around them to hurl at each other. The lochs and streams are a result of their gouging and scraping of the landscape. Pointed, steep-sided hills are all around, and when you catch a glimpse of a sheered, rocky cliff completely in shadow, the landscape has a more menacing, unforgiving tone.

The local gardeners keeping the grass surrounding the Sligachan Hotel trimmed

As my ferry to Raasay is not until midday, I have time to take in some sights and decide to head off to the fabled Dunvegan Castle – seat of the chief of the Clan MacLeod. Two things interest me here: firstly, the current Chief can trace his ancestry back over 800 years, and secondly, what credence or, rather, how much relevance do clans have any more?

---

1 - Standing is Norman Collie and seated is John Mackenzie. The two spent 50 years in the latter part of the 19th century climbing, mapping and often naming the hills, mountains and Cuillins. The cynic in me is fairly sure these already had names…

My surname is extremely uncommon, not just in Scotland but anywhere. It isn't really known if it originated (and worth pointing out that Stirk means young bullock or heifer) in North England or the Fife area of Scotland. On my mother's side, I have Stephenson lineage (amongst others), which is a mix of Scottish and Irish. I seem to recall a relative suggesting that we are direct descendants of George Stephenson, famous for being the father of railways. But then I am also sure that another family member suggested we are descendants of Robert Louis Stevenson, the Scottish novelist. This could be believable due to Stevenson's slight resemblance to my late grandfather; however, as Robert Louis died in 1894 (at just 44) and had no biological children, I will go out on a limb and dismiss this completely.

The point of my ramble is that Scotland and Ireland have a side industry in tracing the roots of all those, and we'll narrow this down to mainly those coming from North America,[1] with a pinch of Scots-Irish heritage. From the castles and 'homes' of clans to the gift shops in airports selling tartan book markers, this pandering with provisions is not for the home market. I have to tread carefully here as names, heritage, and history always bubble under people's feet. It's never hot enough to notice until someone says the wrong thing, and suddenly, it becomes a thorny issue. Having said that, I believe I am on safe ground in suggesting that my Scottish neighbours have less interest in their family's history, which clan they are part of, who their 'Laird' might be, or where the family seat is, than those coming across the pond. Because I have spent much of my life within the UK, I have absolutely no desire to research the Stephenson clan and adorn any part of my life with the relevant tartan.

I'm sure there is a dissertation on this subject, but I suggest that this lack of interest in clans, family history and traditions has allowed a shift towards a more united country. There's a lot to unpack there, and this is a light-hearted book, so I'm not going to even attempt it. There is always a little bemusement when an obviously transatlantic accent claims any sort of heritage – especially when accompanied by a proclamation of being a 'Scottish-American'. Trust me, you'll make more friends if you word it as an American with Scottish ancestry. We're all originally from East Africa anyway.

Alas, my drive to Dunvegan Castle is in vain as it is closed, and with no chance to add weight to any of my points above,[2] I am forced to turn around and head back. I still have time for a quick trip to Talisker Distillery, situated at Carbost, a short drive along the southerly shores of Loch Harport. Talisker is owned by Diageo, the largest of the Scotch whisky companies, and whilst Talisker Distillery is fairly inauspicious from the outside, easily mistaken for a large fish processing plant, inside the visitor centre and shop is a lesson in not judging a book by its cover.

---

1 - Not to dismiss the Antipodean islands, it's just that Americans and Canadians greatly outnumber you.

2 - Or counter any of my points.

Types of Whisky Drinkers

I have more bottles than I will ever have time to drink, more whisky books than I will ever likely read,[1] and have visited well over 150 distilleries. I'm not boasting, far from it; I am merely offering you an insight into that 1% of people that so many hobbies attract. Be it Hi-Fi, wine, model railways, well, models of anything, comics, bird watching, fishing – any pastime, hobby, sport, hedonistic pursuit and even academia; there is always that 1% of participants that live in the deep end. You know who they are; they take their passion too far, have only one topic of conversation (and will always steer it back to their favoured topic). They will have t-shirts, mugs,[2] and even tattoos of whatever they are into. Some will even go so far as to name their children after their hobby (mostly tastefully done, such as Islay or Skye in the case of Scotch whisky fans – I haven't come across a child named 'Hornby' or 'Airfix' yet).

What I and the other 1% often forget is that over 98% of all Scotch drunk around the world is not consumed by the 1% that are obsessed. I was going to put over 99%, but this group, myself included, does drink more than their fair share (although we are, often, a very responsible lot). So, when you are in a group with a member of that 1%, and someone just by chance brings 'whisky' into the conversation, you will watch them come alive with facts, figures, trips, drams and all manner of trivial content. This is not a criticism; most of us have that one topic we feel comfortable with. Yours might be East Berlin composers between 1946 and 1989. Or farming techniques pre-industrial revolution (limiting subjects that take much manoeuvring to get going in any normal conversation).

But even within the whisky world, we have subdivisions – naturally, we are not happy just being labelled whisky drinkers. There are those who only drink blends, or old blends or just malt whisky and then those who spend all of their time and money on just one distillery. Sure, they will drink other whiskies, 'but [insert distillery name] whisky cannot be beaten'. Where we have geek-level interest, we, of course, have the collector and the completionist. The collector will seek out whiskies that interest them and often buy more than one: one to drink and one to look at. The completionist often buys with the intention of drinking but then realises that as the whiskies are being released in a series (sometimes a never-ending series) to drink one would ruin the 'set' – thus begins the task to try and 'complete' the series.

As someone who fits into all of the above categories, I have to psychoanalyse introspectively. But frankly, that would likely lead to buying habit changes, and I haven't

---

1 - And thank you for getting this far along with this one...

2 - Ahem...

quite finished that last series I was hunting down. Once I get that final bottle, I'll have a long, hard talk with myself. Ooh, look, there's a new series after this one. After I've bought that set, I'll reign in the buying. Maybe.

This does lead me onto a much-repeated joke within the collecting fraternity (be it fishing rods, comic books, cars or whisky):

"When I die, I hope my partner does not sell my collection for the amount I told them it cost."

It is also worth noting that none of us are taking any of this hoarded loot with us. Memories are made from sharing, and whisky, amongst those who wish to partake, is the greatest drink to share the world has ever known. But good luck getting that collector to open one of their cherished bottles...

If you're heading to Skye and you're a fan of whisky, particularly smoky whisky, you are likely planning on visiting Talisker Distillery. But, and I'm in danger here of dating this book, I would try and dissuade you. Don't get me wrong, the whisky is fantastic (although considerably cheaper in just about every other outlet than from the distillery shop), the distillery is worthy of a trip, and the staff are all excellent. My call to boycott is due to Diageo's respect for its surroundings – or rather, lack of respect. Other than the few locals who come and go on the B8009 road that more or less ends at the distillery, all other traffic, be it tourists, delivery vans, trucks and all other heavy machinery that aids the distillery and its processes, is, in reality, Diageo traffic. That the Scotch whisky industry's largest company does not maintain the road, ensuring visitors do not lose wheels in potholes the size of prams, is a disgrace. Once you have circumnavigated the bunkers and arrived at the distillery, all of their 'local' and 'Skye' signs, banners and messages seem rice paper thin in sentiment. Rant over, and I hope that when you are reading this, the right thing has already been done, and the road is a beacon of pristine tarmac.[1]

Despite my detour,[2] I still have plenty of time but decide to head to Sconser, the ferry terminal to Raasay. The day is slightly overcast and each peak in view has its own crown of cloud. When the sun does get through, it is amazing how teal in appearance all of the water is – as if Skye is on a painter's palette, and rather than a deep blue, the colouring has leaned towards turquoise and highlighted each wave with spots of white. It is hard to describe Skye as anything other than rugged. At times, it has a barren, lonely feel, but I half expect to find a 'Braveheart' Highlander standing astride every crest or on every hill holding an enormous claymore, watching me with suspicion and misgiving. I get why people come here in their droves and why so many return – often several times.[3]

_____

1 - A Scottish invention.

2 - You guessed right. All they had was a horrible tin cup - no ceramic mugs.

3 - Not to mention those English-speaking immigrants.

I'm met at the ferry terminal by Alasdair Day, co-owner of Isle of Raasay Distillery, who has very kindly travelled from Livingston to accompany me during my time at the distillery. I learn that Storm Kathleen changing my plans has meant a change for Alasdair, too – my taking an early ferry resulted in a very early morning for the poor man. The ferry journey is just 25 minutes, and during it, Alasdair points out an old pier and the concrete remains of what was a viaduct to an iron ore mine. Several German POWs were interned on the island and worked at the mine. It is hard to imagine such a peaceful place being a bustling contributor to the Great War effort,[1] but the fact is that several POWs worked and died on the island – many of the deaths from an outbreak of influenza. As the ferry reaches the terminal at Churchton Bay, Alasdair points out the distillery on the hill to the right. The sun is catching more than a glimmer of gold in the middle of the building.

"When we originally submitted our plans, we wanted a material that would rust for that part of the roof, giving it a dark copper appearance," Alasdair informs me. "This was rejected, so we thought, 'Why not go for the most outlandish material – something that will get thrown out immediately, and then we can go back to our original idea?' Well, that plan spectacularly backfired as they loved the new idea and hence the gold roof."

The view from Raasay's residents lounge

1 - The pier, mine and outline of several tunnels can be seen on Google maps.

Isle of Raasay Distillery

www.raasaydistillery.com
Open to visitors

The Island of Raasay is comparable in size and shape to Manhattan Island in New York, and that is where any comparison would begin and end. The last census noted just 161 inhabitants of Raasay (this has leapt to around 200 today) – there are several times more sheep than people and whilst it is possible to cycle to its north-west tip, there is little evidence of any human habitation. Manhattan has more than twice as many billionaires as Raasay has inhabitants but no sheep. I must stress if you are on the small, sky-scraper-riddled island in the US, it is best not to go looking for any sheep.

During the peak of the tourist season, visitors will outnumber locals three or four to one. Nearly everyone living on the island is clustered around the town of Clachan[1] but even so, at no point do you feel anything but isolated and free of any bustle and certainly in no mood to hustle. When Alasdair points out that the Raasay Distillery & Experience now employs at least one in every five inhabitants, I am reminded of telling Anne at Torabhaig

1 - Clachan is a small village or hamlet. According to Bruichladdich Distillery, who previously used this phrase in their marketing, 'Clachan a choin', translates to the 'dog's bollocks'. In reality, Clachan in this use means 'stones' – it is unknown whether the Gaelic people ever referred to their pet's genitals.

that I live in a small community in the Lowlands; "Just 2,000 people live in my village." This does not impress in quite the manner I had hoped - in the Outer Hebrides, 2,000 people is a major centre of population.

"When Bill [Dobbie] and I stood outside Borrodale House and looked across the Sound of Raasay with [the hill] Glàmaig to our left, the Red Cuillins in front and the Black Cuillins in the distance, it was not hard to make the decision to build our distillery here," Alasdair tells me standing on the exact spot he stood in 2014. Alasdair had spent a number of years building a whisky brand from a long-lost family company, and when realising that to lay down sufficient stock for growth was to be a financial commitment akin to building a distillery, he changed his tack and began looking for a partner. A chance meeting with Bill, who had already acquired Borrodale House and the decision became an easy one.

"It's funny looking back on the building process as the hurdles of island life were just problems to solve. We knew everything would take time, careful planning and clever design. The hardest part of the build was the visitor centre and accommodation. We knew we had to make the distillery a destination – the distillery build was a much simpler task as we could design the building to fit all of the brewing and distilling apparatus. What was much harder was to ensure that when people visited, we had enough space and reason for coming."

Alasdair had a vision for the spirit before any drawings were made. "I wanted a big fruity distillate; less apple, pears and bananas and more dark fruits, black cherries and blackberries, and lots of body. I knew that the spirit had to stand out from the crowd. The whisky had to show well at a young age but also mature well." Alasdair also had no regional 'style', perceived or otherwise, to dictate what his whisky should taste like. Like many other newly-built distilleries featured in this book, there are no records of any local whisky or its production, taste and style that could in any way guide the planning of the distillate. "We knew we wanted a 'Hebridean' style whisky, but in truth, that did not hem us in any way. There are so few Hebridean whiskies that with Jura making a non-peated whisky, Talisker making a peated one, and Tobermory making both; we decided that to give us the greatest choice in the future to determine our style, we would make two styles, peated and un-peated and use three different types of wood[1] for each – this gives us six different styles for future bottlings."

I remark that these casks are not cheap and that there are less expensive options such as ex-Bourbon and STR.[2] "True, but we were intent on ensuring our style was different. We are not tied to these three wood types." Alasdair explains that he held

1 - Chinkapin oak (a specific species of oak from North America), ex-Bordeaux red wine casks and ex-Rye whiskey barrels.

2 - Used ex-wine casks that are Shaved, Toasted and Re-charred.

onto some used hogsheads from his blending days and filled these with Raasay spirit. "These have turned out to be fantastic whiskies, but don't tell William [Dobbie, Raasay's Managing Director] as these casks cost very little, and he'll question all the costly wood we have." I nod in agreement.

A brisk five-minute walk heading east from the distillery brings us to two custom-built warehouses with an area for a third to be erected shortly. William joins us, and Alasdair opens a cask with a bung extractor. The casks are made of a Colombian oak called Quercus Humboldtii[1] and are classed as 'virgin'.[2] Typically, you would expect the oak to be totally dominant. Due to the nature of this oak species, the tannins and vanillas imparted are very different from what we normally expect from American oak.[3] This species of oak is a first for me, and I am surprised by the distinct lack of tannin, vanilla and general woodiness that can often be detected in virgin casks. Notes of crème brûlée, cola-flavoured sweets, Bakewell tart and a sweet minerality all pop up. The whisky is still young but shows remarkable promise and maturity for its age. Alasdair then opens an old hogshead, one of his leftover casks from his blending days. The whisky is full of ripe fruit, bread & butter pudding and mild spices. Everyone agrees that the distillery character is shining through from this cask. "And these casks cost so little." I chime in, immediately remembering my promise not to mention this fact in front of William. "You weren't supposed to say that in front of William," Alasdair says, laughing at me. No, I wasn't, but good whisky makes me say a lot of things.

Raasay had no established 'whisky' tourism that newly built distilleries on either the Isle of Islay or in Speyside could tap into. Whilst Skye could boast a million or more visitors a year, the small island of Raasay was attracting a tiny proportion of those. "We're not sure of the exact numbers visiting Raasay before we were open, but we received over 12,000 visitors to the distillery last year, and our accommodation is filled about 97% of the time," Alasdair explains. The distillery's guest house has five rooms and is fully catered for by a restaurant, a resident's lounge (with an honesty bar), an additional bar open to all visitors, a shop, and a tasting room. "We believe that people are looking for experiences in life more than just products. With this in mind, we want Isle of Raasay to be an experience from getting the 25-minute ferry from Sconser on Skye to staying in our ensuite rooms in the distillery, dining in our restaurant or bar, visiting the maturation warehouses, seeing the whisky and gin being bottled and exploring the island. Much of the building has been designed to allow the view back onto Skye."

Frankly, a view it would take a lifetime to tire of.

---

1 - Named after Alexander von Humboldt a Prussian explorer who discovered the trees in the late 1700s.

2 - A virgin cask is one that has not held anything prior to being filled with spirit, beer or wine.

3 - American oaks come from the family known as Quercus Alba or 'White oak'.

The weather today has treated us to cloud ringlets above the hills on Skye. This is followed by rain so heavy that the Sound of Raasay (the strait between Raasay and Skye) has disappeared from view. Just a short while later, glorious sunshine breaks through, interspersed with clouds, as if the sun is being switched on and off. Every weather pattern offers a new view, and you can count the hours by watching the ferry head out and return. But counting time should definitely be avoided on this little island. Instead, I sit in the lounge with a dram of Raasay whisky and just admire the view.

It is simply staggering what Alasdair and Bill have achieved. I cannot help but admire the fact that their efforts have created a destination. It is not an overstatement that the Isle of Raasay and Torabhaig Distilleries and their visitor experiences have put each of their locations on the map. 'You are so lucky to live here', I overhear a tourist say to one of the employees. But that statement should be reversed; 'we', the visiting public, are so lucky that these people live and work here, providing us the amenities for the location. We are the lucky ones.

As we walk to Raasay House Hotel after an excellent dinner in the distillery restaurant, the lights of the distillery fade, and the dark of the night sky begins to sparkle with celestial bodies. It strikes me that whilst big cities and ancient towns can offer more relatable history, the natural state of Raasay's surroundings, the tangible ground, fauna and air feel like a walk amongst our ancestors. The fact that they would have walked under these very stars, gazing up in wonder as I am, adds to the moment. This part of the world regularly gets the aurora borealis and is internationally known for having 'dark skies', allowing phenomenal night vistas. As I retire to my beautifully presented bedroom for the evening, I am quite sure that no one's ancestors ever had a day to match mine – and none will have slept in such a grand room. But then, no one, even in recent history, could ever imagine how much the island would progress.

Raasay House, which is just a few minutes walk from the distillery, was originally home to the Macleods of Raasay, and whilst the original house burnt to the ground in 1746, it was quickly rebuilt. Tragically, the hotel burned down again in a devastating fire in 2009, just weeks before a mult-million pouned refurbishment was completed. Only the library remained untouched.[1] The great essayist Samuel Johnson stayed there in 1773:

"...such a seat of hospitality amidst the winds and the waves, fills the imagination with a delightful contrariety of images. Without is the rough ocean and the rocky land, the beating billows and the howling storm, within is plenty and elegance, beauty and gaiety, the song and the dance."

The gaiety, song and dance were not on display for my stay, but as I drew the curtains, I could not hear a thing; not a bird, or wind, sea, road, people – nothing. It was

---

1 - I made sure all of my electrical equipment is switched off before retiring.

not an eery quiet – it was a peace that is so rare in today's rapid world. I wondered what Johnson would have made of Raasay Distillery had he been alive today:

"Were this an inner-city project, it would stand proud against those vain, high, wide, architectural, aesthetical and fashionable designs that sprawl our streets. People would bypass grander buildings, scorn more expensive projects and instead seek that place that reeks of its location, embodies passion and fills each and every visitor with a lifelong affair for its product."

I'm sure Johnston would have put it better. Or maybe he would have preferred the bleak stylings of modern hotels? Who knows.

Alas, my time on Raasay and Skye, at least for this trip, is over, and once off the ferry, I head back along the A87 towards the Skye bridge. Once again, the teal of the surrounding waters around Skye is impossible to miss, and before long, I am heading over the Loch Long Bridge. I drive quite slowly, spending more time than I should, looking at Eilean Donan Castle, possibly Scotland's second most photographed castle after Edinburgh. The road is not busy, and after the castle passes from view, it continues for several miles along Loch Duich.

As I make my way back, past sporadic reminders of civilisation amongst Scotland's terrain, I am reminded of Alasdair telling me that Raasay has no police officers. There is no crime on the island, so there is nothing to 'police'. On one occasion, a couple of rogues in a van attempted a spate of thefts and were no doubt feeling they were free birds as their ferry pulled into Sconser. However, there are police on Skye, who, having been alerted, had no difficulty arresting the two and returning all of the stolen goods. It is a 'happy ending' little anecdote, but it reminds me that the more remote and rural parts of Scotland are communities of like-minded people. My first time in Dufftown, I stayed at a local bed and breakfast. When I asked for a key to the house and room, I received a quizzical look from the host. "We have no need for keys in Dufftown." She replied. That was over 25 years ago, and things have changed, but not too drastically. Small communities still look out for each other and crimes are thankfully few and far between.

CHAPTER 4

THE PENINSULAS

"[Scotland] is one of the most hauntingly beautiful places in the world; the history is fascinating, the men are handsome, and the whisky is delicious."
J K Rowling

I barely have time to drop off my bottles before packing to head west again. I am thrilled, though, for several reasons. Firstly, I will see the A82 in better weather than when I headed to Skye, and secondly, Nc'nean and Ardnamurchan have been high on my list of distilleries to visit for several years. Better weather means easier driving conditions, and I'm soon passing a placid and inviting-looking Loch Lomond. Replacing the waves and rain of my last passing are water skiers and sailors. The Loch Lomond cruise boat sails past me, and a joyful scene of activity on the water passes me by.

Less concerned with the treacherous road, I can enjoy the drive and take in the local village names. One makes me chuckle; 'Stuckindroin'. I wonder if the village was originally called 'Droin', and until the A82 road was built, the locals really were Stuckindroin? Soon, I am into the true Highlands and join the queue of tourists marvelling at the sites. As I approach Glencoe, it strikes me how a place associated with a tragic event, even centuries old, can sometimes never shake that attachment. If I were to name Chernobyl, Hillsborough, Pompeii, or Gettysburg, most would immediately associate the place with a tragedy. For Scotland, there is Dunblane, Lockerbie and, of course, Glencoe. This might have little resonance to anyone, or possibly few, outside of Scotland, but Glencoe, despite being one of the most beautiful places in the country, is synonymous with a massacre.

The Massacre of Glencoe has lived on in the consciousness of Scots and the wider world since its occurrence in 1692. The MacDonalds of Glencoe paid a heavy price for not pledging allegiance to William III and Mary II. Around 120 Clansmen from the Campbell clan, as part of the Earl of Argyll's regiment, unexpectedly, for the MacDonalds at least, tore through the area, killing anyone they came across. Some 38 people lost their lives, and Glencoe has lived with a cloud over it ever since.

Just beyond the town of Glencoe is the Inchree-Corran ferry. This is a roll-on, roll-off ten-minute ferry that reduces the journey time to the Morven Peninsula by around 2 hours. I barely had enough time to get out of my car (I was the only one that did) to take a photo of the Lighthouse before we docked at Corran. The road south along Loch Melfort is quite an epic journey with rising, rugged hills to my right and the calm, blue waters to my left. As I turn a corner, and as if on cue, a red stag stands proudly on a boulder as if posing for a 'Monarch of the Glen' style painting. It watches me pass and then leaps off into the distance – hopefully a sight afforded to all tourists to Morven.

The road then heads into the centre of the peninsula, and vast plains, woodland and sheep grazing fields replace the coastal beaches and blue waters. I had already noticed that the single-lane road was disconcertingly marked by the tell-tale signs of skidding cars forced into a sudden stop. Several dual, black treads are here and there, and at first, I assume these are people stopping to look at wildlife or photograph one of the many stunning views. When a sheep, hitherto unseen, suddenly decides that it prefers the look of the grass on the other side of the road, I realise that these skid marks are evidence of drivers avoiding the ingredients of Haggis from being splattered over their bumpers. I contribute to the road artwork with my fine braking display and am glad that the only skid marks are from my tyres.

When arriving at the tiny village of Lochaline,[1] my hotel is almost the last building on the road. My room looks out towards the Isle of Mull and Ardtonish Castle - the old seat of the Lord of the Isles, now a ruin. Just about visible in the distance is Duart Castle, where the Clan MacLean moved in the 15th century. I am told that porpoises, otters, red squirrels, sea eagles and golden eagles abound, but alas, other than the solitary red stag and some skid-inducing sheep, I will have to make do with a cormorant or two diving in the distance. I'm not complaining; this view and the tranquillity are more than sufficient.

The hotel owners are still up, so a dinner can be prepared and as there is nowhere else to eat for miles (and miles) I am lucky with my timing. Nursing a very good local beer I sit out at the head of the loch and soak in the view. The midges, and I'll discuss these later, are not yet about in numbers and the placid waters let my mind wander as I sip the beer. I enjoy the company of people too much to allow the tranquillity and view of places like this tempt me from where I live. I've already mentioned how visitors often fall in love with places they fleetingly visit. Frankly it's not hard to understand as the sun reflects off the loch and the castle ruins in the distance. But I'm not falling for it – tomorrow is Nc'nean and I am excited to visit and meet with Annabel Thomas.

---

1 - Pronounced 'Lock-alan'.

The view from the Lochaline Hotel

The next morning I retrace my route to the eastern part of the peninsula. I pass a sign stating 'Clacna Criche 250m', so with a few minutes to kill, I park and walk up to a hole in a wall of volcanic rock protruding from the banking hill. Local legend has it that anyone passing through this hole without touching its sides would have their wish granted. I'm not superstitious, but I see no harm in the tradition. My first thought is to wish for the agility I had in my youth to climb through the blasted hole, but eventually, I manoeuvre my ageing carcass through. As it is quite a large hole, I successfully managed not to touch the sides. If all of those horror movies have taught me one thing, it is that any wish for something selfish or personal will result in some horrific or debilitating side effect. I keep my wish simple.

The single-track road continues, and due to the scarcity of anything suggesting 'industry' (or even human presence), I pull over more than once to ensure I am heading in the right direction.[1] Eventually, a reassuring sign directs me up a dirt road to Nc'nean Distillery. The sign also states 'No Loads Over 1.5 tonnes' – there is no way this distillery build was without complication. Although not situated on an island, the area has a remoteness that adds to its charms. The entire peninsula is home to around 350 people, and whilst that may sound a lot more than, say, the Isle of Raasay, in reality, due to the space between homes, it feels considerably less accessible. A few hundred yards up the hill, a reassuring cask has been placed and signed to keep any intrepid traveller continuing.

---

1 - Without a phone signal or any paper maps, this is just me looking one way down the road and then the other, realising as there is only one road, I have a good chance I am heading in the right direction.

Clacna Criche - looks to me like a fist with a thumbs up

Roads? Hardly

"Please Drive on the Left"

A quick search demonstrates that we Brits are odd regarding which side of the road to drive on. Parts of the world, once part of our colonial past, have remained equally as stubborn. In Europe certainly, we are pretty much on our own regarding driving on the 'wrong' side of the road' (to which a Brit might reply, 'No, we drive on the right side of the road' with the response from almost every other nation: 'No, WE drive on the RIGHT side of the road').

Left being right, or right being right, aside, we are not likely to change soon so best to pay attention and keep to the right side, which, of course, is on the left. In my experience, continental drivers and those renting cars tend to be more considerate, often not in a rush, and wary of others. Instead, those who should know better can frequently be the tearing-weaving-maniacs that scare everyone else. That said, and I tread lightly here as it is a delicate, divisive subject, one mode of transport has grown to such epidemic proportions in recent years as to warrant a little attention.

I speak, of course, of the motorhome: the diesel chugging, maximum 50mph, lane hogging, car park choking, home from home on wheels. I remember, and it is not that long ago when seeing a motorhome anywhere in the UK was quite a rare sight. There are now a quarter of a million of them registered,[1] and it feels, at times, that all of them are in front of me. While on my travels for this book, I had several near misses, and every single one involved a motorhome. Notice I am not including campervans in the same category, being much smaller and more manoeuvrable, but there is some blame for these, too.

The idea is great. Isn't it? You can drive around Scotland, park up, sleep, cook for yourself, stop at every attraction, get every angle of nature and the surroundings or if you get a good vibe somewhere, just stop and enjoy it. Indeed, it is hard to argue with that. But here is the rub: our country roads were barely designed with cars, never mind motorhomes, in mind. The numbers now clogging the scenic and rural parts of the country are a hazard to the locals, businesses, emergency services, the roads themselves and other road users. 'Ah, but I am a careful driver!' I hear you cry. That may be the case, but you are still enjoying wide open roads with a trail of traffic behind you. You are also visiting tourist areas, and other than using the local water, rubbish, and supermarkets,

---

1 - And those numbers swell during the tourist season.

little is often contributed to the local community. No hotel or guest house is benefiting. Quite often, the only businesses that receive these tourists are the oil companies filling their guzzlers and supermarkets – neither of which is a great help to the local community.

This is becoming a significant problem for those living in the western Highlands and Hebridean islands. Accidents and blockages can cause food and supply trucks to not get through, problems on ferries, and chaos for emergency services. This little rant will not stop those whose dreams involve tootling around nature's best bits in a mobile home, but just maybe, if you don't need to, you could stay in one of Scotland's many small hotels. You may find that the hotel, guest house or B&B opens up a whole new world and insight into the area.

Whichever mode you use to self-propel around Scotland, and certainly if an engine is involved, there are a few more points for consideration. Firstly, the Traffic Police are a finely-honed group of efficacious individuals devoid of humour and starved of generosity. One of their most preferred pastimes is to sit as close to a change in road speed as possible and 'nab' anyone who has dared to begin accelerating in anticipation. Where the Traffic Officers seem to have the most fun[1] is where speed signs are non-existent, roads are clear, and you could only hit something if it fell out of the sky. Recently, the 20mph zones that can suddenly and without much (if any) warning pop up on a 60mph road have added an extra string to the Police's bow - fore-warned and all that.

Secondly, if the slamming on of breaks due to an unexpected 20mph zone, an idiot overtaking on a bend, or a Motorhome creeping into your lane isn't bad enough, the wildlife seems to have a death wish. Too numerous to count were the badgers (much larger than you think), sheep and deer, all in some state of post-collision, lying either in the road or at the side. Badgers, foxes and hares will cause some bumper damage, but sheep and deer are large enough to cause a major collision. Often, you have little time to react, but should the road be busy, remember to pull to the left – if not from these shores, you will tend to swerve to the right, which could mean oncoming traffic. Not that I am speaking from experience or anything...[2]

A word also on what must be the stupidest animal on the planet: the pheasant. Somehow, this creature has evolved to know the exact moment to either step out in front of a car or change its direction whilst crossing. Pheasants possess a sixth sense for when a driver will swerve to avoid collision and thus ensure it plucks certain death from the jaws of survival. It is possible that pheasants have evolved to understand their intended demise is

---

1 - And by fun, I mean the extraction of hard-earned money from already overly-taxed drivers.

2 - I am. I once had a collision in Italy due to my tendency to swerve to the left and the poor sod I hit, whose tendency was to swerve to the right. I remember receiving a letter from Hertz Rental Car stating that they would ban me renting from them again. I have rented from them since – perhaps they realised that genuine accidents are, unfortunately, part and parcel of rental cars.

being chased by dogs and then shot, in mid-flight, by a group wearing woolly socks, tweed trousers and flat caps. Maybe being hit by a car bumper is their way of a premature death on their own terms?

Finally, it is worth remembering that the drink-driving laws in Scotland are some of the strictest in the world. Most, if not all, distilleries will now offer 'driver drams' – a small taster bottle of whatever whisky is available on tours. Some tours will even ask drivers to identify themselves so as to prevent whisky from being needlessly poured for them. This is a welcome move, and I am quite sure that in the future, all festivals and distilleries will make it easier for drivers to visit and safely enjoy their trips.

I have been spoiled by my views at many distilleries, and Nc'nean is no different. Turning left before the warehouses and rounding a gravel road bend, the hill drops away as the Sound of Mull comes into view. Tobermory is almost directly opposite and a cruise ship is loitering. The Oban-Mull ferry, which looks like a child's toy in comparison, can be seen plodding on its journey back to the mainland. Watching all of this, I wonder if, by the end of the writing of my tour, I will be able to pick a favourite view – no doubt it will be as challenging as picking a favourite whisky.

Quinten, my tour guide, is there to greet me and three others joining the morning tour, and with a warm drink of our choice poured, he sets off on his story. My touring companions are a couple from Orkney and a tourist from Amsterdam. They are perfect touring companions, not novices nor nerdy, and Quinten finds just the right level of information to delve through all things Nc'nean. Whilst the sustainability and 'green' credentials are explained and highlighted, they do not come before the most crucial aspect – the whisky. And, as if to bribe us into unwavering, undying loyalty, a delicious piece of cake is offered before we delve into the whisky being poured.

Just after my tour and right before lunch, Annabel Thomas arrives at the distillery She looks remarkably fresh having taken the sleeper train from London before then driving for much of the morning. Annabel is a charming, chatty, and informative afternoon companion. I learn that we are both not native Scots and have a strong Welsh element to our lives ('Thomas' being one of the most common Welsh surnames). We both also share a desire to reduce any stuffiness within the industry – either perceived from the outside or existing within.

Nc'nean Distillery

www.ncnean.com
Open by appointment

"I have to admit, I didn't often drink whisky before the idea of Nc'nean Distillery came to me." Annabel Thomas, Nc'nean's founder, admits to me. "My husband would occasionally take a dram, but I often found the strength of the alcohol too much at times."

Annabel and I are sat on a wooden bench in the courtyard of the distillery she built on her family's small estate. The sun is shining down on the Sound of Mull, onto the two of us and also sparkling through a couple of drams sitting invitingly on the table. We each have to slightly squint in the bright sunlight, but knowing the inclement weather we have had for about six months, there are no complaints.

Having taken a sabbatical from her busy London job, Annabel found her taste and love for whisky and a germ of an idea turned into a serious project. Investors were eventually found, and nearly £8 million later, work began in 2016 on the distillery. "My mission was very simple – create something truly sustainable and innovative within the Scotch whisky industry, with the aim of bringing the drink to the wider audience," Annabel continues. "We also wanted this to be as positive as possible for anyone working for us."

The easy part was the location; the land & buildings were owned, ready and willing to be utilised. "We had two key challenges: one was the remoteness of the site – which brought its own difficulties getting materials in, accommodating (and feeding) the build team; and lack of anything or anyone nearby to address any ongoing problems. The second challenge was more specific to some of our sustainability initiatives, which added complexity to an already difficult build."

I take this to be a wonderful example of understatement: "Getting our large biomass boiler and related crane along the single-track road, trying to get our cooling pond water, and renovating and installing complex machinery into an old building instead of a new one were just some of the challenges we had to overcome." Annabel tells me, were just some of the difficulties that had to be overcome.

The biomass boiler, which is fuelled by sustainable wood from the estate, arrived at the Corran Ferry in one solid, massive mass of machinery rather than three manageable pieces. The ferry was incapable of transporting it, so it was returned, dismantled, transported back and then rebuilt at the distillery.

I asked Annabel about the packaging and marketing of Nc'nean, which is very much their own, and whether that was a conscious effort to stand out. "Weirdly, to begin with, not at all," Annabel reasons. "Because I wasn't 'part' of the industry, I just proceeded in a way that I thought was right, and that turned out to be different. I think the more immersed in the industry I become, the harder it is to remain different."

Even the name of the distillery is a departure from the normal. With the local area named 'Drimmin' (far too close to Drymen near Loch Lomond), it was eventually decided that an abbreviation of Neachneohain, a fairy queen from Scottish folklore (also known as Nicnevin) was the favourite. Thought to mean 'daughter of the divine' this mythical goddess was deemed suitable considering the strategy and folks behind the distillery.

Having now released several expressions, I wondered how it has been for Annabel to watch her spirit mature and presenting it to new markets. "It's been so cool," Annabel beams. "I think it's such a long journey for anyone who starts a distillery. It was seven years from leaving my previous job to the launch of the first whisky and so to finally have a product in a bottle was amazing. The reaction has been better than I could ever have imagined. We've won lots of awards and had tonnes of support from within the industry but also from those people I started out wanting to attract – the people who thought whisky wasn't for them."

Everything about Nc'nean tells you that this company is different. For most consumers, it will be the unusual flowery packaging and lack of any usual 'whisky' talk on the labels that makes the company stand out. But for those that can venture out to the Morvern Peninsula, it will be the location, view, boutique distillery, and, most importantly, the people and product that will imprint that specialness.

Annabel has taken on sustainability within the whisky industry and challenges points I felt were safe ground. For instance, in 2011, the Scotch Whisky Act was changed to make it mandatory for all single malt Scotch whisky to be bottled within Scotland. I suggested this was a great move and wished they had gone the whole hog to include all Scotch whisky – as this safeguarded jobs and ensured a certain level of quality, etc. Annabel, however, challenges it on the grounds of carbon footprint. Much of the glass, the bulk or weight of whisky exports, is imported, meaning the glass has travelled a long way to get to the bottling lines before being sent back to the markets. It would make more environmental sense to send the bulk products to the markets for bottling. This I had not considered. I guess it is a question of whether securing local jobs is as important as carbon footprint. It is far too long and complicated a debate for this little book.

Annabel guides me through the warehouses and bottling hall which are situated a short walk above the distillery. The entire site has a 'farm distillery' feel to it – not showy or pretentious. Funds have been spent carefully and with full understanding that the remoteness of the distillery, at least for now, is the major factor in smaller visitor numbers than other distilleries can boast.

We end the tour trying several single-cask selections of Nc'nean bottled for England, Germany, a famous chef and, well, I forget some of the other details. Time here, just like on Raasay and other remote parts of Scotland, doesn't seem to matter. I don't check my phone or watch as would be my usual habit. Instead, I bask in the sun, take in the view and soak in the tranquil atmosphere of this truly craft distillery. I don't even hesitate at the word 'craft' – a term that has become slightly too ubiquitous and has stretched thin its definition at times.

Drams of Nc'nean with Mull in the distance

My time with Annabel and Nc'nean Distillery is up, and as the distillery is very much at the end of the road that hugs the south-eastern coast, I head back towards Lochaline and the centre of the peninsula. I pass a car and continue the tradition, which is prevalent in much of the remotest parts of Scotland, to wave to the oncoming driver – a sort of 'thanks' for a harmonious passing. This harmony is nearly broken when a tourist in a rental car, heading in my direction, pulls over to the right into a layby, and at the exact moment, a car in front of me pulls over to their left with a near head-on collision. The hand waving is replaced with fist shaking. Occasionally, trying to do the courteous thing can lead to disgruntlement.

My first junction would give me the choice of heading back to the Corran Ferry or the road I take that will head towards my destination of Strontian. Had I been in any way mourning the loss of my spectacular view from the Lochaline Hotel, I needn't have worried. Strontian Hotel sits at the head of Loch Sunart and is every bit as stunning. The sun is beating down now, and having checked in, I order a beer and revel in the majesty of the view. A couple sit next to me and we quickly realise that not only do we live in neighbouring villages, but originally, and quite recognisable by their accent, have spent much of their life in Hertfordshire. It has struck me, thus far on my trip, that so many of the voices have been of a more Southerly accent. The gentrification that so horrified Sir Ian Noble is quite alive and not going to stop any time soon.

The view over Loch Sunart

Strontian is such an odd name, but it wasn't until one of my companions on the Nc'nean tour mentioned its relation to the element Strontium that the penny drops. Few small villages can lay such a worldwide claim to fame as Strontian can, being the home, or discovery place, of Strontium by two scientists in 1790. The name of the village is Gaelic for 'nose of the fairy hill' which doesn't sound very 'tough Highlander' to me, but I'm sure the rugged, quarrelling clans had a poetic side to their nature. That blue paint wasn't only used for smearing across faces you know.

The next morning is another glorious day, and although there is beaming sunshine, the cold wind keeps skin exposure to a minimum. The road to Ardnamurchan is even more eventful than the one to Nc'nean and I have two realisations: firstly, anyone having had a good night of liquid refreshment and a solid Scottish breakfast would at this point be regretting their choices. Secondly, just how difficult the locations of these distilleries must have made their building and continual operations. At one point on the road, a bridge, just 3.5 metres wide, is the dictating factor in how large Ardnamurchan's mash tun could be – this, I learn later, had a knock-on effect on how much whisky they could make.

Some of the pot-bellied humps have me imagining trucks stranded with wheels dangling either side - and the tell-tale signs of road scraping must fill delivery drivers with dread. This is a genuinely barren part of the world. Perhaps as few as 800 people live on the five peninsulas: Moidart, Ardgour, Sunart, Ardnamurchan and Morvern. Like Skye, tourists often outnumber the local inhabitants.

Whilst I am here to spend the day with two friends, Graeme Mackay and Connal Mackenzie, I am unexpectedly greeted by Jenny Karlsson who I haven't seen for a number of years. Jenny, Ardnamurchan's Marketing Communications Manager, is Swedish but has lived in the UK for so long that she now pronounces more words in an English, Irish and Scottish slant than anything resembling a Swede speaking English. Naturally we try and remember the last time we saw each other but cannot recall. Part of the beauty of working with a globally respected and exported product is that you never know when you will see an old friend or colleague at one of the many functions, festivals, and tastings - or distilleries.

About a third of the way into painting this sign, the idea of calling the whisky AD was formed.

Ardnamurchan Distillery

www.ardnamurchandistillery.com
Open to the public

To trace the lineage of Ardnamurchan Distillery, you need to understand how a connection to a part of the whisky industry's history can have a knock-on effect generations later. In 1880, Archibald Walker & Co. gained ownership of the Adelphi Distillery in Glasgow to add to their existing distilleries in Liverpool and Limerick (possibly the first time a company had owned a distillery in England, Ireland & Scotland). The newly owned distillery ran afoul of the general downturn in Scotch whisky in the late 1890s and was sold in 1903 to the Distillers Company Ltd. In 1932, the very last spirit was produced at the Adelphi Distillery.

Aerial view courtesy of Ardnamurchan

Fast-forward to 1993 our story truly begins. Jamie Walker, the great-grandson of Archibald Walker, began bottling whisky under the name Adelphi Distillery Co. The newly formed company set out to uncover outstanding casks of whisky, and Adelphi started to gain an excellent reputation amongst the growing malt whisky aficionados. This reputation led to a chance meeting for Jamie with Keith Falconer, an Asset Manager and his neighbour in Argyll, Donald Houston. What began as a friendly enquiry about buying a cask turned into the sale of the Adelphi Distillery Co.

As Keith and Donald had no intention of running a bottling business, they hired Alex Bruce, a wine merchant in Edinburgh who had previous experience working with the Scotch whisky brand J&B. Alex's charisma and work ethic took Adelphi to new heights, and the company quickly became one of, if not the most, respected independent bottlers of Scotch whisky. The success of the single malt sector in the early part of the 21st century resulted in a slowing of supply. This led to many independent bottlers looking for a business model that ensured greater control over quality and growth. For Alex and his partners, that meant only one thing – their own distillery.

The team were determined to build a distillery that would operate within a circular economy built on Donald's farm on the Ardnamurchan peninsula. Several sites were discussed before deciding that a boggy field in the hamlet of Glenbeg was the perfect location. "We had three main reasons for building our own distillery," Alex tells me. "Primarily, we wanted to make our own whisky. We wanted to create something not only for the growing consumer base around the world but also as a long-term employer in a remote area of Scotland that was fast losing its population and the infrastructure to maintain those remaining. Behind these two fundamental reasons, we were witnessing first-hand the decline in the supply of mature third-party malts for our Adelphi bottlings. We were keen to ringfence our own supply to the company for the future along with potential bulk trading for other distiller's malts." Site work began in 2012, and the distillery began operations in the summer of 2014. What possibly separates Ardnamurchan from many of its peers is the team's openness to cooperation and collaboration. Alex, having spent over a decade building the Adelphi brand around the world, decided to view independent bottlers as a positive for the industry and has actively encouraged their participation.

Similarly, the distillery, its design and staffing have been implemented with the peninsula and the locals in mind. There is currently no restaurant or even a café that might have impacted any nearby businesses. The staff are all as local as possible, with opportunities for training and advancement. Whilst it was not practical to move the bottling facility from the existing site in Fife, all of the casks are matured on-site and the distillery has a permanent team of 12. "The distillery was designed to benefit from and give back to its local surroundings in what is a very remote part of the Scottish west coast," Connal Mackenzie, Ardnamurchan's Sales Director, tells me. "Wood chip is our local fuel source, delivered by tractor and trailer from just two miles away and harvested from woodland on the peninsula that is being replanted as it is felled. We are also very fortunate to have a large hydroelectric generator on the river that supplies our cooling water, and have recently added 138 solar panels to one of our warehouses. Making the most of what we have around us is a fundamental part of our pragmatic approach to long-term sustainability."

Again, thanks to the company's philosophy of 'flavour first', decisions were made to ensure that Ardnamurchan spirit would not blend into the background against other malt whiskies. The washbacks were made in both stainless steel and Douglas fir (the original ones installed were oak but struggled to keep shape in the Scottish climate), and the condensers were placed outside the building, promoting a quicker-than-normal cooling period and resulting in a heavier spirit. A mix of peated and unpeated and, at times, heavily peated barley is used to give Connal and his team the greatest variety of flavours to choose from and help keep customers interested in the offerings from the distillery.

As great as the product is (and amongst whisky aficionados, Ardnamurchan is one of the most highly regarded new wave distilleries), the team behind the product are equally well respected. As I have made my way through the whisky world, I have asked everyone which Scotch distillery they follow most eagerly. By far, the greatest response has been Ardnamurchan, and most of those asked have been keen to stress that they look forward to meeting up with the Ardnamurchan team just as much as they look forward to the new releases.

It is a worthy reminder that, at the end of the day, whisky is just a drink. It is a stellar, world-conquering enigma of a drink, but without fine humans behind it, singing its praises and making the environment it dwells in a harmonious, welcoming, and inclusive place, it is just a drink. From the founders Keith and Donald to Alex Bruce, Connal Mackenzie, and the entire team, Ardnamurchan is more of a welcoming cousin or old friend than just a distillery.

Graeme, Ardnamurchan's Sales Executive, greets me; we first met when he was working at The Good Spirits Company in Glasgow.[1] Graeme shows me the new staff accommodation – built specifically for flying visits by the sales team. "This," he claims "is life-changing". One can only assume the previous arrangements were rudimentary. Connal arrives with much-needed supplies (living in these remote parts means stocking up as often and whenever possible) and shows me around the distillery. Despite its location, the distillery is getting well over 8,000 visitors a year, and this number is growing year on year. So much so that I am devastated to learn that the 'Distillery Exclusive Bottling' is currently sold out; great for the distillery but not for me. I guess I'll have to return soon - every cloud has a silver lining...

I get the full tour as this is my first visit – which sadly coincides with a broken boiler and a silent distillery. If general supplies are hard to come by on a remote peninsula, specialist boiler parts are an age to arrive, and the distillery has been dormant for over a week. Connal jokes that the washbacks, filled with the mashes prior to the enforced shutdown, may now be getting close to breaking fermentation records, although he ponders if good friends the Thompson Brothers up at Dornoch Distillery have that record sewn up.

---

1 - A fantastic independent Whisky and Spirits specialist shop situated on Bath Street in the city centre.

The downtime for the distillery allows the team a chance to provide much of the machinery with either a service or a good clean. As we approach the mash tun, we can see signs of activity through the open hatch; the lights are on, a water hose is draped over the side, and a tuneful whistling from within accompanies the sound of rushing water from the hose. Clearly, someone is inside the mash tun, hosing it down. Without making a sound, the hose on the outside is grabbed and bent so as to prevent the water from coming out. There is audible disconcertment inside the washback on seeing the water dribble to a stop. True to every cartoon I have ever watched, the first instinct is to look down the hose and see if there is a blockage. At this point, the grip on the hose outside the mash tun is loosened, and a fresh jet of cold water sprays the unsuspecting recipient, who utters grunts of surprise and bewilderment. Having worked at a distillery, I know that it is this type of harmless hijinks and camaraderie that makes the days fly by, even in such a remote area.[1]

Connal, Graeme and I head out to explore the peninsula. At times the two are a comedy double act. By pure coincidence they went to the same school near Inverness and also worked their way through the drinks industry via sojourns in the Antipodes. It is hard not to enjoy their company; both love their work and enjoy a good laugh. Dry humour is especially on the cards, and references from music, books, movies, TV, or history often garner continued laughs as they are thought out and expanded.

'Maclean's Nose' - no matter how hard I squint, I can't see a nose

1 - I must add that I had no part in this other than to laugh. I'm sure I can't remember who bent the hose...

Our first stop is a place called Maclean's Nose. The Ardnamurchan peninsula is a result of volcanic activity, and Maclean's Nose was formed as the molten rock made its way from the highest point on land to the sea. Connal and his team had recently released a premium and award-winning blend of the same name – partly due to the proximity of the point of interest but in part as a bit of fun with a certain Charles MacLean, who has been Adelphi's honorary 'Chief Nose' for over two decades.[1] From there we head to the small but spectacular Mingary Castle. This standalone and recently restored mini stronghold is now a five-star restaurant, hotel and venue. Although out of my budget for this trip, I want to return one day as it will be the closest I could get to feeling like a Lord of the Isles.[2] We then head to the Ardnamurchan Lighthouse, the most westerly point on the Scottish mainland. From this vantage point, and the weather is continuing to play nice, the isles of Muck, Coll, Eigg and Rum are all in view. Just about visible in the distance, is Skye. Beyond is the Atlantic and Canada – but we can't see that far.

On the drive back, there are few signs of human life, but one house we pass has a few red deer in the garden – I count six. Apparently, the owners found a pair in their garden one day and fed them, and they stayed, or at least continued to return. It's not until we pass the house and see the rear garden, which is home to well over forty deer, that I realise word of free food must have spread.

Back at the distillery, we have time for a quick jaunt through the warehouses to taste some work in progress. Ardnamurchan has had a fairly open policy towards cask sales and swaps, and many of the casks are marked with companies and names I recognise, and for any private owners reading this, you will be pleased to hear your whiskies are coming along nicely...[3] Connal pours me a sample from an ex-Bourbon barrel of unpeated whisky distilled in 2014. "This is some of my favourite distillate." He informs me. "It really shows off the quality of the spirit." It is indeed fantastic, but my pick is a cask of their peated whisky maturing in an ex-Pedro Ximenez.[4] This whisky is full-bodied with a funkiness that reminds me of some great Springbank whiskies. Connal approves of my comparison. I'll have to keep an eye out for that release.

"The blending team are all in-house," Connal informs me. "All are passionate about quality whisky and their time served in the industry. There are no white coats or AI interventions, just the constant search for flavour." Quite right, I agree. Blending multiple

---

1 - Charles MacLean is one of the world's leading authorities on Scotch whisky. He has written too many books to mention and nosed more whiskies than he can ever remember. He is also fabulously good company should you be lucky enough to meet him.

2 - For more information visit www.mingarycastletrust.co.uk and www.mingarycastle.co.uk

3 - Just in case anyone is worried, at no point are private casks ever opened without the explicit permission of the owner(s).

4 - A fortified raisin wine from Montilla, Spain.

distillates to create a consistent product is not an easy or light-hearted task, but, as with so many of the new wave of distilleries, there is a definite self-belief in being able to put out fantastic whisky.

A cheeky wee gift from Glenfarclas Distillery to mark the opening of Ardnamurchan Distillery.

Alas, my time on this majestic peninsula comes to an end and back along the Humpty-Dumpty road I drive, sad to be leaving such a beautiful part of the world. I arrive back at the Corran Ferry, and once onboard, a car pulls up next to me. Glancing over, all I can see is a large male driver and a dog sitting on the passenger seat. The man appears to be having a full-blown, and possibly heated, discussion with the dog. The dog is just staring straight ahead, never wavering from its gaze. I glance into the rear of the car, but it is empty. Perplexed, I put my passenger window down, and the driver, noticing, puts his down, too.

"Are you having an argument with your dog?" I ask.

"I might as well be." He replies, "She's the only bitch that listens to me."

At that point, a passenger sat completely hidden by the driver's profile, unleashed a fairly competitive left hook into his chin.I laughed, he laughed, the passenger sulked, and the dog continued staring into the distance, no doubt wondering what flavour of tinned dinner was to be served.

Build Your Own?

The giant elephant in the room when considering building your own distillery is money. You will need pockets so deep you can scratch your ankles without falling over. You'll also need a lot of patience, especially regarding planners, site surveys, SEPA (The Scottish Environment Protection Agency) and just about every Health & Safety body, executive, legislator and enforcer.

Still not put off? Well, you'll require a site which in turn will require adequate water and power. Both can be brought in-house with generators or boreholes; both are hugely expensive. But maybe you're a lucky so-and-so, and the site is not a problem. Well, in addition to the problems and costs of the site, you'll need to purchase the equipment, receptacles, mash tun, washback, stills, and receivers, which will set you back well over seven figures.

Once we get past the site and its legal requirements, installation and commission are costly and very time-consuming. You could be looking at a year's wait just for the stills and possibly two or three years of build and installation time. During this period, costs have escalated again, and your budget has been blown to Smithereens. But others have broken through these hurdles, so assuming I haven't dissuaded you thus far, let's continue.

You've secured the site, dealt with the planning committees, power providers, and water authorities, and even managed to get all of the kit fitted. You are now at the 'Ribbon Cutting' moment. The first spirit runs off your gleaming copper stills, filling your very first cask, and all of the trials and tribulations of the build are behind you. You now need somewhere to store these casks, which may be filling at over fifty a week. Perhaps you have allowed for your first year's production, and an on-site warehouse is racking up nicely. Excellent, except you now have a minimum of three years to wait until you legally have a product... and during that time, you'll likely be another seven-figure sum into staff wages, heating bills, cost of raw materials and, this is the one expense every distillery will take their time to convince you about; the cost of empty oak barrels. And during that time, the cost of building warehouses has risen exponentially, perhaps another seven-figure sum to ensure you have somewhere for the next three year's production?

And remember, you still don't have a whisky yet.

Still thinking about it? Well, good for you; many have got this far, proving what I have just described is not insurmountable. But herein lies another problem. Scotland is heaving with new distilleries. I have only visited 25 of the more than 40 built in this millennium, and more are coming. You might have found a site, had the funds, and convinced SEPA and everyone else to do their best to convince you otherwise that your distillery is viable. You may also have commissioned the stills and equipment, had it all installed and begun distilling. You may be at the point now where time has turned that spirit into whisky and are at the stage where you can finally bottle and promote your liquid. But in the swilling mass of available whisky in the market, you're only special for a short time. You're new and different, granted, but most whisky drinkers out there have never heard of your product and can almost certainly buy their tried and tested brand of whisky for a chunk of money less than you need to sell yours for.

It is worth also noting that Scotland has not been an isolated case for the explosion of new distilleries. Prior to 2007 there was not a single English whisky distillery. Now there are well over 30. Ireland could only boast three until the 21st century and can now boast a similar number to England. From Canada and across most of the continents to New Zealand there has been a scramble to build local distilleries (there are over 60 distilleries in Tasmania - granted many are just making spirit, but many make whisky). Whilst many of these are rapidly expanding the consumer base interested in whisky, they all contribute to a watering-down of Scotch's prominence in the sector. In other words, the cachet that came with being 'Scotch whisky' has lost some of its shine around the world as more and more 'other' whiskies become readily available. And, as already alluded to, they are not bad. Not bad at all.

Still considering it? Well, that's what makes you a pioneering spirit and worthy of inclusion in this modest little book. I could write an entire book on just one distillery's start-up, cataloguing the day-to-day trials and tribulations, hurdles and legal wrangles that slowed their progress and delayed their spirit from being filled into casks. Building even a micro-distillery is not for the faint-hearted or easily dissuaded. You need to be a tour de force; an obstinate and motivated 'doer'. Someone who can find a way to solve problems, source funds, wait and then wait some more before finally travelling the world to convince the buying public that your product is worthy of their hard-earned coins.

And at the end of the day, after all this headache, effort, expense, stress and perseverance, there is no guarantee that the finished product, your whisky, will be received well. You'd have to be slightly mad to even entertain the idea of starting a new distillery...

But don't let that stop you – we are all a little mad, aren't we?

CHAPTER 5

DOONHAMERS AND REIVERS

"There is a myth that Lowland whisky is the best region for those beginning their journey into appreciating Scotch whisky. That's akin to suggesting the first book someone reads is 'War & Peace'."

Like Glasgow, the south-west of Scotland was a region desperately bereft of any notable malt whisky production. Both areas could boast a large grain distillery, Strathclyde in Glasgow and Girvan on the coast in Ayrshire. Other than those great factories, there is not, nor has there been for a long time, much Scotch whisky worth seeking out. The county of Dumfries & Galloway, bordering England, could at least boast Bladnoch Distillery, having been recently taken over and revived. On the other hand, tasting a whisky from Ayrshire was only possible via a few independent bottlings of Girvan grain whisky or the equally rare bottlings of Ailsa Bay – a malt distillery housed within the Girvan complex and given very little promotion.

My route to Ayrshire is north-west on the A76 from my base in the Lowlands. Most travellers would likely be heading out on the M8 from Glasgow to the M77. The two motorways, as is often the case, offer the least inspiring route. My journey takes in sweeping glens, the River Nith and some spectacular views out towards Wanlockhead (once an area renowned for gold mining). I pass Drumlanrig Castle, Scotland's Pink Palace and Dumfries House, owned by King Charles III. Whilst the King owns around 91,000 acres in Scotland (and virtually all of the seabed), the Duke of Buccleuch,[1] whose ancestral home is Drumlanrig Castle, owns over 200,000 acres stretching across the country. It's not that surprising, given the history of Great Britain and how the land was gifted and carved up over centuries to certain families. Indeed, the Buccleuch Estate's greatest land acquisition occurred when the 3rd Duke inherited the Dukedom of Queensberry in 1810.

What may come as a greater surprise is to learn that the largest land owner in

---

1 - Currently Richard Walter John Montagu Douglas Scott. He is also the Chief of Clan Scott and Chancellor of the Order of the Thistle. No, I'd never heard of it either.

Scotland is not Scottish nor a native of Britain. The centuries-old tradition of Danes marauding and taking land in Scotland has been updated to a more informal, less pillaging, method of buying up great swathes of countryside. Denmark's richest man, Anders Holch Povlsen, has, in not much more than ten years, acquired over 220,000 acres, including several formal estates and castles. What is perhaps more surprising is that it appears his intentions are purely naturalistic. Povlsen's plans are to adjoin his land and re-wild it.[1] As his estates are running at a considerable loss each year, it would certainly appear that for the Dane, this is very much a passion project.

International ownership of land does not make the headlines often but is worth a brief consideration, especially within the Scotch whisky industry. Scotland is roughly 19 million acres and around 750,000 acres are estimated to be owned by non-residents. Additionally, of the total £22 billion of residential property in Scotland, some £3 billion is attributed to off-shore ownership. Whilst this is relatively small compared to, say, London's off-shore issue, it is on a worryingly upward trend. I bring this up solely as it is quite relevant to the Scotch whisky industry itself. Most of the new-wave distilleries are Scottish-owned and mark a trend away from multi-national overseas conglomerates. In other words, for the majority, taxes on profits are applied for and collected within Scotland.

Prior to this recent explosion of smaller, Scottish-based distilling companies, nearly 70% of all Scotch whisky distilleries were owned by multinational or overseas companies. This international involvement goes as far back as the 1930s and is the result of a period of conglomeration in the latter part of the 19th century. Distillers combined forces to prevent industry-wide issues such as price-fixing, imported products affecting domestic price & quality and over-production. From the beginnings of an industry where it was not normal to have more than two, maybe three, distilleries under one company banner, larger firms began acquiring existing distilleries and brands to the current situation where eight companies contribute over 75% of the total production. Those eight companies own 68 distilleries, which leaves around 65 distilleries owned by a further 53 companies; some large, like LVMH (owners of Glenmorangie and Ardbeg), and some tiny, such as Daftmill.

I appreciate that this is all getting technical and in-depth, but it does illustrate several points that have driven my desire to seek out these new companies and distilleries. The first, as has been pointed out, is that most are Scottish-based. This, at least to me and I'll wager most of my fellow residents, means larger investment into the country and economy, and that is always a great draw. Secondly, it means we are seeing a disbursement of choice away from the great industry drivers and suppliers. Never before has the consumer had a wider array of whisky to choose from, especially single malt whisky, and can now support local in a way that was never an option before.

---

1 - This is a form of ecological restoration that attempts to increase biodiversity and restore a natural process to land reformation and development - removing the human intervention.

I have pondered all of this whilst taking the one-hour drive to Lochlea Distillery. I'll no doubt swing back around to this topic later, but for now, I've got to tackle a road closure that my hi-tech yet completely backwards navigation system is adamant I must drive through. Eventually, and by looking at the map, I realise I could take a slightly different road and come from the north to turn into the distillery. I am a fan of new technology but especially enjoy those moments when we beat it or can blame it. For instance, car maps will often show accidents and delays on journeys and there is always that little moment of triumph over technology when either the queues have dissipated or there is no evidence of any delay. Likewise, the estimated arrival time becomes a challenge to ensure that minutes are shaved off. Small victories, I realise, but ones that keep you human against an ever-growing mass of technological advances.

Lochlea Distillery.

Lochlea Distillery

www.lochleadistillery.com
Not open to the public

For anyone passing, there is little evidence that Lochlea Farm houses a distillery at all. Remove the small sign at the entrance, and you'd be none the wiser. Even once on the grounds, it is only when I park and turn towards the distillery sat amongst inconspicuous warehouses and farm buildings that I spy the tell-tale gleaming copper stills through the large glass windows. When Neil & Jen McGeoch bought the farm in 2006, it was, as are most of the farms in the area, a dairy and cattle business. The McGeoch family were known for the clothing retail chain M&Co., and Neil had worked there until the pull of farming brought him to Lochlea Farm.

The farming of pedigree cattle was becoming an unstable, and at times unviable, business model, and in 2014, Neil and Jen decided to change tact and plant 50 acres of barley. Speaking at the time, Neil showed how tough the decision was. "I just love the whole farming way of life and the people. Letting the cows go has been a heartbreaking decision." Barley had historically been grown on the farm but predominantly as livestock feed – this was the first time it had been grown with the intention to supply distillers. The next natural step was to distil their own barley, and conversion of the former piggery, byre and midden[1] began in 2017. The larger cattle sheds were converted into warehouses, and the distillery was commissioned in August 2018. Lochlea, being a farm distillery, grows all of its own barley.

In 2021, John Campbell, previously Laphroaig Distillery Manager, joined the Lochlea team, bringing his decades of experience with him. "The whisky really comes from the DNA of Ayrshire; we are integrated into South Ayrshire and want to deepen the roots in our community," John states. "Ultimately, the goal is to become a single-site distillery as that is the best way for Lochlea to reach our environmental, quality and sustainability targets. But the pressure is that we don't have 200 years of heritage to fall back on, and we need to keep improving all the time."

In a way, though, that lack of distilling heritage allows Lochlea to be their own category. The nearest distillery of any note is Lochranza on the Isle of Arran, to the west. Further afield is Auchentoshan at Clydebank in the north and Bladnoch in Wigtown in the

---

1 - A byre is a farmhouse in which the living quarters are combined with the livestock. A midden is an area on a farm used for waste products.

south. Lochlea needs not, and is not, anything like these other whiskies. This suits the team at the distillery just fine.

"The spirit is developing different characteristics as it ages," John continues. "This is part of the fun right now in understanding the development." The public's response to Lochlea's whiskies cannot be ignored, and whisky drinkers in the know have hotly anticipated each new release. It is a testament to the work put in by John and his team and the array and quality of casks used for maturation.

John and I talked about his last position and how important it was for those visiting the distillery and that sense of place combined with the product. "That's the wonderful thing about single malt," John replies. "You can generally visit a distillery and get under the skin of the place, which allows for a different level of connection." One can only hope that Lochlea will be open to visitors soon as the only Ayrshire single malt distillery.

Lochlea's Stills

Robert Burns, Scotland's national poet, is an inescapable constant when living and travelling in this part of Scotland. Burns lived at Lochlea farm from 1777 until his father's death in 1784. Every town and many villages in the surrounding counties have monuments and statues. The English are just as guilty with our permeating and ubiquitousness of William Shakespeare, but as I've never lived in or near Stratford-upon-Avon, I have little to compare the plethora of effigies that abound in this area. A quick search shows that Burns' memorials outnumber Shakespeare's by a considerable number. Perhaps 50 to one, but much of this will be due to the fact that Burns was alive 200 years after Shakespeare and as the Scottish emigrated in such numbers, his words went with his kin.[1] Perhaps also, it is the insistence on English and Drama departments worldwide that everyone study and discuss either 'Macbeth' or 'Romeo & Juliet' ad nauseum that restricts a greater love for England's national poet.

Burns' writing, without any Scots language knowledge or training, is an almost foreign language. Certainly, during my schooling in Hertfordshire, there was little to no coverage of his work (we didn't even sing 'Auld Lang Syne' on New Year's Eve). I was, therefore, terrified when asked to perform the 'Address to a Haggis'- a self-explanatory poem penned by the Ayrshire bard in 1786. It was not that I couldn't give it a go; it was being asked to perform it in the middle of a whisky festival in The Netherlands surrounded by a throng of my peers – most of whom hailed from Scotland. I had two choices: perform it in a comically English way, mispronouncing most of it, and almost certainly emphasising the wrong parts. Whilst some may have found this funny, others may have felt a certain level of disrespect towards a rather important Scottish figure. My second option and this was what I decided (ensuring that a peaceful festival ensued), was to chicken out completely. "Surely," I reasoned emphatically, "one of the Scottish contingent could perform this?" The irony was that the organisers replaced me with the most English-sounding Scot one could ever encounter and the recital ended up being fairly close to how I would have performed it.

> *"Fair fa' your honest, sonsie face,*
> *Great Chieftain o' the Pudding-race!"*

For most travellers to Annandale Distillery, the route will involve getting on and off the M74 motorway. This crucial section of road starts at the border with England (taking over from what is the M6), next to Gretna and continues up to Glasgow. As I've mentioned, motorways are often not the most scenic route to any destination, and again this journey is no exception. For my route, I am first heading directly south towards the town of Dumfries (or, as my niece once referred to it, 'Stupid Chips') before heading west along a magnificent stretch of the A75.

I feel I've already spent a fair chunk of this book describing roads, and yes, there's more to come. Scotland is, after all, renowned for its scenic routes, but I must offer a few words on the A75. Stretching from one side of Dumfries & Galloway to the other, the A75 is a crucial artery from the M74 motorway to the ferry terminals on the West Coast (that brings goods and people in and out of Ireland) and all of the small towns in between. Once past Dumfries, the road climbs up above the most southerly lands of Scotland and, weather permitting, offers spectacular views over the Solway Hills, the Solway Firth and beyond that, Cumbria in England.

Today, the weather suits me just fine. The sun pierces the scattered clouds,

---

1 - There are more statues of Burns in Canada than all of the known memorials of Shakespeare put together.

highlighting sections of the scenery like a random set of spotlights. The road to the wonderfully named village of Mouswald (pronounced Moose-ald or Mouz-ald) will take you to the equally splendidly named Caerlaverock Castle (pronounced wrongly no matter how many times you attempt it). This uniquely triangular, standing castle is complete with a moat and drawbridge and is worth a quick detour. Few castles, anywhere in the world, give a greater sense of impenetrability but then few also demonstrate how weak a position of defence is if surrounded. The forces from Caerlaverock sacked nearby Lochmaben Castle; perhaps it was then that the phrase 'the best form of defence is attack' was coined.

Much of the county I call home is farmland and is not blessed with an abundance of any major industries, let alone many distilleries. When Bladnoch Distillery was resurrected, or plucked from certain doom, in the late 1990s, it was the only distillery the county could boast. And until Annandale was built, Bladnoch remained the sole producer of whisky – not that the distillery was easy to get to or often visited (nor was it that easy to find any Bladnoch whisky in a shop). It would take more research than I am willing to invest to truly understand why the bordering counties between Scotland and England are so devoid of a Scotch whisky story. But it neatly brings me to the distillery closest to England and, therefore, the most Southerly situated in Scotland.

One of the gloomier days of my trip but shows how traditional Annandale Distillery is in appearance

Annandale Distillery

www.annandaledistillery.com
Open to the public

For David Thomson, a simple gift of a book would change his and wife Theresa's lives forever. Teresa had bought David a book titled 'Scotch Missed' by Brain Townsend which catalogued and explored all of the derelict and closed distilleries in Scotland. In this book was an entry for Annandale Distillery, built in 1830 and closed in 1921, situated just outside the Royal Burgh of Annan, just 15 miles from where David had been born and raised.

"For some reason, I misread the entry and thought it had been demolished. After reading the article, my late uncle suggested to the contrary and he was able to confirm that some of the buildings still existed." David states. "We eventually tracked down the owner and convinced him to sell."

Annandale was originally a small farm-based distillery built by George Donald, a former excise officer. Distilling commenced in 1836 and operated for over 40 years before being leased to John S. Gardener in 1883. Gardener was a retired businessman and son of the former Mayor of Liverpool who had looked north for his next business venture. Despite extensive improvements and equipment upgrades, the distillery was bought by John Walker & Sons in 1886. We know of this company now as Johnnie Walker, and no doubt Annandale was a significant contributor to the world's most famous blend until the distillery was closed in 1919. Having purchased the dilapidated buildings in 2007, David and Teresa spent the next seven years battling the listed status of the building, excavations of parts of the site, floods and the painstaking process of restoring and protecting crumbling bricks and walls. There was nothing simple in the re-build and the pair spared no expense in creating something they were truly proud of.

In November 2014, the very first cask was filled. I was lucky enough to have been invited to the event. I marvelled at how much David and Teresa were able to waive away all of the troubles, expense, and sheer stress of this build as they joyously filled cask No One. Most of the guests witnessing this historic occasion were oblivious to the summers of mud, winters of non-stop rain and hours upon hours of restoration, much of which was brick by brick.

"I doubt that I'd have taken the plunge if Teresa hadn't pushed me." David continues. "Working with Teresa throughout the Annandale project and experiencing her enthusiasm, commitment, and sacrifice has made me very proud of her (especially since she's teetotal). Without her, there would have been no Annandale."

David's vision for the distillery was one of tradition. Historically, the distillery had been making a peated, smoky whisky. The distillery thus alternates production during the year. One month, it makes a non-peated whisky called 'Man O'Words' in tribute to Scotland's great poet, Robert Burns, and the next month, it makes a peated whisky called 'Man O'Swords' in remembrance of Robert the Bruce, who was once Lord of Annandale.

In 2018, Annandale welcomed its first whisky in over a century and the only known bottle of Annandale single malt in the world. What had taken twelve years, thousands upon thousands of man hours, and over £17 million investment finally had a bottle, label, and cork. Annandale was firmly put on the whisky map in a way it had not been for centuries. It would have been so much simpler for David & Teresa to have just built a new distillery or even a couple, but their belief in tradition and giving back to the area is now evident for all to see. When you visit, ensure you stay long enough to examine every nook and cranny. From the welcoming gate to the nod to the local breed of cow, the distillery has delights at every turn.

My tour guide, Joe, is much like me in possessing an English accent (his being a soft Lancashire lilt - mine being much more southern) but never calling anywhere 'home'. This results in an oration that is carefully explained and enunciated well. Only two others are joining us for the tour: visitors from France and Joe clearly tailors the tour to their ears - something he does with skill and ease.

As I've explained, I am no stranger to Annandale Distillery. My first trip, sometime in 2011, was a damp and muddy affair. David Thomson and project manager Malcolm Rennie took several precious hours out of their day to show me around. I was struck with David's vision and passion for a project that looked to me like a Titanic struggle. My second visit a year or two later found the site transformed. Whilst the excavation and preservation of the old direct-fired stills were ongoing, and the chimney was being repointed, brick by brick, the old malting floors (now the café), visitor centre and offices had been completed. Work had also begun on the extension to incorporate the new boiler, toilets and gift shop. Today, the site looks like it has never been anything but a traditional, purpose-built distillery. My advice, if and when you do the tour, is to ask to see the complete set of photos from the restoration and build project.

A 'Doonhamer' is someone from Dumfries, although the term has been extended to include neighbouring areas. This was supposedly a self-appointed alias by Dumfries locals working or travelling around Scotland. Therefore, it is not derogatory by any means; it simply means down home, as in 'I live in the south'. The border counties of both Scotland and England are a mix of people and lifestyles that are quite determinable, or at least detached from the counties[1] and much larger cities that exist above and below them. Dumfries & Galloway, The Scottish Borders, Cumbria and Northumberland sit like a vast buffer between Scotland's industrial and political centres of Glasgow and Edinburgh and England's northern powerhouses of Manchester, Newcastle and Leeds.

These neighbouring counties have a rich history in cross-border mixing, migration, and trading. Although I can only suggest this, they are more closely related and relatable than their countryfolk living to their north and south. It is especially true, when it comes to local sporting rivalries, that folks from Northumberland are more likely to visit the Scottish Borders than they would Cumbria. Likewise, living within the heart of Dumfries & Galloway, having told a local I was visiting Hawick for the first time, I was not surprised to hear him state, 'You're not missing much' in response. I can assure you a similar point would have been made had I been travelling in the opposite direction. Thus, soft, inter-country borders can sometimes be more pertinent than lines between countries. This, naturally, goes out the window when it becomes a national sporting event – in particular when it is either Rugby or Football.

Hawick is the home of Tweed, that itchy, hard-wearing fabric worn only by a certain class or those wishing to appear a class above their station. Few materials have worked harder to reinvent themselves, and like, say, Doc Martin shoes, Tweed is often in and out of fashion. It is currently out. Cashmere, Hawick's other claim to fame, is currently 'in', and the town remains the home of Hawico and, confusingly, Johnstons of Elgin. Whilst I do own several Tweed jackets, all gathering dust in a wardrobe, I do not possess a single item of Cashmere – not even a lonely sock. Like most tourists visiting Edinburgh, I have seen the swanky shops but have never felt the need to go inside.

Intrigued, I pop into Johnston's of Elgin (in Hawick) to see what a Cashmere jumper might cost me. The charming lady on the desk had only just finished welcoming me in before she opened the door, allowing me to exit. I'll leave the Cashmere jumpers for those less likely to spill a Latte down a single piece of attire that cost more than my entire outfit (including shoes and sunglasses - and it was reduced to half-price). The faddy world of fabric and clothes goes someway to explaining why Hawick has not been at its best in the last few decades. Many factories have closed and unemployment is still a major concern for the area.

The Borders Distillery is only a half-hour's drive from Annandale Distillery and is topographically a simile of the lands in the neighbouring county. That is not much of a surprise, but what is different, or at least feels different, is the greater emphasis on industry. The southwest of Scotland has a much more dairy and cattle-driven economy, whereas the southeast has a much greater nod to mills, works, and fabrication.

---

1 - These are designated as council seats. I am sure some inhabitants shudder at the mass collectivism, but for my purposes, it makes writing about the area much more straightforward.

Hawick is not a large town. It has around 13,000 inhabitants and is about half a mile from one side to the other. Thus, it does not take much navigation before I turn in and through the wrought-iron gates of the distillery into a small courtyard. Immediately, I was struck by how much grander the distillery was than I had expected. The Borders team have quietly been getting on with laying down stock of maturing spirit, and as such, I had very little preconception of the setup. In my head, I assumed it was just a small concern with probably a skeleton crew. My lack of awareness was simply due to not seeing the whisky in shops, festivals, or the brand advertised anywhere.

The Borders Distillery

The Borders Distillery

www.thebordersdistillery.com
Open to the public

"We chose Hawick for several reasons," John Fordyce, Borders Distillery Founder and Managing Director, tells me. "There wasn't a distillery in the Borders; the last one, Kelso Distillery, had closed in 1837, and the area had an industrial background. Hawick is a manufacturing town, so we knew how to find staff who understood how to work in a factory and were used to shift work, health & safety regulations and the general day-to-day operation of machinery in an industrial environment."

John and I are sat in a large and comfortable tasting lounge above his office and the distillery's shop. "This was originally built for the Hawick Urban Electric Company." John continues motioning to the buildings around him. "The part we're in is a Tudor Cotswold building dating back to 1903."

I am struck by just how perfect the restoration and re-purposing of the site has been. The buildings had not been used since 2010, when the last tenants, Turnbull & Scott Engineering, left. Whilst the Cotswold office and shop building adds a touch of architectural class to the site, it is the older warehouses complete with original glass roofs, several kinds of brick and stone work and the tracked steel pully system (complete with ropes and winches) that hammer home to visitors its history. John is visibly appreciative of my praise.

"The site needed complete restoration when we bought it," he informs me. "We were very keen to retain the historical features. The brickwork, for instance, shows how the materials changed during different eras. I'm very happy with the industrial feel of the distillery."

Around 2013 four friends, all veterans of the Scotch whisky industry, came together to build a distillery. John was joined by Tim Carton, Tony Roberts and George Tait and after initially considering a bid on Bladnoch Distillery in the town of Wigton, decided to look to the Scottish Borders.

"Dumfries & Galloway, where I'm from, was becoming well established with its distilleries at Wigtown, Newton Stewart and Annan [in addition to Moffat and Auldgirth], and we really didn't want to be just another distillery in an area. The idea of the Scottish Borders did not take long to discuss, and Hawick was our first choice for location. We knew there was other interest in building a distillery in the area so a race developed to see who would be the first and here we are."

What also sets The Borders Distillery apart from many of its contemporaries is the insistence on making one style of whisky. "We can make 1.6 million litres of alcohol a year, although ongoing troubles from recent work on the River Teviot have reduced this to around 1.2 million. We don't make a peated spirit, nor do we experiment with different yeasts or barley strains – we are happy to use what is provided. And because we want a distillate-driven whisky, we are predominantly using ex-Bourbon barrels for maturation."

This was a strategy the company had from the outset, meaning that despite the oldest whisky in casks soon turning six years old, it may be a couple more years before we see a core product released. In the meantime, visitors to the distillery can buy bottles of experimental whiskies, including some that contain Rye whisky. An early decision was also made to include a Carterhead still to enable gin and vodka production using the single malt distillate as its base.

The Borders Distillery is fully geared for tourists, and whilst Hawick is not on the tip of most tourists' tongues, a visit for any whisky enthusiast travelling through the Scottish Borders is a must. All tour guides are distillery workers, each schooled in every aspect of the distilling process. What has been built for the town's future prosperity is a striking embodiment of Scotland's past and present.

The impressive stillls of The Border Distillery

John is an amiable, well-travelled and knowledgeable host. We chat about Thornhill, where I live; as it turns out, John grew up there and went to the same school as my children (granted, not the new 'Academy' that was completed in 2010). John's career in the whisky industry began in Hong Kong, working for Wm Grants, owners of Glenfiddich and Grant's Standfast blended Scotch whisky. Several years were also spent in the wine industry in Portugal. Eventually, a pull for home brought him back to Scotland, and he sank his considerable knowledge and experience into The Borders Distillery.

We share a very similar opinion on the whole 'Scotch Whisky Regions' debate, as John shares my belief that it is a lazy way of lumping together distilleries in a region of such incredible diversity. "We are not making a Lowland-style whisky," John states emphatically. "The region is too large and too diverse to collectively just stamp as one style." I nod in agreement.

Heading home, I revel in having met a kindred spirit within the industry in John. He was not what I was expecting, although I wonder what my expectations were. Nothing about funding, planning and starting a distillery is easy. Once again, I realise that John barely mentioned any of the trials and tribulations he and the team went through in establishing the mightily impressive Borders Distillery. Just possibly, to bring a project like this to fruition, you must be someone who not only sees the bigger picture but can shake off adversity like a wet dog drying itself.

I realise I haven't explained where the term 'Reivers' comes from. 'Reiving' was the practice of raiding or plundering livestock or goods from anyone around you (but not family). Much of this occurred in the wasteland or lawless areas that separated the Scots and English, especially during the wars of independence (1296 – 1346). Essentially, 'Reivers' were bandits, and one story goes that the wife of an infamous Border Reiver, to show her husband that there was no food in the larder, served him his spurs instead of dinner. Ergo, mount up and go 'reiving' or go hungry. It's certainly a tougher nickname than 'Doonhamer' – but then it's not a contest.

YOUR OWN CASK? WHY NOT

If there is a single recurring question I am asked more often than others, it is about buying a cask of whisky. There are several reasons why this has become such a prevalent possibility for the casual drinker, but one reason above the others has really ramped up interest: return on investment (ROI). In recent years, there has been a slew of news pieces about casks of whisky fetching astronomical prices and, therefore, offering on a plate an attention-grabbing click-bait headline for the more unscrupulous salesperson. This was heightened when Ardbeg, foolishly in my opinion, proudly released news of the sale of a single cask of 1975 whisky for £16 million – twice what the distillery had been bought for twenty-five years earlier. Those eager for a good investment pricked their ears up, and those boasting nonsensical returns on mediocre casks they owned revised their ROI claims.

This is nothing new, nor is it restricted to any luxury or desirable good. Folks will queue for hours for a limited edition Swatch watch, knowing that they have a good chance it will rise in value. Ferrari buyers are asked to sign an agreement that they won't sell their car within the first year of ownership. Likewise, many of those distilleries selling casks of whisky to the public and wishing to control this onward trading have water-tight agreements, meaning that the cask of whisky never leaves their warehouse.

There are quite a few things to consider if you are pondering the parting of hard-earned cash for something not yet made, nor matured. Time is the first factor. How long are you prepared to leave the spirit in the wood? Three years? Ten years? More? Very few three year old whiskies are worth bottling, so I'd suggest you consider a while longer. Too long and you'll likely be outside of the distillery's maturation agreement (usually not longer than ten years) which means additional storage costs and insurance. After that, what is your intention with the liquid? Are you looking for a return on investment? If so, does the contract of sale allow a transfer of ownership? If the contract of sale does not allow the cask or spirit to be removed in bulk then I would suggest very few parties will be interested in it other than the distillery owner.

My advice regarding buying a cask is always the same: do it for fun. Maybe get a small group of friends together to ease the pressure of the purchase. Agree beforehand how long you intend to mature it (often the distillery's terms will dictate this period) and then once bottled, divvy it up and do with the bottles as you see fit. If, and I must stress that this is a big IF, the cask goes up in value in the ten years or so you have owned it, and assuming the cask has not leaked nor turned bad (and yes, that happens) and the contract of sale allows it, you could find a willing buyer from one of the many independent bottlers out there. Don't be too surprised, however, if your cask is worth very little more than what you paid for it. No distillery should be legally selling you a bona fide investment vehicle. Should you need a second opinion about the quality of your matured whisky, please reach out to me. I am always happy to oblige with a second opinion (the larger the sample the better).

Can you spot your cask?

CHAPTER 6

ARRAN: SCOTLAND IN MINIATURE

*"An island with a rich distilling heritage,
although most of it only recently legally."*

For just the second time on this trip, I'll head to one of Scotland's 790 islands. Raasay being the first, with Harris and Islay to come, but today, it is the volcanic rock that sits between the Firth of Clyde and the Kintyre Peninsula. For those searching for it on a map, you may notice that the Kintyre peninsula has a certain, let's say, phallic shape, and I probably don't need any fancy words to allude to what the adjacent Isle of Arran may be representing.

Once again, I have been blessed with one of the best days to travel, certainly weather-wise. The doom and gloom of my chosen weather app promised rain and possible thunderstorms, but in reality, it is calm, mostly blue skies and pleasantly warm when the sun is out.[1] I am accompanied by my mother, who jetted in from Texas a few days earlier to see friends and family on the other side of the pond. This negates the need for any music, podcast or audiobook in the car as we spend the journey discussing family and, as almost always, religion. I am an ardent atheist; my mother is a devout Christian. How did that happen, you ask? How long have you got? My mother (Carol, for those interested) is an ideal companion as it worth remembering that the vast majority of tourists that Arran receives are casual whisky drinkers at best. Some will not be advocates of smoky whisky and may visit purely out of curiosity or for the fantastic café and views.

We are also lucky, blessed, you might say, that the ferries are all running as promised. The ferry from Ardrossan to Brodick takes just under two hours. Ardrossan and its surroundings are an area I know well, as my first whisky warehouse was in the neighbouring town of Stevenston. It is a fairly run-down part of Scotland, as so many of the port towns are. Ardrossan is also the port for ferries to Campbeltown but this route runs less reliable than a 1980s printer.

As the Arran ferry slows on its approach to the port, you can get a good look at Holy Island, the small isle off the east coast of Arran. Incredibly there are around 30 inhabitants

---

1 - Obsessed with weather...

on this tiny rock – I guess for those that found Arran 'just too busy'. The fact that there is a 'Centre for World Peace and Health' based on the tiny island suggests that life there is for those who enjoy quiet contemplation. Very quiet contemplation. Arran boasts a population of just over 5,000, with around a fifth of those living in the village of Lamlash and slightly less in Brodick. I don't know how or where they all fit in, but Arran receives nearly one million visitors annually. There is no bridge, no airport, no tunnel, no hovercraft and you can't walk to it when the tide is out. Island life hangs on the thread of a lifeline that is the ferries. Just thought I would get that in there if anyone from the government has been given this book and is reading it...

I am in danger of running late for my pre-arranged meeting at Lagg. My mistake was to assume that once on Arran there would be no delays (I hadn't even allowed for getting off the ferry – something that can eat up a lot of time depending upon the number of lorries that are in front of you). I certainly didn't allow extra time for any road closures as there are only four roads on the whole island. As I pass the main island village of Lamlash, the fastest route is to leave the A841, the road that travels the full circumference of the island, and head across on a minor 'B' road. This road is unfortunately closed, and there is nothing for it but to continue around the south of the island. It is a much nicer drive, and as we round the southern tip of Arran, we are treated to a stunning view of the Pladda Lighthouse and beyond the tip of Ailsa Craig; both are shrouded in mist.[1] It is hard to be stressed about punctuality when the view is this spectacular.

Eventually, we can see signs of industry and turn into the car park for Lagg. I realise I keep stating how blown away I am with so many of the distilleries I visit, but Lagg is another jaw-dropping moment. The modern buildings are perfectly in line with the environment. The theme of Arran's Lowland/Highland lines, two angles, one larger than the next, frames the distillery and is replicated in the frames of the neighbouring warehouses. The roof is turfed and seeds each year, not just allowing it to blend in with the surrounding hills but also helping with capturing heat. This was not a design requirement from any local planners but demonstrates how much the Isle of Arran Distillers Ltd wanted a building that blended in with its environment.

My mother and I are greeted by Fred Baumgärtner, Visitor Centre Manager, and Graham Omand, Distillery Manager, who is also waiting for us. I apologise for being late and hope they were not waiting long. "Not long at all," Fred says. "We guessed that the road must have been closed." We are guided upstairs to the distillery café with spectacular viewing windows out towards Ailsa Craig. Fred is a local and, were it not for the distillery, would have had to seek employment elsewhere. Graham is yet another Illeach[2] drawn into the industry that surrounded his childhood.

---

1 - Another moment when I lament the fact I am photographically challenged.
2 - You are correct, a native of the Isle of Islay – you have been paying attention!

"It's funny," Graham tells me over a cappuccino. "When I was a lad on Islay, if you weren't doing well at school, then working at a distillery was used as a means of encouragement. 'If you don't work hard at school', a teacher would tell us, 'Then you'll end up just working a still.' This was in the 1980s when the industry was in the doldrums. Hard to imagine when you look at the industry today." I shake my head, amazed - how times have changed.

Graham has been on Arran since 2011 and had a big say in the building and style of Lagg. Whilst Graham talks about the spirit, Fred pours each of us a sample of the current 'fill your own bottle' available at the distillery. There is an undeniable 'saline' quality to the whisky.

"This has surprised us," Graham admits. "The peat we use is Highland and is not associated with a sea-salty quality. But the distillery is just a few hundred yards from the coast, and it must be coming in as part of the micro-climate. We get none of this sea breeze with our sister distillery, Lochranza."

Arguably when it was first released, the Arran whisky was hard to distinguish, in any meaningful way, as an island malt. As explained earlier, Lochranza Distillery was the passion project of Harold Currie. Sadly, Harold Currie did not live to see the completion of Lagg Distillery in 2018, as he passed away in 2016.

Fred passes me a bottle that contains merely a teaspoon of clear liquid. From the label, I am informed that this is their heavily peated distillate. The peat is not overbearing to my nose, and there is no evidence of the saline quality. For my mother, this is an abomination and should be destroyed. But then it is a new distillate that contains well over 65% alcohol, and she is not a fan of either high alcohol or overly smoky whiskies.

Harold Currie and the Lochranza Distillery

Harold, or Hal as he preferred, had an extraordinary life. Born in 1924 in Liverpool, he was a child war evacuee in 1939 to North Wales. As soon as he turned 18, Hal enlisted in the army, taking part in the D-Day offensive. He was fascinated by engineering and joined the 7th Armoured Division, otherwise known as the Desert Rats when they returned from North Africa. He trained as a wireless operator at Bovington[1] and then fought at Villers Bocage in a now infamous tank battle. Hal also spent time in Berlin after the German surrender.

After his service, Hal joined the wine and spirits firm Rigby & Evans in Liverpool, specialising in importing and selling Jamaican rum. By 1961, and after a move to Scotland, he was made the Managing Director of Chivas Brothers. His marketing and communication skills suited the role, and it is believed that he came up with the slogan 'Come to Chivas Regal when you can afford it' – reaffirming the quality and superiority of the Chivas brand.

From Chivas Brothers, Hal joined Pernod Ricard briefly in the mid-1970s and, despite retiring in 1982, was kept on as a consultant until an architect friend with land on Arran suggested a distillery on the island. The build was not without its problems, as it was delayed by four months due to the discovery of a Golden Eagle nesting on the site. It was then further delayed by a rare dragonfly. Even in the 1990s, the local habitat and wildlife preservation were paramount.

Arran cost around £1.2 million[2] to build and was completed in June 1995 before being officially opened in August. The distillery is much changed today from what was first opened. Expanded in 2016, it can now make 1.2 million litres of alcohol a year. The distillery also receives well over 100,000 visitors a year, making it one of the most visited distilleries in Scotland and Arran's top tourist destination. The whisky is highly sought after and prized worldwide and is perhaps the most fitting tribute to Harold's legacy. After all, without great whisky, it's just a great story.

---

1 - Now a tank museum.
2 - Although rumoured to have cost twice that – regardless, a drop compared to the Lagg Distillery costing £18 million.

Lagg Distillery

www.laggwhisky.com
Open to visitors

"The idea for Lagg arose from a discussion about additional warehousing for Lochranza on the island," Euan Mitchell, Arran Distillers' Managing Director, tells me. "A site was identified on the south of the island, and the Board of Directors mooted that we should consider a micro-distillery and warehousing to allow for some experimental distillation. Architects were summoned, and suddenly, the vision for the Lagg Distillery began to emerge. The idea of the micro-scale distillery was discarded, and a discussion began around the concept of a second single malt brand from the Isle of Arran."

The warehouses were indeed built first and enabled Arran to keep all of its stock on the island. "We actually brought back our casks from the mainland," Graham Omand tells me. "As Euan said, in the early days of the vision for Lagg, it was to be a small craft distillery in conjunction with the bonded warehousing. The small, craft idea grew arms and legs as demand for Arran malt whisky soared and it was then decided to build a fully-fledged, distinct distillery with a large visitor centre to accommodate the ever-growing tourism industry on Arran."

Graham joined Arran Distillers aged 22 and pretty much straight out of completing his degree in Biotech and Applied Sciences. "I've been on Arran for 13 years and wouldn't want to live anywhere else," he confirms. "You get the island community feel here without the desolate remoteness; just being a couple of hours from Glasgow central was mind-blowing for a boy from Islay." Having worked his way up to distillery manager, Graham was a keen advocate of the new site. "Historically, the site was perfect for a distillery – the last documented legal Arran distillery, before Lochranza opened in 1995, operated just a mile down the hill, closing in the 1840s." Arran has a long and documented history with legal and not-so-legal distilling. We both stop on the tour to discuss one of the placards in the visitor centre, describing the history of Robert Armour & Sons, a coppersmith based in Campbeltown. I was aware of Robert Armour due to my research into the Campbeltown book I wrote in 2004, but from the placard, I learned that he supplied much of the apparatus that kept illicit stills thriving on Arran.[1]

"The idea for Lagg to become a heavily peated distillery was an easy choice. Arran was traditionally a non-peated malt, with just the Machrie Moor distillate coming from one month's peated mashing each year. As soon as we knew we were building Lagg Distillery, we ceased the production of a peated Arran malt." Graham continues. "Lagg now makes the island's only smoky whisky, and whilst most mashes are heavily peated, we do the odd distillation with lower peating levels and a few with a much higher peat content."

As with anything build-related on one of Scotland's islands, weather and transport were the main stumbling blocks for the building of Lagg. A particularly bad winter and impacted ferry services delayed or prevented contractors from attending or completing jobs. This often caused a domino effect as one stage held up another, but in the end, the attention to detail and overall impact of the distillery is simply astonishing.

"The day the inaugural release arrived, wrapped on a pallet, was a momentous moment, not just for me, but for all of the staff," Graham beams. "Three years of hard work, not knowing what the final outcome will be like. My spirits, along with the entire team's, I believe, were lifted when we all had a glass of Lagg whisky together. Everyone just nodded in approval. Helping to create a never-before-seen spirit and seeing people enjoying it as whisky, there's no feeling quite like it."

Like so many other newly built distilleries, the fact they are there means much more than just a new drink on the market. Lagg offers full-time employment to many who may otherwise have been forced to leave the island and the small community that they would prefer to remain a part of.

"Fred [Baumgärtner] would not have stayed on Arran had it not been for Lagg Distillery," Graham tells me. "Lagg, like Arran, has become a part of the island and is providing a reason for people to stay on the island." From what was deemed a madcap notion from a retiree, has since become a world-famous and quite revered single malt Scotch whisky. From that initial effort, perseverance, and pioneering esprit de corps, the island of Arran can now boast two fantastic distilleries and its place firmly on the Scotch whisky map.

---

1 - I also learned from the placard that people from Arran are called Arranachs. Not to be confused with Anoraks.

Graham takes us on a private tour, albeit the same one available to everyone visiting the distillery. There is a surprising amount of space. The distillery, built with a larger than-normal footprint, has allowed a layout so free of pipes, valves and exchangers to make it look like an unfinished project. It has clearly been built with expansion in mind. There are spaces for more washbacks and an additional set of stills – lessons have been learnt from the building of Lochranza.

Fred has to leave us to look after a delegation from CalMac,[1] a most important group to the islanders, whilst Graham takes us to Warehouse One – teeming with a group of Danish tourists photographing the racked casks. "This warehouse and the next one were built before the distillery as we needed space for the casks we were filling at Lochranza," Graham informs us. "We previously had to take filled casks off the island for maturation as we did not have enough space and could not build warehouses on the site of the other distillery." In front of me are some 1996 ex-Sherry butts of Lochranza whisky - some of the oldest and most valuable distillate they still have. Had the warehouse been empty, I might have been cheeky enough to ask for a sniff; I'll just have to wait for them to be bottled.

Graham, too, now has other commitments, and my mother and I thank him warmly for his time and personal tour. A quick bottle purchase of the salty 'fill your own' single-cask Lagg whisky we tried, and we are back on the road. Although situated on the other side of the island, we have just enough time to make a flying visit to Lochranza Distillery and remark on just how different it is. Whereas the Lagg whisky is still a work in progress, Arran is now a mature and formidable force. There are no less than five distillery-exclusive bottlings available and a 'fill your own' single cask bottling – and if that isn't enough, there are several in-house blends and numerous expressions of Arran whisky and even Arran Gold – a cream liqueur if that is your thing. It's not mine, so instead I buy a couple of the distillery exclusives - and no coffee mugs...

Our journey back is on the ferry to Troon, and as the boat chugs along at what feels like six or seven knots, we experience one of the calmest ferry crossings ever – barely a ripple on the water, not a breath of wind. Again, just a little reminder: if you should experience Arran and the ferries on a day like I've just had – don't suddenly sell everything and move there. You're missing out on ferries being cancelled, on swells that send seasoned travellers green and on island life that can send some folk cabin crazy. But don't let me put you off if you're truly determined – there are worse places to live and who knows, maybe Lagg will need some new tour guides soon – definitely worse gigs than that.

---

1 - CalMac is short for Caledonian MacBrayne, the owners and operators of the ferries.

CHAPTER 7

ONE ISLAND – TWO NAMES

I don't need a witty quip or quote here.
One day you will visit Harris, and you won't regret it.[1]

In a strange sort of way, Storm Kathleen has done me a favour by rearranging my trip to Harris. Well, two favours actually; firstly (as I was going to avoid using this mode of transport), I am forced into flying from Glasgow to Stornoway to get to Harris. Secondly, the weather app tells me my timing could not be better as I will hit a mini heat-wave. I wanted to avoid flying for no other reason than I dislike it. All of it. The extra time you have to arrive at the airport, the airport, the security, getting on the airplane and most of all the flying bit. I'm not alone – the fear of flying (and all that comes with it, as I've just described) is one of the most common fears in the developed world.

However, being forced into flying allows me to discuss a most puzzling tradition – a hallowed, religiously followed rite of passage. I am referring to the 'airport pint', or pints (or glass(es) of wine, but mainly pints). Having travelled extensively, I have come to realise that this is not an exclusively Scottish tradition, but I'm convinced that the Scots are the most common practitioners. The rules are simple: regardless of when or where you are flying to, if the bar is open, you must have a pint before boarding the plane. Or two. Or three. Or many. Governing bodies are complicit with this practice as, unlike the high street bar or restaurant, alcohol can be sold at any time in airports and on airplanes. This means a 6 am flight to Valencia or Majorca can begin with a jar or two of Stella Artois before boarding.

For 99% of the time, I have no issue with this hallowed custom. Indeed, as someone who does not enjoy flying, I have been known to have a Gin & Tonic or three on flights longer than a few hours (assuming I am not driving upon landing, of course). But we have all witnessed that one traveller who has had too much prior to boarding. And whilst we remain silent, we are all in chorus repeating the prayer of 'please don't sit next to me' as they weave their way through the cabin. They are often singing a song no one has ever heard before, obliviously bumping into every person as they try to find their seat (invariably

---

1 - I reserve the right to backtrack on that statement should you be visiting during one of the rare storms. Assuming that storms aren't your thing.

next to you as you begin the other silent prayer: 'Please have the wrong seat'). The other problem with these pre-flight pints (and this trait covers a wider age demographic) is not fellow passengers drunk to obnoxious levels but to the point of needing to visit the facilities regularly. They are never sat in the aisle, and you thus spend much of the flight getting up and, with a look of resignation to everyone sat behind you watching your game of musical chairs, wait to repeat the motion. And then wait to do it again.

As I am driving upon reaching Stornoway, I do not partake in this tradition. In truth, I am looking forward to this short 35-minute flight as the path will take us over Skye or the West Coast, and I've yet to see this part of Scotland from the air. My joy of not having either a 'singer' or a 'dancer' sit next to me is short-lived as cloud cover means I see nothing until we are halfway through the descent to our destination. Once we break the cloud, the plane passes North Lewis on our right and the Point Peninsula (or An Rubha in Gaelic) on the left.

Stornoway has very little 'island' feel about it, being somewhat more like a small town similar to what you might find throughout Scotland. But it is not long before the scenery completely changes, from green and fertile lands to rising hills and rock. Lewis and Harris are one island, but they are geographically quite different. The two names for the one island came about as a means to differentiate the north (Lewis) and the south (Harris) due to two Clan MacLeod's creating a boundary sometime in the 14th century. Approximately nine times more people live in Lewis (less than 2,000) than in Harris, which is quite evident once Stornoway is behind you.

A few miles past the last outposts of Stornoway lies the Pairc Land Raiders Monument – built in memory of around 200 Lewis inhabitants who defied the laws by shooting and eating the landowner's deer. It is yet another reminder of how two things have shaped the Highland landscape more than anything else: sheep and potatoes. As landowners realised that livestock (predominantly that meant sheep) was a more profitable venture and with less potential for trouble, many of the Highlanders were driven from their homes. Had the potato not thrived in the harsh lands of the Hebrides, the population would have been forced to thin even further.

Scotland's Most Terrifying Predator

The midge, whose Latin name is Cullicoides impunctatus, is a little shit and demonstrates more than any lack of miracles that there was no such thing as intelligent design. What is truly frustrating about this abominable little blood-sucker is that it much prefers some people more than others. This tiny little speck, no longer than a few millimetres, is attracted to some as if they are wearing 'eau de Midge'. Attempting to talk to someone whose hormonal excretions do not work like catnip to midges is one of the most slow-burning irritants known to humankind. Whilst they swish away the odd one that has got lost on its way to whichever piece of skin you've left exposed, you battle like a flailing Godzilla or King Kong against an army of creatures often too small to see until they've landed and bitten you.

Those agents at Guantanamo Bay accused of 'water-boarding' inmates needing to extract information missed a trick by not simply filling a room with midges and just waiting until the poor sod trapped inside could take it no longer. With minimal physical damage (although perhaps a lifetime of avoiding Scotland as a holiday destination), I am sure that a full written confession, possibly to anything, would be achieved after just a few minutes. The name 'Midge' is likely derived from the Swedish Mygge or the Dutch Mugge. Only the females bite; the males are vegetarian – take from that what you may, but I wonder how anyone can tell the difference?

Although midges have likely been in Scotland for over 8,000 years, the first mention isn't until the 18th century. In his diary of the 1730s, a certain General Wade reported from Fort Augustus while resting from road construction, "I have been vexed with a little plague... swarms of little flies which the natives call Malhoulakins." Even Bonnie Prince Charlie, after his defeat at Culloden, was blighted by the pest as one account stated, "...we greatly suffered by mitches, little creatures troublesome and numerous in the highlands... to preserve Him from such troublesome guests we wrapt him head and feet in his plaid, covered him with heather where he uttered several sighs and groans."

For decades, many hardened campers swore by a product called 'Skin So Soft' distributed by the direct-to-consumer cosmetic company Avon. Nowadays, there are several more effective repellents, and it would appear that darker clothing attracts the midge. One repellent brand is called Smidge and their website (smidgeup.com) forecasts, using traps and mini-weather stations, where the worst likelihood of an attack is. The last I looked, it appeared that everywhere was at risk. Ardnamurchan Distillery recently teamed up with Smidge, releasing a limited-edition whisky. Whether one is to drink enough that the reek of the whisky repels the airborne little monster, or you are to douse yourself like a cologne is not clear. Perhaps it is just a reward for putting up with being bitten?

The other flying blight is the cleg (also known as 'gleg' or 'horse-fly'). The cleg flies in complete silence and is barely detectable once it lands. What makes this micro-flying vampire much more of an irritant is that it is often only detected after having had its fill of blood, and pain is felt only upon departure. The puncture from feeding can result in an itchy, painful welt for hours or even days after the bite. Clegs have a particular penchant for exposed skin on golfers preoccupied with their next shot. Many a time I have been concentrating on a putt to then notice just a momentarily sensation of something and instinctively swat at a calf or upper arm. By that point, the damage is done, and the rest of the round is spent rubbing the red spot of the bite and in paranoia of further attacks.

But if you really want to avoid either, head out on the open water, or near concentrations of people and when there is a firm breeze. It could be argued that the midge and cleg does more than any fence, sign or public order to keep the wild campers to a minimum. Perhaps for this honourable side-effect they should be lauded rather than maligned.

The landscape of Harris reminds me of the rock pools I used to play in as a child. Except these are pools for a giant, and instead of looking for small crabs, fish and other tiny sea creatures stranded as the tide goes out, the giant would find the odd bathing human, stranded sheep or cow. With about five miles to go, I stop to collect two hitchhikers, making their way back to Tarbert, which is also my destination and, frankly, the only destination for quite a while. One is a Canadian but has lived on Harris for several years, and the other is a Liverpudlian just up for a visit. I learn that a misjudged leap across what appeared to be a solid peat bog resulted in the lad from Liverpool sinking waist-deep. Apologies were made for any mess or smell, but as peat is not overly odorous, and my passenger appeared mostly dry (and more importantly, the car was a rental), I was not bothered – it is a helpful reminder, should you stray from the path, that what looks like a solid place to stand in a peat bog can often be a lot deeper than anticipated.

Tarbert, which means crossing place, is a tiny sliver of land that prevents South Harris from being its own island. One side is the local school looking out onto the West Loch – arguably the most picturesque school in Scotland. On the other side, homes, hotels, shops, and the ferry port to Skye are all looking out over the East Loch. The entire isthmus is less than one mile long and was used by Norse sailors during the Viking period, who would carry their smaller boats from one side to the other. As I make a sharp bend and the port comes into view, I am struck by just how perfect the setting is for the Isle of Harris Distillery. Not even the newly opened Port Ellen Distillery can claim to be as close to the ferry terminal as Harris Distillery is to Tarbert.

I am staying at the Hotel Hebrides, a fine establishment that is clearly well-liked by the locals as the restaurant is full and the bar is also busy. The sun wakes me around six in the morning, and when I hear a noise, I poke my head out of the small bathroom window. Not more than a hundred yards from my bathroom window I can see the door closing on the ferry, having discharged its cargo and now loaded, preparing to leave. By the time I was out for a morning walk, the ferry had gone, and the harbour had just a few small boats.

Back at the hotel, I ordered the famous Stornoway black pudding with eggs, haggis and a potato scone. While haggis is arguably Scottish in origin, Black Pudding is from Yorkshire, England. However, this is a moot point, as Stornoway's version is the best. Made with rich beef suet, it has a wonderful texture rather than being slightly lumpy with chunks of fat. And yes, for those wondering, it is indeed made with pig's blood. And again, yes, for those wondering, haggis is traditionally made with some sheep offal, and the stomach or sexcum is the sack that it is cooked in (but you don't eat that bit).

Those who turn their noses up at the idea of sheep offal or pig's blood will get a bemused look from the locals, especially if they are happy enough to eat eggs or sausages. I heard a funny exchange between a group of Americans at breakfast discussing the ingredients of some of Scotland's favourite foods. That was until one of them pointed out that an American hot dog was made with the very last remnants from the carcasses of whichever animals were available. All nodded in agreement that hot dogs were filled with disgusting ingredients; all agreed that they ate them, and none ordered the haggis or black pudding from the breakfast menu. I took great delight in ordering both.[1]

As I'm early, once again, I have time to order a coffee from a small caravan that has popped up on the road next to the distillery. The owner is an Australian who, having spent over thirty years in London, decided to get away from it all and settled on Harris – about as 'away from it all' as possible. I make him laugh by asking for a 'Kiwi Flat White'.[2] Over an excellent cup of coffee (seriously, what is it with Antipodeans and excellent coffee?), Shaun, the owner, educates me on life in Harris.

"Staff, that is the problem," he tells me. "The distillery has made a large impact on the area, as before, the jobs available were not paying well enough to encourage anyone to stay and work here." Shaun admits he can only work his coffee van for six months a year due to relying on tourism. "The local population is too small to keep me working throughout the year. And I rather like the months off work."

I finish my excellent coffee and see signs of life at the distillery. Blair Sterrick, Isle of Harris's UK Sales Manager, greets me at the entrance. "Would you like a coffee?" he asks. I laugh, pointing at the coffee van, and we head inside. As has often been the case, Harris Distillery shatters any preconceptions I may have had.

---

1 - The combination of haggis and black pudding is akin to me swallowing a flare. My culinary pleasure was short-lived as indigestion festered for several hours. Don't let my sensitive digestive system put you off. It is a culinary delight and more than worth a few burps.
2 - Perhaps more than any sporting event, the question that riles Australians and New Zealanders the most is, 'Which country invented the Flat White?' I'm staying neutral on this one.

Isle of Harris Distillery

www.harrisdistillery.com
Open to visitors

"We really wanted the distillery to feel like a home away from home." Shona Macleod, Harris's Blender, tells me. "Burr [Anderson 'Burr' Bakewell, Founder of Isle of Harris Distillery] was adamant that the visitor centre would be a warm, cosy and welcoming place. This went so far as having a log burning fire that we always have lit."

'Burr' Bakewell is a slightly enigmatic figure which I find adds to the story of Harris in a charming way. An American who fell in love with the island's remoteness, Burr was keen to help with the thorny issue of long-term and meaningful employment in the area. A new distillery seemed the logical choice and once the site at the port of Tarbert had been decided upon, he set about finding the right partners to begin the work. These partners became known as the Tarbert Ten, which makes them sound like a Cowboy gang of guns for hire in an old western. The analogy is not far off the truth, although we'd need to replace the guns with various marketing, sales and business expertise.

"We were extremely fortuitous in that the site had been infilled from the sea a number of years ago and had not been developed." Simon Erlanger, Isle of Harris' Managing Director, tells me. Frankly, it couldn't be more perfect. "Located by the terminal for the ferry to Skye, in the heart of the main village of Tarbert and a few hundred metres from reservoirs containing some of the softest water in Scotland, it was as if it had been destined for us.

"Our first challenge was to design a building which would sit comfortably in the heart of this traditional village and yet stand out as a symbol of optimism and hope for the island. Additional foundations were required to protect against a once-in-a-century flood risk. Building during the storms of winter 2014, when gales exceeded 120 miles per hour, tested the building's resilience, which it thankfully passed with flying colours."

Looking out past Tarbert's small harbour into the deep blue and calm sea waters beyond, it is hard to imagine storms and floods. But then, once again, I am getting caught up in the trap so many tourists fall into. This is a remote island which experiences just about everything Mother Nature can throw at it.

From the original ten employees, the distillery now boasts a team of over 40. The impact on the local economy has been perhaps the distillery's greatest achievement – offering careers that were few and far between on Harris. Shona Macleod, a Harris native, was initially hired as the Customer Experience Manager and part of the original Tarbert Ten.

"I was involved in the sensory and quality work behind the gin from the start and really enjoyed it," Shona tells me. "Over time, I developed a keen interest in whisky production. As our whisky stocks developed, so did my sensory skills and I became involved with new make spirit quality control, whisky recipe creation and cask selection under the guidance of our sensory consultant, Dr Gordon Steele. As we approached the launch of the whisky, we knew there was a need for an in-house blender, so I threw my hat in the ring, and here I am! I now work closely with the distillers and warehouse team."

What sets Harris apart, other than the quality of the product has been the incredible marketing success of the gin. Simon's decades of experience working with some of the whisky industry's largest brands, such as Glenmorangie and United Distillers, alongside Ron MacEachran, previously Whyte & Mackay's Chief Financial Officer, helped to shape the product. "The success of the Isle of Harris Gin afforded us a lot of time to not have to release our whisky too early," Shona proudly informs me. "It gave us the chance to mature the whisky for longer than it may have otherwise. It set the scene for us in terms of quality and brand awareness and put a spotlight on Harris during these early years."

Whereas other brands of gin are struggling (and for all those that state packaging isn't essential, they are wrong),[1] sales of Harris Gin continue to be a large part of the business. And had anyone been concerned that the gin was a fluke or somehow lucky, they would

---

1 - I suggested that the team should set up an online site where anyone can upload a picture of the Harris gin bottle being used as a vase or water bottle in a commercial environment. The site would be inundated such is the success of the bottle design.

have had their frown turned to astonishment when The Hearach[1] single malt whisky was launched - a launch unlike anything the industry had witnessed before.

"The sales launch saw hundreds of people queuing outside the distillery," Shona tells me. "Some waited for over three hours to get their hand on these precious first-release bottles. Our online sales were an enormous success, resulting in the sale of 28,000 bottles in four and a half hours."

Both the gin and the whisky are unique to the island. They represent the natural beauty, remoteness and ruggedness of the area - it is little wonder that more than 70,000 visitors make a pilgrimage each year to the distillery. You might come for the beaches, sea life, wildlife, fauna and views, but you'll definitely appreciate it all a little more with a dash of Harris spirit in a glass.

Blair and Shona take me on a private tour of the distillery, which produces around 200,000 litres of alcohol annually. I am impressed with how every room, every display, and even the filling store are pristine - everything has a place and is where it should be. I remark that I've never seen a cleaner filling store in any warehouse. Blair and Shona laugh; there is clearly a slight obsessiveness to order and presentation, but to a tourist, the image is one of care and pride.

Row upon row of private owner's casks at one of Harris's warehouses

1 - Hearach means a native of Harris.

After a short drive out to the warehouses at Ardhasaig, the orderly nature of the business continues. Pretty rows of private casks line one of the warehouse walls, all adorned with the red, blue and grey colours of the distillery logo. The views from these warehouses are likely unmatched by any warehouses in Scotland and perhaps the world. Again, the weather is spoiling us, and the views out over West Tarbert Bay are as far as the eye can see and bathed in sunshine. It makes me think of the massive industrial estates, warehousing millions of casks in row upon row of uninspiring buildings.

Blair drives me out towards the North Uist Ferry terminal just south of the tiny village of Leverburgh. Here, the Isle of Harris Brewery has opened a restaurant and shop, and we sit outside basking in the sunshine and enjoy a beer. Well, I do; Blair has a soft drink, as is the driver. Usually, I would feel some guilt, but just like drinking a whisky at the distillery enhances the experience, so does drinking beer at the brewery – and I've been driving a lot lately.

The Isle of North Uist is soon to boast its own whisky from the North Uist Distillery Company. As if Harris wasn't remote enough, this tiny island with just over 1,200 inhabitants will reward the most intrepid traveller. Just below South Uist, and only accessible via the Eriskay Causeway, is the Island of the same name. Those who have read Compton Mackenzie's book 'Whisky Galore' may be more familiar with Eriskay's fictitious name – Great Todday. The true story of the SS Politician (named SS Cabinet Minister in the novel), from which Mackenzie based his novel, was grounded in 1941, with around 22,000 cases of duty-suspended Scotch whisky. Unlike the book, where the Islanders get away with their stolen loot, no less than 19 of those caught stealing the bounty ended up incarcerated in Inverness.

No trip to Harris is complete without a visit to the beaches. From Tarbert, the main road takes us past the Seilebost and Nisabost beaches. These have golden sands and light turquoise water and could easily be the setting for a movie set in the Caribbean (if the weather would always play along). I try my best to capture some of the views with a panoramic shot, but really, you're going to have to visit the place one day.

Back at the distillery, I am amazed at how busy it now is. As each ferry from Skye or bus from Stornoway arrives, more and more tourists enter and mill around the shop, waiting for their time to tour the distillery. My arrival is rather well-timed as it coincides with the management team also being present to entertain a group of Scottish parliament members and employees. I realised that two of the passengers on my flight I had mistaken for Jehovah's Witnesses were, in fact, a member of Parliament and his secretary. This reminds me once again not to judge books by their covers. Perhaps MSPs and Jehovah's Witnesses buy from similar tailors?

Far too soon I am heading back towards Stornoway to get my flight to Glasgow. My journey to the airport allows me enough time to resolve that I must return and for a lot longer than a night or even two. Harris has an almost tangible magic to it. Its beaches, water, rock pools, and people are an intoxicating mix of, or a distilled essence of, what the islands of Scotland offer. I am shaken out of my resolution by a house near Stornoway airport. Mostly, the houses on Harris are a mix of traditional Scottish bungalows, two-storey builds and several amazing dream homes, but this house, albeit on Lewis, stuck out like a burnt-out car on a pristine playing field. I was immediately reminded of a line from one of my favourite movies, 'Hot Fuzz'; 'Hardly in-keeping with the village's rustic aesthetic'. Perhaps a retired Football player built it?

I was quite happy for that to be my final word about Stornoway, but having been warned about Stornoway's airport security, I'd like to add my solitary experience with the overly cautious security detail. I had one bag – a small leather holdall. Granted that, along with my one change of clothes and meagre toiletries, there was a bottle of Harris Gin, a bottle of Hearach whisky and a few sample bottles, it may have warranted a quick check. But no check was deemed necessary, and through security I went without a hitch. Only to then have my name called out to return to the security area, where a gloved officer was waiting for me with my bag.

"Mr Stirk? You have an e-cigarette in your bag, and we asked you to remove it before checking your bag."

This wasn't posed as a question, nor was there any mention about an e-cigarette at check-in. There was not a single part of the tone that allowed for any possibility of error. I assured the officer that I did not smoke, did not possess an e-cigarette and had packed the bag myself. The officer was having none of it and systematically went through every single nook and cranny of my bag. My used underwear, socks, and shirt were all pulled out. My toiletry bag, containing just soap, toothbrush and toothpaste was emptied and checked, and my small leather holdall was padded down into the corners several times. Again, my protestations that I did not smoke and have never possessed an e-cigarette fell on deaf ears. The supervisor was called, and the entire process was repeated, again without a word to me. I even suggested at one point that they put the bag and contents back through the machine. No acknowledgement of what I felt was a sensible suggestion. Accusations then came from the first officer that I had removed it - despite the fact that I had not moved from the first officer's side since being summoned.

Long story short, and after much embarrassment as every other passenger on my flight passed me, watching as my few possessions were again shaken, padded and spread out (and with both officers still refusing to put my bag and contents through the x-ray machine), it was decided that an essence dropper was the offending article. Mercilessly, I was left to re-bag everything whilst the first officer, perhaps in the hope of nailing me for something, swabbed me and my bag for a drug test. I recall having a considerably easier time flying into Moscow with a suitcase filled with whisky. I was warned, and now you have been too because you're going to go to Harris one day, and you might be flying there.

My photo does not do Seilebost beach justice

CHAPTER 8

THE WEE TOON. FAR, FAR AWAY.

*"It's a sea loch.
If Campbeltown Loch had been filled with whisky, as Andy
Stewart famously sang, all marine life would be pickled."*

I can almost trace the journey from Glasgow to Campbeltown in my head. I say 'almost' as I find that much of the road is new, and some parts have been completely rebuilt. I moved there in January 2002 after a fortunate break with a new job. But I'm racing ahead of myself, so let's get beyond Glasgow and over the Erskine Bridge, heading west through Dumbarton along the majestic Loch Lomond.

Loch Lomond will always have a special place in my heart. Not only because it is one of the most beautiful parts of Scotland but also because I attended a summer camp on its banks almost every year from the age of eight until my early twenties. I learnt water skiing, fencing, archery, riflery, paragliding, and rock climbing, fell in and out of love and had more meaningful, moon-lit bonfires with friends than I can remember. The Loch keeps many of my childhood secrets, and due to the water having no memory, we have a special bond. I turned 13, 18 and 21, all on the banks of the loch (and local pubs in Drymen). When I turned 21, I was bought what was referred to as a 'dirty pint' – effectively a pint of everything on the back bar: gin, vodka, whisky, schnapps, Bacardi, rum, Uzo – it all went in.[1] I was then egged on to drink the lot in one go and duly complied. Supposedly, all of my 'friends' had a wonderful night whilst I was comatose under a table. However, on returning to the camp, I emptied myself of the 'dirty pint' in the car park, and the next day was as fresh as a daisy. Everyone else in attendance suffered a prolonged hangover under an unusually strong Scottish summer sun.

My reminiscing on childhood halcyon days is interrupted by a Traffic Incident Support van flashing past me and the car in front on a blind bend. Clearly, incident support work has seen lean times recently, and this van driver was attempting to create additional

---

1 - Since made illegal. May have been at the time come to think of it.

work for their unit. The road to Campbeltown is, at times, magnificent but quite long. Often upon returning from some international whisky festival, I would thumb a lift home from Glasgow with Euan Mitchell (then Sales Manager of Springbank); he used to joke that the most depressing sign in Scotland was the 'Campbeltown 95 Miles' sign as you enter Kintyre. It was not that Campbeltown was a depressing destination, just that despite the long journey you'd already taken, you still had 95 miles to go.

In my last book, "Independent Scotch", I hinted at having taken the Glasgow to Campbeltown bus once (possibly twice) and vowed never to do it again. Perhaps now is a good time to explain some of that journey and why it left such an indelible impression on me. I was on a fairly late bus. Opposite me was a very numerous family that clearly had a father who often asked and a mother who rarely declined. Their clan took up at least four rows of seats and with the combined volume of two or three simultaneous discos. The mother had prepared well for the journey, and by 'well', I mean she had brought enough food for the crew of a transatlantic crossing of an ocean-going liner in the 1800s. The food, which included numerous different sandwiches and baked goods, was not dished out so much as forced into the hordes of already hyper and vibrating children. I am assuming they were all her children – it didn't take the greatest piece of deduction considering how similar they all were; each had one eye staring vacantly, dark curly hair and a dialect for which no dictionary existed. I think anyone nearby would have assumed a close-knit DNA.

All of a sudden, the children began to show some ill effects of their feeding. At first, whimpering, then belly-clutching accompanied by 'Mummy, Mummy', repeated with growing urgency. Many around me began to grasp the likely outcome, and a wave of panic rose from neighbouring seats. Those seated near any of the children had little time to react to the first retches before all in view were treated to a cacophony of sloppy, wet, chunk-riddled projectile hitting the floor. Children are the very worst at preventing one instance of vomit from turning into a medley of vomiting. This family of overly stuffed, travel-sick, look-alikes needed only the slightest nudge of encouragement as one after the other began to make their last meals reappear. All bar one, the youngest, a cheeky little fellah that squealed with delight as he watched each sibling produce their innards left, right, up and down. I am fairly confident that this little chap was the only one enjoying the spectacle.

Eventually and reluctantly, the bus driver stopped, allowing everyone to hurriedly exit for some fresh air. Had we been less than 20 miles to Campbeltown, most passengers would have walked the rest of the way. The driver, in his infinite wisdom, and having made the best with the meagre cleaning apparatus to hand, reorganised us, seating the 'vomiting family' (now much, much quieter and a lot stiller) at the back and the rest of us as close to the front as possible. This did not stop the stench of bile from hitting our noses, but at least most of us could not see the paper napkins piled in layers as their absorbing ability was tested. Some five and a half hours after leaving the Buchanan Bus depot in Glasgow, I arrived in Campbeltown. The runway at Machrihanish suddenly had an unrivalled appeal as a mode of transport in and out of Campbeltown. I recalled all of this as I continued my drive from Thornhill, taking just a mere 4 hours in a comfortable car (and without any vomiting little companions).

During my time living in Campbeltown I was hugely into Mike Oldfield.[1] Frankly, if you can suggest a better album for touring the western coast and the Hebrides or the Highlands of Scotland than Mike Oldfield's "The Voyager", I want to hear it. The general Celtic feel of this album is a perfect soundtrack to the winding, climbing, and, at times, breathtaking A83 Loch Lomond to Campbeltown road. [Interesting, well to me at least, is that the longest distance signpost in the UK is that for Glasgow when leaving Campbeltown – 136 miles]. Much work on the road is clear evidence of dealing with the constant issue of landslides. I recall that when I lived in Campbeltown, the first indication of a landslide and subsequent road closure was that anything fresh in the supermarkets was suddenly unavailable. Broccoli, bread, milk, eggs and the like would vanish from shelves as everyone stocked up, not knowing when the next truck would arrive. It made me wonder what the local diet had been like before trucks made daily deliveries and long-life containers such as cans and cartons had yet to be invented.[2]

As I enter the town, I have much less sense of a distillery graveyard or ghost town than when I first visited. The place seems bustling, busier – active and changing. When I first arrived in January 2002, I felt a real foreboding about the place. Jobs were hard to come by, shops lay empty, and perhaps saddest of all, the newly refurbished ferry port was still a thorny issue. Ferries to Northern Ireland had begun in 1970 but had stopped by the time of my visit. I hope that the ferry fiasco, as it is now known, gets sorted for the sake of the entire region of Western Scotland and the Hebrides. Perhaps then the stresses on the roads can be lightened slightly.

On my first day living in Campbeltown, my boss informed me that there were only three things to do in the 'Wee Toon': drink, play golf and fornicate.[3] I was already well aware of Campbeltown's famous whisky history, of which more later, and that the Machrihanish golf course had just received the accolade of 'Best first hole in the world' by a prestigious golf magazine but the whole 'fornicating' bit? That seemed an odd activity to bring to my attention. That was until the first weekend I returned to my flat on Bolgam Street, having frequented one of the local pubs only to find access blocked by a couple that had exhausted the first option of drink, ignored the possibility of a round of golf (it being night and all) and were trying their hardest to attempt option three. There is a look my dog gave me when it first accidentally nudged the toilet door open, observing me doing what it does wherever there is grass. It was a look of confusion, disgust, and captivation, but mostly disgust. This is the expression I must have had on my face as the sound of my approach caused the two

---

1 - Although I am not a fan of his best-selling album 'Tubular Bells'.
2 - Another reminder of how crucial the ferries are to this part of Scotland.
3 - I believe a different word was used.

writhing, partially clothed creatures to stop in their unholy act and spy me. This presented me with three options: pretend I hadn't seen them and walk away; stop and stare, hoping they might magically vanish into thin air; or casually step (well, 'leap' would be a more apt way of describing it) over them as if this was a daily occurrence. I chose option three, and incredibly, thankfully, I never saw either of them again – or if I did, I couldn't recognise them standing up (there are only 4,500 inhabitants in Campbeltown, so this is quite likely).

Campbeltown Whisky: It's Rise & Fall & Rise

Should you be lucky enough to visit Campbeltown, I would like you to do something for me. Weather permitting, take a seat anywhere with a view of Campbeltown Loch, then try to imagine this thriving little town over 100 years ago. It has changed quite a bit, so imagine the supermarkets weren't there anymore, the row upon row of modern bungalows and wooden frame houses are all gone, and the modern gym, pool and football fields are all removed. With these gone, now consider that area with double the population of today. Children running around in shorts with muddy, grazed knees, ladies in corsets and bonnets and all of the men in heavy tweed suits with some cap or hat.

Now imagine that Campbeltown has not three, like today, but 24 working distilleries. All with belching kilns and solid fuel fires boiling the water and keeping the stills heated. Twenty-four. Try and place them around the town, bearing in mind that these were not built near the owners' large, plush stone houses on either side of the shore. Pretty soon, you are placing them next to each other. And that is how it was. 9,000 people working and living amongst 24 distilleries. At times, the air would be thick with the peat reek. The reclaimed land that runs beyond Lochend Warehouse at the top of what is known as Mussel Ebb and as far as Springbank Distillery was awash with discharges from the distillery – decades before anyone had thought of Health & Safety. Around the Mussel Ebb were the Glen Scotia, Dalintober, Benmore, Lochead and Kinloch distilleries. All side by side, amongst flats, houses, shops and other businesses in a way no other part of Scotland has ever experienced.

I have often wondered how this must have been to anyone not brought up amongst it. Perhaps a modern-day example could be visitors to Wolfsburg in Germany or Boeing in the US, but these are modern cities and factories – built with people, safety and comfort in mind - with as little intrusion into lives as possible. Campbeltown is a town where the industry was thrust upon it, thrived and then exploded to the point where distilleries were as synonymous as, say, cars in Detroit or diamonds in South Africa.

I bought a flat in the building that replaced Dalintober Distillery; out of my kitchen window was the unappealing view of the backside of Glen Scotia Distillery, and out of the lounge window, I looked directly onto the green, the town and the harbour. I often wondered how dreadful the Mussel Ebb must have been for the inhabitants. Shocking newspaper clippings of children playing in the streams when boiling effluent was discharged would likely now destroy an industry but, back then, barely made the front page of the Campbeltown Journal.

I want you to now time-travel forward to the late 1920s, when all but a few distilleries have ceased to operate or even exist. Around Kinloch Park, only Glen Scotia Distillery struggles along with a skeleton staff. The stills at most of the other distilleries are silent or long since removed. The town's population has shrunk by half due partly to the Great War and through migration. Businesses are closing, buildings are empty, the steamers no longer bring the daily parade of life, and Campbeltown slowly falls away from the whisky blender's consciousness. Within a short space of time, just two distilleries will remain, and even these will work sporadically for decades.

The revival we see today is one born out of a stubbornness, a refusal to allow the once mighty Campbeltown region to fold or be forgotten. Instead of scratching around making a meagre existence relying on other companies wanting Campbeltown whisky in their blends, the owners of Springbank decided that their product was good enough to put the region back on the map. And this they have achieved with a singularity and independence that is wholly theirs. Just as we will never see a return, and probably rightfully, to the industrial mayhem of 20-plus distilleries in the town, never again will the region of Campbeltown be overlooked. On the contrary, should there only be one region recognised, for some whisky drinkers Campbeltown takes the prize.

Today, Kinloch Park is a real asset to the town. A state-of-the-art Swimming Pool and gym and all-weather outdoor sports facilities were built, which have given Campbeltown a much-needed modern look. We'll ignore that, at first, the newly finished site began to sink into the reclaimed land and instead concentrate on the fact that it is still there and looking entirely operational. There are still signs of Campbeltown's past. A short walk around the perimeter of the park and you can still see the now condemned buildings of where Dalintober used to be, the old and floorless Lochend Warehouse, next to a supermarket, and opposite Glen Scotia the bus depot still looks very much like Benmore Distillery.

Whilst Glengyle Distillery was the only newly built distillery that I could include in this book the town is witnessing a renaissance that was unthinkable a decade or so ago. There are several distilleries being planned but it appears the first independent distillery for over a century will be Witchburn Distillery owne by Brave New Spirits. The owners of Raasay have plans for an additional distillery at nearby Machrihanish and severl other plans have either been lodged or approved. Campbeltown, despite its location, is a buzzing whisky mecca.

I had some spare time on the morning of my tour of Glengyle, so I drove the short distance to Machrihanish Golf Club. Having checked the weather reports (all were promising non-stop rain), I never bothered bringing my golf clubs. Frankly, I've lived here long enough to know better than to trust any weather apps over simply waking up and looking out the window. I was, therefore, pining for my clubs as I woke up to blue skies and a not-unusual wind cutting in from the Irish channel. Ideal for a round of golf had I brought the right tools with me.

When I lived here, I was not a golfer, but I remember being at Machrihanish Bay when a certain Greg Norman flew in with his son on what was a spectacular helicopter. A small crowd gathered and watched as Norman sent his tee shot so far into the sea that no doubt someone on Northern Ireland's Antrim coast discovered it near the Giant's Causeway. I'm delighted to add that, having taken up golf in 2012, I played Machrihanish ten years later and sent my drive screaming down the middle – with not a single soul watching. Golf is very much a game where your best work will go unnoticed. It's a lot like fishing.

I also took the time to explore the changes in the town brought about by J&A Mitchell and was, frankly, in awe. 22 years ago, the odd rambler, or importer, and occasionally a Scandinavian or European whisky club might venture to the end of the peninsula[1] seeking out Springbank. These visits were a welcomed diversion for me. I can recall very happy occasions when I presented some formidable whiskies in the small office underneath the flat I rented from the company. Now the office is a plush café/bar called 'The Tasting Room'. Around the corner, the old sandwich shop called Eaglesomes is now the Wm Cadenhead shop. Wm Cadenhead is Scotland's oldest independent bottler. It is an incredible thought, considering how famous Springbank whisky is worldwide, that when the distillery was struggling to sell its wares, it was the output of Wm Cadenhead that kept the distillery and bottling staff in jobs.

Between the shop and my old office is a blending room where you can spend an hour and thirty minutes blending your own special concoction from eight different whiskies (and you get to keep 70cl of your final product to show off your blending skills). At Springbank Distillery, a fairly new shop greets you at the entrance – and now with a convenient car park next to it. In the small store are old ledgers, old bottlings and, more importantly to those in the know, a 'cage' system whereby duty-paid bottles are pulled out of casks and sold with nothing more than red and white sample stickers for labels. Such is the scarcity and desirability of these bottles that they are limited to one per person per trip (not daily, per trip). As I was there on the exact day of the 20th anniversary of Glengyle's opening, I was able to pick from a trio of Kilkerran's that had been specially bottled.

One of my reasons for writing this book is that I was an employee of J&A Mitchell during the build and the eventual opening of Glengyle Distillery. Being young and lacking

---

1 - I used to joke that Campbeltown wasn't in the middle of nowhere, it was the end of nowhere.

any sense of occasion, I did not grasp how momentous the build was – nor, really, how single malt Scotch whisky was rapidly shifting the spotlight onto itself as the most exciting spirit in the world. In hindsight, I should have got more involved and recorded the entire build, but alas, when you are young... I was extremely lucky to not just be at the opening of the distillery but also the first person to try the new spirit.[1] I would often visit the distillery as it was being built and wandered up one day, with the knowledge that the plant was ready to begin producing distillate. Frank McHardy, J&A Mitchell's Director of Distilleries, was there with several of the distillery staff. As the first liquid appeared in the Spirit Safe, Frank filled a glass and passed it to me.

"Here," he said. "You're a writer; what can you taste in this spirit?" I couldn't believe I was going to be the first person to taste the spirit of Glengyle Distillery. I eagerly took the glass and took a large swig. And swiftly spat it out. Frank and his colleagues roared with laughter. Apparently, the first few distillations are full of copper sulphate and other undesirables that work their way out. Sure, it was vile and a lesson learned, but that doesn't stop me from being the first person to taste the distillate of Glengyle – and no one can ever take that away from me.

Across from Sprinbank's distillery shop is the Washback Bar in what used to be the joiner's workshop. Here, you will find all of the available Springbank[2] and Glengyle whiskies. Beyond that is a small museum dedicated to Hedley Wright, the previous chairman, and beyond that, is the Springbank blending room where you can take part in the 'Barley to Bottle Tour'. This culminates in being able to blend your perfect Springbank dram from several aged whiskies. As if that wasn't enough, you can also join a Cadenhead Warehouse Tasting, tour Springbank and/or Glengyle, and stay for three nights as part of the 'Eat, Sleep, Dram, Repeat' package (including a guided historical tour of Campbeltown). And for those that want a truly immersive experience, you can even wait several years to join the 'Whisky School' and learn how to make whisky the Springbank way, from malting to bottling. I feel like I've just written a promotional piece for the company, which I have, but in reality, J&A Mitchell has created a whisky Disneyland for enthusiasts. An adult's playground – just so long as they like whisky. And if that hasn't exhausted you, just a few minutes walk from Springbank is Glen Scotia Distillery – here you can choose from a Distillery Tour, a Dunnage Warehouse Experience, a Distillery Manager Tour, a whisky heritage walking tour and The Warehouse Journey. It's a far cry from the occasional and never more than once-a-day tour (only of Springbank) that existed when I lived there.

Dizzy, after taking in all the changes and options, I retired to the Ardshiel Hotel just up from the ferry terminal where I am staying. I'm not allowed a moment's respite from

1 - And here I must add a huge apology to the tens of people who have read my last book or have already heard this story.
2 - Just to ensure the whole 'Glengyle/Kilkerran' name is not confusing enough, Springbank Distillery makes three whiskies: Springbank, which is lightly peated and distilled two and a half times; Hazelburn which is triple distilled and unpeated; and Longrow, which is distilled twice and heavily peated.

the whisky ferry-go-round ride that I've just got off, as the bar is stocked with excellent whisky. I befriend a trio of Germans on a whisky pilgrimage who have, in turn, made the acquaintance of a Lancastrian - also here for the whisky. Being a Yorkshireman, there is a quick and friendly joke about how the best feature about each other's county is the road leading out.[1] I find it a little amusing that the broad accent and colloquialisms of my new Lancastrian friend are not tempered or dialled down for our new German friends – for whom English is evidently a very second or even third language. When the server behind the bar asks if anyone wants a drink, this is translated by the Lancastrian for no one's benefit as "D'ya want 'owt?"[2] To which at least one of the Germans replied, "No, we just got here".

Silent but soon to begin distilling, Glengyle Distillery's stills

1 - This area of England is known as 'up North'. And to the Scots as 'down South'.
2 - In this instance 'owt' means anything – as in 'would you like anything'.

Glengyle Distillery

www.kilkerran.scot
Open for tours

Glengyle Distillery's introduction was one of completing circles, rejuvenating lost sites, giving back to a community and sticking two fingers up at an association that had planned to wipe Campbeltown's whisky importance from a map. Like all great anecdotes, the latter must be taken with a few grains of salt but, the story goes that at some point, a map began circling, showing only four Scotch whisky regions; someone had lumped Campbeltown in with the Highlands & Islands. Hedley Wright, the owner of J&A Mitchell (the parent company of Springbank & Wm Cadenhead), felt this was not-on – especially when you consider that at this time, the Lowlands could only boast one additional malt distillery to that of Campbeltown. The decision was therefore made, as three distilleries had been proven to be sufficient to ensure a 'Scotch Whisky Region' Hedley was going to re-build Glengyle Distillery.

The original Glengyle Distillery had been founded by William Mitchell, who had previously helped his brother, John Mitchell,[1] run Springbank Distillery. A family dispute erupted, and William left to build his own distillery, which opened in 1872. Glengyle ran intermittently until 1919, when West Highland Malt Distilleries acquired it before closing it in 1925. By the time Hedley Wright purchased the buildings in 2000, there was little evidence the buildings had ever been useful to anyone – other than a public loo for local pigeons.

The build took four years, and whilst it was not a case of cutting corners, compared to similar distilleries in this book, the costs were considerably less. Much of this can be credited to Frank McHardy. Frank's first job within the industry in the mid-1960s was at Invergordon Distillery. Invergordon was built in 1961 solely to provide grain whisky to blending firms, but in 1965, a malt distillery was installed and named Ben Wyvis. The usefulness of having the Ben Wyvis Distillery within the Invergordon complex was limited, and it never made a huge amount of spirit before closing in 1976. Frank's links saved the redundant stills, which were brought down for a new lease of life in Campbeltown.

Glengyle not only marked the first new distillery built in the new millennium and the first new distillery in Campbeltown for over a century (and silencing the discussion of whether Campbeltown was a whisky 'Region'), it also holds the accolade of being the

---

1 - The 'J' in J&A Mitchell.

very first distillery since whisky brands existed that was built with the intention of 100% of its output to be bottled as a single malt. That was the intention, however, David Allen, Kilkerran's Director of Sales & Marketing, informed me:

"Although Glengyle was built to make malt whisky for bottling as single malt whisky, we do use a fair bit of the unpeated distillate in Campbeltown Loch. It's a blended malt that we take great pride in, and the ingredients are top-notch whiskies."

The reason why the whisky is called Kilkerran? Well, it's a simple matter of brand ownership and money. As the distillery is built in the same location and buildings as the original Glengyle Distillery, there was never any other choice for the name. The brand name, however, belonged to a different company, and no agreement was achieved - probably to neither party's benefit. This odd name arrangement, coupled with Hedley Wright's way of doing things, just added another line to this fascinating story. So much so that a distillery with a capacity of around 750,000 litres of alcohol each year has never made much more than 100,000 litres in a single year. This means it is generally operating seasonally from September to December. This tiny output allows the company to keep all of its stock for their own products – ensuring a greater control over the future of the distillery.

And, just in case you've yet to visit Campbeltown and see for yourself, the logo is not the view from the local prison out towards the Longrow church (and possible salvation). Rather it is the view through a barred window in a remnant wall that once formed part of the distillery. Why barred? Well, you probably wouldn't be surprised to hear the lengths some folk will go to get an illicit dram.

As I am in Campbeltown just before the tourist season begins, I am privileged to have a private mini-tour of Glengyle. I note that now tours start in the Springbank courtyard and walk through the distillery to a walkway ending directly at the back of Glengyle. This allows a walk past the old warehouse window that silhouettes the spire of Longrow Church[1] - the logo for the new distillery. In truth, neither Springbank nor Glengyle are much to look at. They were both built with functionality over aesthetics and as we've already discovered at Glasgow Distillery, there is no correlation between a distillery being pleasing to the eye and how good the whisky is. Little has changed in Glengyle's twenty years of production, and the distillery has a damp, fermenting odour as currently not in use. Despite much of the industry ramping up production over the past decade or so, J&A Mitchell has carefully laid down what they feel are adequate stocks of malt spirit. Lessons have been learnt from decades of ups and downs, and no doubt the life out on a limb - on the Kintyre Peninsula - has engrained a spirit of 'we will do it our way'. Seeing how buoyant the town is and how sought after the whiskies are, the philosophy is working.

---

1 - The Lorne & Lowland Parish Church.

CHAPTER 9

THE KINGDOM OF FIFE

"Fife is too short.
Spend it with people who make you laugh and feel loved."
Misprinted inspirational quote.

As I head east for the first time on this little adventure, I am reminded once again about this concept of Scotch Whisky Regions. These new distilleries that I am visiting are raising (whether they like it or not) a very valid question about regionality. Sure, there are occasional similarities in spirit with nearby distilleries, but it can and should be argued that this has as much to do with what spirit the distillers are trying to produce over any greater regional or climatically influenced contribution. Scotland's geography and topography are so varied that having great swathes of the country supposedly possessing some similarities is like suggesting that the New England beaches of the US are similar to the West Coast beaches of Ireland because they are in the same sea.

The hardest to fathom is this idea of a Lowland/Highland line. Historically, this line was intended as a clear distinction between the two peoples. The more Norse/Pictish group of the North and the more Norman/Saxon and Irish group of the South. This may have meant something several hundred years ago, and whilst there will always be a north/ south, Highland/Lowland (and Island by Island) divide, I think it is fair to say that Scotland has never enjoyed a more harmonious 'completeness' – a unison of voice and people if you will.

Back to my point... the idea that Bladnoch is in any way similar to Glasgow, Lindores or Glenkinchie because of some imaginary line is bizarre. It lumps together a product in a way that is more than just simplistic for lazy marketing and writing, and it generalises to the point of banality. I feel it is also confusing to those starting their journey – far too many times I have heard people say something along the lines of 'I'm not a fan of Lowland whisky' without realising what this generalisation is encompassing.

As I travel east, my hi-tech map takes me on a journey through several small villages and the occasional farm. I have no doubt it has shaved thirty seconds or even a minute from this two-hour journey, but then I have also had several near misses with tractors, more than a few hairpin turns and muddied my recently cleaned wheels. I know I am not the first traveller following a shortcut from the navigation system as several dog-walkers have given me that weary look of 'couldn't you have stayed on the main road'.

I could have taken the main road; I know this journey well enough, but where's the fun in that? I would have missed the village of Quothquan and perhaps one of the steepest single-file bridges certainly in Scotland – you have no idea if a car is coming the other way until you are just about touching bumpers. To further prove my point about the Highland/Lowland line being obsequious, the landscape flattens into an enormous plain, the likes of which you cannot find in the neighbouring county of Dumfries & Galloway. Slowly the pastoral land changes to large ploughed fields – we are now in barley country. Scotland produces around 1.6 million tonnes of barley a year and contributes approximately 90% of all the required barley to the Scotch whisky industry. With the growth of the specialist whisky distillery, there has been a wholesale move to use a more locally made barley.

I was not schooled in Scotland and, therefore, have definite gaps in my local knowledge. For instance, despite constantly referring to the area as the 'Kingdom of Fife', I had never learned that this was due to its once being an independent Pictish Kingdom. Come to think of it, I don't recall any coverage of Scotland, Wales or Ireland in any of my history classes. Plenty of time covered the two great wars, the Spanish Armada, the Reformation and the French Revolution. Robert Burns never came up; nothing about Scotland's clan wars, kings, queens (other than Bloody Mary, of course), the clearances, and, most surprisingly, I don't believe the Union of 1707 was part of the curriculum.

For most of my generation growing up in England, the first mention to our ears of Robert the Bruce and William Wallace was from the 1990s great Anglophobe Mel Gibson in his cinematic[1] movie, "Braveheart". It is likely that this oversight in English education fuels, at least partly, the rivalry between England and its conjoined and nearby neighbours. For instance, I grew up through the troubled 1980s when bombs were exploding all over England from disaffected Irish republicans. The general, if not overriding, mood of the average Englander was 'just unite Ireland and be done with it'. It wasn't until I moved to Belfast in the late 1990s that I began to comprehend just how nuanced the situation was – many of my compatriots would not have known what caused the partition in the first place.

Inchdairnie Distillery is my first stop in the Kingdom of Fife, and as I approach it, I am not filled with confidence that my navigation system knows where it is going. The system is telling me to take a sharp left turn off the Kinglassie Road (great name), but all I can see is a large industrial estate, a golf course and supposedly 'Fife Airport'. A modicum of trust in my navigation is restored as I approach an electric iron gate with a large grey metal sign and orange lettering stating;

---

1 - As historically accurate, as a one-armed, one-eyed archer with his back to a moving target.

"INCHDAIRNIE DISTILLERY. No Visitors – We are busy making whisky".

This is my first indication that Inchdairnie is set up differently from its peers. Once inside the gates, I slowly bring the car around a bend, and the distillery comes into full view. The site is a hive of activity. Hi-res jackets and hard hats are bobbing around everywhere, some still emerging from white vans that take up many of the precious parking spaces. New stills are about to be installed, increasing the distillery's capacity from two million to four million litres.

Inchdairnie Distillery is an impressive setup

Inchdairnie Distillery

www.inchdairniedistillery.com
Not open to the public

Ian Palmer, Inchdairnie's Founder and, until just recently,[1] Managing Director, has kindly taken time out of his busy day to show me around the distillery. "We were working flat out to reach two million litres. Whilst we can now make as much as four million litres of alcohol with the new stills, we probably won't get to that amount but can if we need to." Iain informs me.

I'm sat in what is a large conference room that Ian uses as his office. He has an impressive CV having begun his whisky career with Invergordon in 1978. When Invergordon became part of Whyte & Mackay in 1993, Ian moved to Edinburgh to oversee the bottling operations. I wondered if he worked with Frank McHardy but he missed him by a few years. "I learnt about 90% of everything I needed to know working at Invergordon Distillery," Ian said considering the number carefully. He is an engineer by training and clearly a thoughtful and methodical man. I tell him my reasoning for the book and stress how Glengyle was the first Scottish distillery, probably ever, to be built in order to be self-sufficient.

"Unlike us," Ian interjects with a wry smile. "We were built to supply customers with whisky. 70% of our output is pre-sold to trade customers." This fact helps to explain not just why the site is so impressive and much larger than most other distilleries built this century but also why there is no provision for tourists.

Having worked with the Glen Turner Distillery and helped them build the Starlaw grain distillery in Bathgate, Ian knew it was time to do his own thing. Wanting to build the very best distillery possible meant an early realisation that he needed partners and ones who understood all of the constraints that come with building a distillery. Taking three years to develop the business Ian then found the perfect location on the site of an old mill next to the river Leven. With contacts already gained within the industry, Inchdairnie sourced its funding and began production in 2015.

"We are a Fife distillery." Ian Palmer informs me. "We use 100% Fife grown barley, we distil in Fife, we use Fife water, and we mature in Fife. Provenance is very important to

---

1 - Just a few weeks after my visit, Scott Sneddon was appointed Managing Director, having been Inchdairnie's Distillery Director since its opening. I'm guessing my visit was the final straw for Ian.

us. We began distilling our own single malt in 2016."

Whilst many Scotch blended drinkers may be unknowingly drinking Inchdairnie whisky, the first single malt has yet to be released. Ian and his team have set the distillery up to offer a multitude of different flavour profiles and to use several different grains. This was born out of the emphasis on the three 'm's' of production: method, machinery and maturation. Ian wanted to do things differently, from how the grain was milled to using a mashing filter and several different yeasts. The first release, called Ryelaw, is a unique product to Inchdairnie, being made from malted rye and distilled in a Lomond Hill still.[1]

"It's not being different just for the sake of it." Ian continues. "There are already established whiskies with certain flavour profiles and were we to make something similar we simply wouldn't stand out. We set out to bring something new to the table."

Sadly it is unlikely that Inchdairnie will be open to the public for the foreseeable future. I say sadly because what is being produced at the distillery is interesting, really, really interesting. I have forgotten how many times Ian Palmer's name has been repeated on my travels, and each time, it has been from a voice of admiration for what he has achieved and produced at his distillery. Perhaps one day, a swanky new visitor centre will welcome eager minds to see just how different his distillery is. In the meantime, I urge you to look out for future releases.

From Inchdairnie, I head deeper into the heartland of Fife and towards St Andrews, one of Scotland's gems. I love travelling to St Andrews. It helps to be a golfer, but I don't think it is necessary in order to love the place. Few single locations in the world can claim to really be the 'home' for any sport, and golf very much rescued St Andrews, or at least prevented it, from a long association with religious conflict, abbey-sacking, and witch-related atrocities – all part of its long history.

Just before entering St Andrews is the turn-off to Gaurbridge. This tiny hamlet on the River Eden has a fascinating industrial history. William Haig, of the famous Haig whisky dynasty, built the Seggie Distillery in 1810. Although several generations of the Haig family operated the distillery, the distillery was converted to a paper mill in 1874. This was a much more successful venture and the village increased around it to support the business's growth. The mill continued until as recently as 2008, when the last operators, Curtis Fine Papers, went into receivership, making 180 locals redundant.

I am greeted at the small cabin/office by Euan Kinninmonth, Eden Mill's Brand Ambassador, who takes me for a walk as close as we can get to the distillery. "The view will be spectacular," Euan assures me. I look out across the firth towards St Andrews on my right and the North Sea beyond. "The building will be split into three sections, and the plan

---

1 - This is a copper pot still that houses six copper plates within its neck. It allows the distiller to create a lighter spirit. It was first introduced in 1955 but is not commonly used.

is to have a café/restaurant at the top looking out." It is a fantastic location, and another reminder that many of the new distilleries have had the luxury of bearing the tourists in mind. A large car park, a visitor and retail area, a café, and a restaurant – all of the facilities that so many existing distilleries, or at least older distilleries, are having to re-create, attempt to fit in or are forced to go without.

Under construction, the Eden Mill Distillery will be a hugely impressive distillery when completed

Eden Mill Distillery

www.edenmill.com
Open to the public

Eden Mill's story is a slight anomaly compared to its peers in this book. In 2012, Paul Miller started a brewery in Gaurbridge, just outside St Andrews. From brewing, Paul moved two years later into distillation and installed the original Eden Mill distillery, housed within the old dispatch building of the Gaurbridge Paper Mill. The stills were Alembic in design and limited to producing just a few barrels per week. Initially the company concentrated on their Eden Mill Gin as stocks of spirit matured.

This business was bought out in 2022, and whilst Paul Miller is a minority shareholder, a new company called Eden Mill Distillers looked to establish a much larger distillery just yards from the original. The site, which looks over where the River

Eden empties into the Eden Estuary, could not be in a better position. The plans for the new distillery, which was well under construction when I visited, are to continue single malt whisky and gin production. It will have the capacity to produce one million litres of pure alcohol annually. The new owners are intent on using only barley grown in Fife and producing a spirit that is lightly floral and fruity - something that will hold up to a variety of wood maturation types.

There will be a small portion of warehousing within the distillery building that is reserved for Eden Mill's "1655 Club" - their first release of private cask owners. Most of the spirit will be just 10 miles from the distillery in new warehouses. Whisky tourism forms a huge part of Eden Mill's plans, with the opening of its purpose-built visitor centre scheduled for spring 2025. They will offer immersive gin and whisky experiences with top-notch food and drink facilities on-site, all offering views across the picturesque Eden estuary and towards St. Andrews.

"Our new building is the old pulp shed of the paper mill and sits right on the banks of the Eden estuary; the location is ideal as we form part of St. Andrews University's Eden Campus dedicated to sustainability. Our neighbours are a biomass plant, and our electric power will come directly from the solar farm just yards away. At the same time, we will capture the carbon dioxide from the fermentation process to be used by the university for research."

From what was one of Scotland's smallest distilleries, the new building will be St Andrew's closest whisky experience and one of the area's most impressive. Coupled with the tourism that St Andrew's enjoys, Eden Mill is sure to spread the word of Fife Scotch whisky to every corner of the globe.

From Gaurbridge it is just a few minutes' drive into St Andrews - home of the oldest university in Scotland and one of the oldest still in existence. The town is still dominated by golf and the university. At any given moment, these two transient inhabitants, or part-time residents, outnumber the locals by three to one. This gives the town a cosmopolitan feel and certainly one of being a class above any other. It also means a level of income, or spending is on display – certainly from the golfing community who love nothing more than arriving at an expensive golf club in a swanky car. A heady combination of students, pubs, golfers and expensive cars makes for large summer traffic jams. As I am off-season, I have avoided much of this but the place is still abuzz with activity.

Golf - A Bastard of a Game

"I used to be young and terrible at golf.
But after decades of practising, I am now old and terrible at golf."
Anonymously, every amateur golfer.

I like to think that a Scot travelled through England and watched for the umpteenth time as a bunch of bizarrely dressed cricketers waltzed off a cricket pitch due to rain. I would say 'ran', but it is hard to imagine anyone who played cricket back then running. The Scot then thought, 'This game is not suited to the English climate. One day, the Southern Hemisphere will take this from the English and beat them at it." He would be right, of course.

On returning to Scotland, the traveller, having thought long and hard about it, realised that Scotland was even less suited to a game that required temperate weather outdoors. Picking up a ball and his curved-handle walking stick, he ventured out along the coast and, in the driving wind and rain, attempted to hit the ball with his stick as far as he could. Thus, the game of golf was born. This is an improbable scenario as golf is likely a considerably older game with references as far back as the 15th century. Cricket would not appear in any literature for another 100 years.

Golf has a sadistic blend of stressful elements - enough to negate any benefits of the three to five-mile walk (depending on how straight you can hit the ball). You are attempting to hit a small ball with a small stick and get it into a hole not much wider than the ball. This, alone, is enough to send most participants into a rage of despair. Still, when you add in the Scottish elements of intermittent but fairly consistent rain, wind that follows you and a terrain that evolution has perfected into a micro-climate of ball-hiding par excellence - well, it is no wonder the country's national drink is whisky.

Einstein once said that the definition of insanity was attempting the same thing repeatedly and expecting different results. I wager Einstein had reached this conclusion whilst trying his hand at golf.[1] I know of no other game where you are on fire one day, hitting the ball where you aim and watching as it sinks down the 4¼ inch hole as if it knows its way. Then, the next day, the club in your hand is some alien technology; the ball mysteriously can avoid being hit, and the hole is now seemingly half the size of the day before. The famous saying goes, 'Golf is a good walk spoiled',[2] but I much prefer the saying, and

---

1 - Which he did whilst seeking refuge in Norfolk.
2 - Almost certainly not coined by Mark Twain.

again not attributable to anyone, "I hate golf. I quit golf. I can't wait to play tomorrow".

This better sums up what the game of golf is; it is that, despite taking over 100 shots to play a course that should only take 71, there was that one shot, just one moment, where all of the stars aligned. When, for some utterly unknown reason, you relaxed, kept your head down, brought the club back on plane, kept the face from opening, reached the top of the backswing without swaying, didn't bow the wrists, brought the club back on the inside, squared the face, shifted your weight correctly, hit the ball first, extended through impact, finished with balance and watched the ball go and do exactly what you hoped it would. That one shot out of the hundred that were sliced, pulled, thinned, fatted or simply never connected is what brings you back. Golf is a cruel mistress, but once under your skin, separation is out of the question.

The apocryphal story goes that golf courses have 18 holes because it took that long to polish off a bottle of Scotch. Whilst sadly not true[1] (the real reason being that St Andrews had 18 holes and most other courses copied or altered to fall in line), it would make the game more enjoyable. I'm not sure how a bottle of whisky per round would go down with some of today's elite athletes, but noting the antics of many professionals in what is referred to as the 19th hole (often the golf club's bar, but any bar will do) it might be a welcome addition.

I am staying just a few doors up from the Dunvegan Inn, a mecca for those golfers seeking the refreshment of the 19th hole, and I dive in for a pint of beer. A bottle of Daftmill 15 year old sits behind the bar and catches my eye, which then more than waters when I'm informed it is £80 a dram. I glance at my watch and mumble something about being late for a prior engagement etc. As a rule when in St Andrews, especially when not busy golfing, a trip to Luvians Bottle Shop on Market Street is a must. I recognise Archie McDiarmid, the manager, and we have a quick catch-up on the great and good of recent whisky bottlings (a dram is poured, naturally). Several pounds lighter, at least monetarily, I leave with a box of bottles. It's easily done and I need little encouragement.

Archie has very kindly recommended a few pubs – one of which, The Keys, also on Market Street, has a better-than-decent whisky selection. Again, I spy a bottle of Daftmill 15 year old and thanks to their ribbon-coloured pricing method I learn that this bottle is £18 per dram. I ask to make sure I've decoded their system correctly and, once confirmed, order that and a dram of Springbank 15 year old. Both come to £26, which, considering the possibility of parting with £80 for one dram of Daftmill just a few minutes walk away, seems a stonewall bargain.

I must, at this point, reveal that whisky people, well, me at least, have a slight habit of using their little knowledge to correct those that often don't give a damn. Two gentlemen

---

1 - I've seen it done in the time taken to play just one hole.

next to me, having spied me buying not one but two drams, begin talking about whisky-related things. "My sister works for [name redacted] distillery. She says that the staff there are always running around with duct tape patching up leaks as they're not allowed to replace anything in case it affects the flavour." One of them tells me and his buddy.

I bite my tongue. This tale is a hangover from when distilleries and their tour guides would often talk about how dents, rivets, seams and imperfections in stills were mimicked in replacement plant to ensure they produced the same results. It is, of course, nonsense but never let facts and science get in the way of a good story.

I do let my tongue get the better of me when someone else at the bar orders a 'Lafrayg'. As the bartender cannot quite hear over the music, I decide to help by correctly pronouncing 'Lafroyg'[1] (or at least as correctly as anyone with an accent like mine can). This, as is so often the case with the best-selling smoky whisky in the world, gives someone else at the bar the chance to ask:

"You don't actually like that stuff, do you?"

I resisted the temptation to suggest that it wasn't ordered because it was the easiest brand name to pronounce.

As it is a glorious evening, I take time to walk down to the famous Old Course and watch a few groups finish their round. One lady makes a 30-foot putt that hangs agonisingly on the edge of the hole - long enough for the small crowd watching to garner some excitement. The ball eventually drops and the crowd erupts. I'm caught up in the moment, and for the briefest of moments, Americans and Europeans delight in a golfing moment without any flag waving.

My night's sleep is rudely interrupted by a few local seagulls having a conversation from the rooftops - at least 100 yards away from each other. As it is just before five a.m. they may be arguing over when sunrise exactly is. I'm not sure why, in the land of stalking, shooting and fishing, seagulls are a protected species. Kill as many as you like of the pheasant and grouse, birds that stay away from humans, rarely call to each other and can barely get off the ground; but don't shoot any of these cackling, sleep-depriving, food-stealing and highly-accurate shit emitting terrors of the sky. Makes no sense to me. They've clearly got a good PR manager – pheasants and grouse should hire the firm. Those who claim to love 'birdsong' must not live near the coast or within 50 yards of a Fish 'n' Chip shop.

The road from St Andrews to Kingsbarns takes you out towards the coast and past the ruined cathedral and the Castle Golf Course. The East Coast of Scotland is a golfer's

---

1 - Laphroaig from the Isle of Islay. No whisky divides opinion more. For some, it is as if the remnant fluids of a long-dead and badly burnt animal were squeezed into a bottle. For others, it is simply nectar.

fantasy road. It is almost a non-stop golf course from Berwick-upon-Tweed on the border up to Dunbar near Edinburgh, on to Aberdour over the Forth Road Bridge, Dumbarnie outside Leven, Kingsbarns and St Andrews and plenty more before one is in Aberdeen, with several more until you get to Royal Dornoch; one of the truly great golf courses in the world. It would require a small fortune to play all of them but many have made the pilgrimage playing several up the entire length of the country. And that is just the east coast.

I have more than enough time to drive into Kingsbarns Golf Course – somewhere I have only ever dreamed of playing. An acquaintance of mine, Doug Clement and one of the main driving forces behind the creation of Kingsbarns Distillery, is a caddie here. As I have not made an appointment to see him, and this being the beginning of the golf tourist season, I send him a message with a picture of the view out of the small but tasteful clubhouse window. My beautiful little golf course[1] in the village of Thornhill costs under £600 for annual membership and just £45 a round for visitors. Kingsbarns costs £418 per round,[2] and if you're playing for the first, and for maybe the only time, you'll want a Caddie, which is a reasonable £65/round - oh, and you'd better tip the Caddie too. And if you get Doug, you'd better tip very well.

I am very kindly let into the clubhouse, as it is usually exclusively for paying patrons. I have my 'writer's face' on and a laptop, so perhaps I am excused as a consultant or something. Whilst cold and overcast, the golfers forking out a small fortune today will have a fairly pleasant day of it. One day I'll make it here, but it's probably best I keep it from the wife. How much will it cost me I wonder…

Despite my detour I am still early when I arrive at Kingsbarns Distillery. Punctuality is an obsession of mine, especially when it is someone else's time – and the problem with punctual people is they expect it from others. But, and here is a great little tip, when you're early at a distillery, this can mean you sometimes get to see or even taste something not 'on the tour', so to speak. It might be the filling of the draff trailer by the farmer eager to fatten up his cattle. It might be the delivery of the grain tipping into a silo, or it could just be a cup of tea or coffee with the visitor guide as they warm up for the tour – which is today's early-bird treat.

The distillery is a magnificently restored old farmhouse that incorporates several rooms that were originally intended for farm animals.[3] George is our tour guide. I say 'our' as I've been joined at the last minute by a family from New York who, having managed to get a last-minute tee time on the old course, have bused down to the distillery to kill a few hours before their bucket-list moment. The mother and son are not whisky drinkers and the father likes Jack Daniels (so not a whisky drinker either).[4] George, having discovered they

---

1 - I don't own it, but all good members take some ownership of a course when they join.
2 - All figures correct as of August 2024.
3 - Cattle and other farm animals were far too valuable to just wander away or get rustled.
4 - That is a joke. Nothing wrong with Jack Daniels.

are from New York, shares a story about running in the famous NY marathon. Afterwards I ask the mother if she can understand anything George is saying (he has a rather 'rural' accent, let's say). "Not a word," she replies. I promise to try and translate, but with a jet-lagged yawn, she makes it clear that that won't be necessary.

Later I am treated to a one-woman comedy show when we get to the tasting stage. Starting with the new-make, she pulls such a face that I have to stifle a proper out loud laugh whilst George is informing us of the notes they look for when making their spirit. Someone out there will suggest to me otherwise, but I've never encountered anyone turned onto whisky, who otherwise did not care for it, through drinking new-make? Her expressions do not get any less constrained as we taste two more expressions. George takes it all in his stride – Kingsbarns' location, and a big reason for being, is to hoover up touring golfers seeking an hour away from the course. Whilst the distillery will welcome aficionados, fans and whisky tourists aplenty, many will be Tennessee sippers with perhaps just enough Scottish ancestry to feel some kinship with the national drink – even if they do not have the palate for it...

Kingsbarns Distillery, the result of a wonderful restoration

Kingsbarns Distillery

www.kingsbarnsdistillery.com
Open to visitors

Kingsbarns Distillery exists from one of those simple eureka moments. Douglas Clement had often thought that a distillery tour after a round of golf at one of the most celebrated courses in the world would go hand in hand, and he set about to make that a reality. Finding the perfect location at East New Hall was the starting point, and it pushed Doug to try to raise enough money to fund the distillery – a proposition that would prove uphill.

The Wemyss[1] family had already ventured into the whisky world with the creation of Wemyss Malts in 2005. Like many other independent bottlers, the question of stock and business growth, when not in control of supply, was at the forefront of future planning. When William Wemyss heard about the plans for a local distillery in Fife, he was intrigued enough to make enquiries before sole ownership was achieved in 2013.

"It was a natural evolution for us to become a distillery owner. It was already a well-trodden path with Andrew Symington [Signatory Vintage] and Lenny Russell [Ian MacLeod Distillers]. The timing was right for us." William Wemyss states. "Having a wine business meant we understood how important it is to engage with the customer. We liked the idea that Fife is the home of golf, and we knew that golfers coming into the area were stating: 'I would like to taste Scotland's other great export, single malt whisky.'"[2]

The existing farm steading was in a terrible state when work began in 2014, but progress was swift, and the distillery opened later the same year. "We had experience in selecting casks, blending, bottling and marketing. Adding on production was the next challenge. The involvement of Dr Jim Swan was key – we couldn't afford to wait 10 or 15 years before releasing a whisky."

The Wemyss family are keen to promote Fife and Scotland as much as possible. "We are a Scottish family owning a single malt distillery when so much of the industry is now owned by international companies. We also wanted to use local ingredients as much as we could, so to have all the barley grown on the family estate was important. Having maturation in the area as well was all part of the same idea of provenance."

---

1 - The name 'Wemyss' means cave and hence can be found in use throughout Scotland's coasts and cliffs.
2 - Quotes from www.scotchwhisky.com.

The original Kingsbarns bottlings were called Dream to Dram playing on Doug Clement's original dreams of a dram for his golfers. The Wemyss family have moved on from this moniker and now offers a core range that includes the 'Doocot' range. A 'Doocot' or 'Dookit' is the Scottish term for a columbarium or room for domesticated doves to nest and breed (and no, I didn't know what that was either). The restoration of this impressive room now allows Kingsbarns' cask No One to sit in pride of place and with little fear of any real doves using it for target practice.

The distillery, as it is approached from the road, is a majestic and fitting addition to not just Fife but the Scotch whisky industry. An inviting small café immediately presents the visitor with somewhere to sit and take in the surroundings and tours are frequent and in-depth. From a moment or spark of inspiration, a proud and beautiful distillery now stands and its product is gaining adulation all over the world.

From Kingsbarns, my next distillery appointment requires a complete re-tracing of my journey back through St Andrews and Cupar before heading north to Lindores. At some point on the busy road, I pass the gates of a driveway to a far-off estate. On each stone pillar at the entrance is a large sign stating "No Through Road. No Visitors. No Camping. No Deer." Much of the rest of the journey is spent pondering the final odd statement. Or was it a request? Just what had transpired that forced the owners to add something so specific? Initially, I wondered whether travellers had, in their droves, traipsed up to the house seeking deer. Had people been arriving with deer as gifts or in the hope of offloading their own unwanted bucks and stags? Were deer turning up with backpacks and camping gear, looking for somewhere exciting to stay? If this is the case, the estate owners are either living in an area with the most educated deer in the world or have completely missed the mark with how effective this sign would be. And should the deer be that literate and self-aware, then perhaps a sign specifically excluding their kind would not go unnoticed. Was the selective, specist, attitude of the estate owners ironically resulting in increasing the deer problem? I had a good mind to go find some deer, round them up, explain the situation and then defiantly drive them straight through the gates into the estate, unleashing guerrilla-style or deer-style warfare against such xenophobia. Thankfully, at least for the back of my car and the estate owners, I didn't see a single deer on this part of the journey. Perhaps the sign was working after all.[1]

Lindores Abbey Distillery, to give it its full title, is just a forty-five minute drive from Kingsbarns, and on first impressions, it has a sort of 'barn-conversion' feel. The impressive size and precision of Inchdairnie, the custom-built and bay-side Eden Mill and the re-purposed magnificence of Kingsbarns are putting Lindores Abbey a little in the shade. I'm a little disappointed.

---

1 - Perhaps a sign at the house in Ardnamurchan would be sufficient to reduce their deer problem?

My spirits are lifted, however, as I walk into the visitor centre entrance into the distillery. The visitor section of the distillery is open, light, welcoming and spacious. An industry friend, John Dorrian, is at the desk and gives me a firm handshake. John has the looks of a 50s rock star with a heart of gold and the strength of someone considerably larger. He calls Drew (Andrew) McKenzie Smith, and moments later, Drew appears and immediately launches into the history and timeline of his family, the buildings and the struggle to get the distillery going. He is a great orator and I feel his days as a chef have trained him not just to present excellent food but also how to pique people's interest in what he does. His stories and tangents are very much like a well-written menu. No need to tell the diner anything that doesn't add to the wetting of appetites.

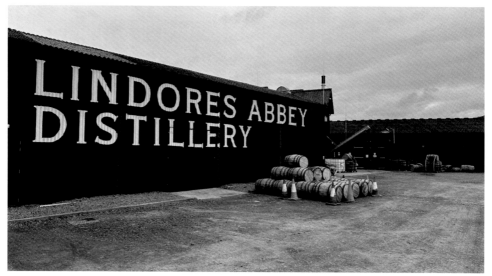

My photo of Lindores explains my first impression

Lindores Abbey Distillery

www.lindoresabbeydistillery.com
Open to visitors

Sometimes, the largest of projects can start with the smallest of nudges. For Drew McKenzie Smith, it was an odd request from an author called Michael Jackson. "Would you mind if I came and had a look at your Abbey?" Michael had asked. Drew was quite used to people wanting to view the ruined Abbey on his family's estate and thought nothing of it. Roll forward several months, and a book titled "Scotland and its Whiskies" landed on Drew's doorstep, and its arrival sent his life on an irrevocable tangent.

"I had no knowledge of Friar John Cor, nor of the reference to the '8 bolls of malt'[1] that were to be sent to King James IV," Drew admits. That set him off on a journey of discovery and realisation that where his family had lived for generations was, until anyone can find an earlier reference, Scotland's spiritual home for malt whisky.

Of course, nothing is simple, and it would take another 14 years before work actually began on the distillery. Some elements were easier than others. Often the most difficult part is heading the distilling team. Early on in the build Drew's wife Helen placed an advert in a local paper looking for an office assistant. By chance, it was read by Caroline Haggart, who mentioned it to her husband, Gary.

"Gary was working offshore at the time having previously worked for Cragganmore Distillery," Drew tells me. "And he sent through a couple of emails; eventually, we thought we should see him and put him out of his misery in that we weren't at the stage of looking for a distillery manager. So, when he came over, we ended up chatting for ages, and we realised we had found the right person for the job."

At times, the build was halted to ensure that any archaeological finds were carefully excavated. Many parts of the Abbey had been buried and, having been carefully removed, are now built within the distillery for posterity. With the dig and Andrew's research came a greater understanding of the size, shape and importance of the Abbey. "I also had a few legal issues," Drew tells me, laughing. "One with a certain 'chocolate bunny' and one with a well-known energy drink, but both issues were overcome, and once we had finance in place, the plans were submitted. The local community were and continues to be, fantastic – not a single complaint was lodged.

---

1 - About 400 bottles.

"The biggest hurdle during the build was power," Drew continues. "I had assumed we would use gas as the mains pipes are about 50 meters from the distillery. I was always advised not to assume anything, and sure enough, when we commissioned (a very expensive) survey, it came back stating that to get an adequate supply, the pipes would have to be widened for about two miles. This obviously would have cost a small fortune and would have caused rolling roadblocks, further setting us back."

The distillery was built with a great deal of help from the Swan Institute and, in particular, Dr Jim Swan. Sadly, Dr Swan passed away before the distillery began operating, but his intervention resulted in Lindores having two smaller-than-usual spirit stills.

"Jim had been working at another Lowland distillery[1] and really felt that the three still setup was the way forward for us – wanting a fruit-forward spirit." Drew continues. "Of course, me, not being from a distilling background, thought 'Well, smaller stills must cost a lot less as they have less copper etc.' I was very, very wrong, and although I acquiesced, as I had promised to follow Jim's lead, it added quite a bit to the build. However, the results are better than what we had hoped for.

"One of my abiding memories of the late, great Jim, who was as much a friend as a consultant, was that he was always immaculately attired. On one of his visits, however, it had been raining, and he had failed to bring any Wellington's [rubber boots]. The only pair we had that would fit him were my eldest daughter's Poppy. Comically, they were bright pink, but Jim was not phased a bit."

The build was quite slow, having begun in 2014, and the first spirit ran off the stills in 2017. Drew and his team took the unique decision to use their new-make and try and recreate Aqua Vitae – a drink that predates what we consider 'whisky' by several centuries (and is likely more akin to what King James IV asked for in 1494). While there is scant information on recipes and flavourings, there is little doubt that local ingredients and traded 'sweeteners' from afield would have been used.

Lindores Abbey Distillery now has a team of 50 employees, some part-time but most fully engaged. Having the product distributed into over twenty markets around the world has been a testament to Drew's vision and perseverance. A friendlier, more engaging owner and team are hard to find, and having built the distillery next to the ruined abbey brings the story of Scotch full circle to its historical home.

1 - Annandale Distillery.

This photo, courtesy of Matthew Hastie, gives a much better view of Lindores Distillery

The centre-piece of Lindores Abbey visitor's area is a great hall with large placards going through the history of the area. It was a clearly thought-out addition replicating the great hall of the abbey whose ruins sit behind the distillery. Gary Haggart, Distillery Manager, takes me on the tour of the distillery. Gary is a perfect match for Drew and the Lindores team. His infectious enthusiasm is matched by his desire to make the best whisky possible. The still house, with its unusual, and as Drew found out, expensive, set up of three stills, looks majestically out over the ruined abbey beyond. My lack of enthusiasm from my first impressions has now long faded. This is an impressive distillery and setup.

Matthew Hastie's photo of the ruined Lindores Abbey

Do I dare bring up the thorny issue of the price of whisky? As Kate Winslet once famously said, "I don't like talking about money. It's a bit vulgar, isn't it?" Money, religion and politics – subjects not fit for the dinner table, or any table. However, at every distillery I have attempted to buy a bottle and, for those without a shop, ordered one from a stockist. Some have been easy purchases, some a bitter pill to swallow and quite a variation between the two experiences. As I have stated earlier, I am trying not to date the book too much, so it is pointless for me to highlight any distiller or bottling for attention. It is clear that well into the third decade of the 21st century there is evidence of a change of habits, preferences and attitudes towards spending. I believe that some distillers whose offerings lean more towards the 'bitter pill' will adjust accordingly. My bottle of Lindores was an easy purchase and I look forward to returning to try the next variation.

Originally, my intention was to only include those distilleries that were open to the public, but I quickly realised that this excluded too many noticeable and important additions. Frankly, a book on Scotch whisky distilleries built this millennium would not be complete without a jaunt to Daftmill Distillery. This has meant that rather than one trip through Fife I have had to return at a later date.

You would think by now I would ignore my navigation system and head out along the main routes, but alas, I have learned nothing. This time, my in-car navigation tries to send me down not one but three closed roads. My record of punctuality is put to a severe test, and I curse not sticking to the motorways that would have got me to the village of Ladybank in good time (despite being boring). My journey is through rush hour traffic, and I resignedly and correctly stick to the 20mph speed limit as kids shuffle their way to school. Once past the villages, the smell of the air fills with burnt kerosene, and I find myself trying to circumnavigate Edinburgh airport – a twisted, sprawling mass of roundabouts, junctions and estates. It is a nightmare to get through, and my arrival time edges ever closer to me being late.

Finally clear, I realise that at least this route allows me to head over the mightily impressive Queensferry Crossing with views of the new and old Forth Road Bridge to my right. The bridge is a masterpiece of engineering, and whilst I can barely admire it as I drive over,[1] I do recall, from when it opened in 2017, that it is over 1.5 miles long and is the longest three-towered bridge in the world.[2] My rural route also presents me with more fantastic place names. I discover Balfarg, sounding like some deep-living demon from Lord of the Rings; Kingskettle, whose etymology is either battle or cat-related; and my favourite, Freuchie.[3] This will be better known to many, especially those that drink specialty Scottish beers, as Fraoch, which is Gaelic for Heather. An old Scots saying, 'Awa tae Freuchie and eat mice', was in reference to the fact that prisoners of the Crown, residing at Falkland Palace just a few miles away, would be held in the village before execution.

Just past Ladybank Golf Course (no thoughts of golf today), I turn right and head towards the village of Bow of Fife (another great name). This is a beautiful tree-lined road and gives a most auspicious and uplifting final leg of the journey – so much so that I miss the small entrance to Daftmill Distillery. Luckily, and despite all the efforts to delay me, I have enough time to turn around and still be several minutes early.

---

1 - I suffer from 'Height Vertigo' which means looking up at tall buildings make me dizzy and nauseous. Not a good idea whilst driving over a bridge.
2 - When I say 'recall' I mean 'looked-up'.
3 - Pronounced 'Froo kay'.

Daftmill Distillery
www.daftmill.com
Not open to the public

"We first had the notion of a farm distillery in 2002." Francis Cuthbert, Daftmill's founder, informs me. These were still the early days in the mad rush for distilleries. "It was Arran Distillery that really got me thinking that we could do it although I wasn't impressed with their first release."

Unusually, certainly, in this industry, the notion of a new distillery took little time to gain momentum. For Francis and his brother Ian, who are both full-time farmers, a swift meeting of minds enabled them to apply for planning in 2004 and begin distilling in December 2005. It was a conscious decision that they kept the planning quiet due to the heavily advertised and extremely local investment scheme, Ladybank Distillery – a project that ended with all speculators losing every penny invested. "We were very mindful that the Ladybank project had problems, and so kept very quiet about our plans as we didn't want to be associated in any way. Once everything was in place, we made it public."

The old kiln that the farm historically used to dry oats for milling, had to be repurposed and a new roof put in – this did allow the Cuthbert's the luxury of putting a pagoda on the top. The set-up certainly places it as one of the smaller distilleries but it suits what Francis had planned.

"We wanted to use our own barley, which at first we had to wheelbarrow to the mash tun. Clear worts were a must so the first waters are poured back over the grist and this naturally filters it. We planned for much longer fermentation times than was standard to extract as much fruity character as possible."

There are certainly some interesting design quirks with washbacks that require their output split in order to feed the Wash Still; condensers that are so large they make the stills look shrunken, and small warehouses that are fit to burst. The family has a long association with the area and has owned Daftmill Farm since 1984. Producing over 800 tonnes of barley a year, the distillery uses 100 tonnes, and mixed crops and cattle allow the distillery to grow, distil and then spread the draff to the cattle, which in turn helps keep the fields fertilised

Francis is, first and foremost, a farmer, and having lived in or around farmers for much of my life, I know how direct and forthright they can be. Francis is no exception. What truly sets Daftmill apart from its contemporaries was Francis' decision to hold back from early releases. "The truth is, I wasn't impressed with our whisky when it was young." Francis candidly continues. "I remember buying the three year old Arran - and really not liking it – and I didn't want to fall into the same trap of releasing whisky before it was ready."

This delay lasted until 2018 when a 12 year old, blended from three casks, was released. Without any marketing, no sales team, no social media or advertising, the whisky caused a fervour of excitement and was massively oversubscribed. A sort of 'Golden Ticket Wonka Madness' spread over any completionist collector or those simply curious about what was going on in this quiet and closed-to-visitors distillery.

Daftmill fills around 100 casks a year, predominantly in ex-Bourbon barrels. Francis, as he has been since he started, keeps a watchful and keen eye over every cask released for bottling. He and his brother have no 'Master Distiller', no blending team, no lab analysis and rely purely on the fact that because the quality was put in at the start, it is quality that comes out at the end.

"We sell what we bottle, and we like keeping it that way. It is incredible how much spirit some of the new distilleries are making, and this requires having a large sales team out there representing their brand all over the world. We don't have enough stock to warrant a sales team and that suits us fine."

Daftmill was Scotland's first mainland farm distillery for over a century and probably a lot longer. The Cuthbert's dream of being a single estate operation, and with a business model that kept supply manageable, has meant Francis and his brother have been anything but what the distillery's name may conjure. Daftmill's decision to delay the release of their whisky until it was ready, granted a decision many other distilleries could only dream of doing, has resulted in a huge demand for what is an overwhelmingly-loved product. Bold, pioneering and daring to be different has put Daftmill firmly in the mind of Scotch whisky drinkers and broken open Fife as a distilling region.

Daftmill's stills are some of the smallest in Scotland

Francis admits that had the notification on his phone not reminded him of my visit I would have been left waiting for quite a while.[1] "I have just had a delivery of seed." He informs me. I thank him for his time in this busy season for farmers. Daftmill, certainly in its present guise, is not suited or set up for visitors. "I used to have two or three a month turn up when we were making spirit, but once that first release hit the market, the numbers jumped. I had no choice but to kindly ask people to leave – showing people around was simply taking up too much of my time." He admits.

The distillery is a truly 'farm & family' operation. Francis and his brother have to work within the farming seasons and this will often dictate how much is produced each year. I'm not sure the terms 'time off', 'downtime', 'R&R' or 'Holiday' mean much to Francis. For instance, he's keen to begin malting his own barley, a time and labour-intensive process, and even wonders about going to the Whisky School at Springbank to learn. "I'm not sure I could justify a week off." He reasons. "Although I guess I wouldn't need the whole week, just the malting part of the course, and I could head to Islay for the cattle sales." I resist the urge to suggest he just book into the Ardshiel Hotel and enjoy a few days of what Campbeltown has to offer.

The distillery tour is like a step back in time. This is perhaps how distilleries looked before the Licensing Act of 1823; small and with a feeling of being squeezed into a space too compact for practicality. The pagoda roof, a rare moment of frivolity from the Cuthberts, is

---

1 - Frankly, I was surprised he had a mobile phone. Nothing about Francis screams technology.

one of the few giveaways that this is a more modern setup.

If you're a hardened whisky aficionado and/or traveller to Scottish distilleries, the pagoda roof is as ubiquitous a symbol and landmark as you are likely to find. The funny part about it is that it isn't Scottish at all. A young architect by the name of Charles Chree Doig re-designed the existing conical cowls that sat atop the kiln floors; these facilitated the drawing of air through the barley, helping it to dry and allowing the smoke to billow out. Doig's new 'Chinese' pagodas allowed the air to draw from all sides and directions and were arguably more aesthetic. The first appearance of the new pagoda roof[1] was its addition in 1889 to the Dailuaine Distillery near Carron in Speyside. The design soon caught on and is now added more for ornamental and heritage reasons than for any practicality.

I can't help but ask the one question that I've wanted to ask since I first heard about the distillery: Why the name Daftmill? "It is the name of the farm," Francis informs me. "So it's where we are but I was not that keen on using it on our whisky. I wanted something that suggested quality, and I thought Daftmill might be seen as gimmicky. But in the 13 or so years from starting the distillery to bottling the whisky, I had not come up with anything better, so Daftmill it was."

Later, in Francis' office, surrounded by bottles of Daftmill releases and samples of future bottlings, I take my time to dissect the latest release from 2011, which has been poured for me (and is indeed very fruity). Francis is in sole custody of what gets bottled, and therefore, it is his responsibility for every drop of Daftmill that is released.

"If I don't like it, I don't bottle it," Francis tells me, scouring his bottles for a particular cask sample. "Quite often, I'll take a cask sample and reject it, only to revisit it maybe six months or a year later and find a completely different whisky."

Few distilleries can boast this level of autonomy and control. There are no committees and no arguments. Francis is self-taught but has been an avid student – and like me, does not feel that any heritage, nepotism or handed-down knowledge is required to make a great product. Unlike me though, Francis never stops. He clearly loves his work and has a restless soul. No sooner have we shaken hands and said goodbye before Francis is off running to his next job, no doubt getting the newly delivered seed into the ground before it spoils. The next batch of Daftmill malt perhaps – after all, if he doesn't plant it, he can't distil it, and I wouldn't want to be the cause of even the tiniest gap in his incredible portfolio.

---

1 - It is worth mentioning that at this time most, if not all, distilleries were malting their own barley.

CHAPTER 10

EAST BUT SOUTH OF THE GREAT NORTH

"Of all the small nations of this earth, perhaps only the Ancient Greeks surpass the Scots in their contribution to mankind."
Winston Churchill

For this part of my journey I am leaving Fife and heading first west and then north across the Tay Road Bridge towards Dundee. The newly opened Victoria & Albert Museum looms on the harbour like some unfinished monotone Lego ship – should giants ever roam the earth, one will no doubt step on this during the night, invoking a large intake of breath. I pass HMS Unicorn, the oldest boat in the water in Scotland, built shortly after the Napoleonic wars. The ship was used for various roles, including a training centre during WWII and is believed to be the third oldest boat still afloat. Sailless,[1] the Unicorn resembles a floating Dutch barn with a modern office roof.

An apology to all Dundonians – I have never really visited your city – it has always been somewhere between me and where I want to get to. Today is no different as rather than stay in Dundee; I have chosen to spend the night in Montrose, a 30-mile drive further up the coast, but considerably closer to my next distillery. The east of Scotland is a valley separated by the Cairngorms and the North Sea. It is a patchwork of thousands of subdivided farms and fields - where mighty forests once covered the land, now a criss-cross of oddly shaped, man-made fences, walls, villages and towns make up this fertile part of the country.

Montrose itself is a rather desperate, medium-sized town home to around 12,000. The locals are nicknamed 'Gable Endies' after the style of buildings (as if somehow gables were unique to the area). It's an odd nickname, but they can probably claim to have gotten off lightly. The locals of Linlithgow were known as 'Black Bitches' due to the town's coat

---

1 - The boat was never rigged.

of arms featuring a black dog. I'd never heard this before and am guessing that its use is minimal. If at all. My hotel is on the northeastern part of the town and adjacent to the 18th hole at Montrose Golf Club – the fifth oldest golf course in the world. Yet again I curse the fact I have left my clubs at home. I reasoned, professionally I felt, that I was touring for a book, not to tick golf courses off my 'not played' list. But, had I played the course and not mentioned it, you would be none the wiser, would you? So, with a bit of time to kill, I perform a quick search for things to do in the area. Number three on the list, and ahead of visiting nearby Arbikie Distillery, is a statue of a dog, which piques my interest. As a dog lover, I wasn't going to miss this and I set out to walk back into the heart of the coastal town.

Montrose High Street is in need of more than a little TLC and some serious entrepreneurial spit and polish. You know businesses are not thriving when the charity shops are advertising closing down sales. It struck me as curious that at each end of the street, there are large white statues on pedestals. One is of Joseph Hume, a politician who seemed to revel in challenging every single public expenditure, and at the other end is a statue of Sir Robert Peel. There is no link between Peel and Montrose – it is quite likely he never once set foot in the place – and he is best remembered, despite being Prime Minister twice, for initiating the first Police force in the UK (the Metropolitan Police Force established in 1829, based at Scotland Yard).[1] I only bring this up because it was quite clear on these pearl-white statues that the local seagulls (and I can only assume that a diet of stolen chips, discarded cigarette butts and dropped iced buns can be the reason for the sustained and voluminous excretion) had fairly uniformly decided that Peel's effigy was their preferred target. Hume's statue shone like a freshly painted lighthouse. Peel's reflective abilities had been diminished rather drastically in a sea of green and brown with every shade in between. From the top of his head to almost his waistband Peel was spattered with seagull shit. I'm guessing seagulls are not a fan of Peel's legacy?

Whereas Peel's statue was beyond tenuous to the town of Montrose, Bamse the dog clearly spent some of its life in the area. There won't be many more dogs that can boast a website,[2] a statue and a book dedicated to their life. But then, no other dog has ever been awarded the 'Norges Hundeorden' by the Norwegian Military or the PDSA[3] from the UK Armed Forces. The statue is as bonny as they come, and I'll not spoil all of the tales of daring and heroism here; as the third best attraction in Montrose, you can discover all for yourself, should you ever mistakenly find yourself in Montrose with a few minutes to spare. Thankfully, it would appear the seagulls are more concerned with scavenging for dropped chips and night-time raids over the Peel statue, thus leaving Bamse looking emphatic.

---

1 - Contrary to urban myth, the name 'Scotland Yard' has nothing to do with any special ability to detect or solve crimes by anyone born north of the border. It was purely coincidence that the headquarters were situated on a street called Great Scotland Yard.

2 - www.bamsemontrose.co.uk

3 - People's Dispensary for Sick Animals – the animal equivalent of the Victoria Cross.

The Scots Language

After the third time of being asked to repeat his question, the hairy, beer-breathed, inebriated local took more than a little offence. In my head, I realised just how English I sounded to him: "I am dreadfully sorry, my good man; I simply cannot understand what you are asking." I might as well have dribbled some marbles and mumbled "Higgins".

You see, there is English, and then there is Cockney, Cornish, West Country, Brummie, Scouse, and Geordie, and that is just in England. Once you head far enough north and north-west, you enter a world of 'hame', 'heid', 'haen', and 'hoora',[1] and that's just a few examples from the letter 'h'. 'Scots' is much more than a dialect and takes quite some time (and a little effort) to get used to. I will not begin to catalogue the many regional differences or go through many phrases, but I will highlight a few memorable instances and a few words that may or may not come up.

I'll begin with what I believe is still the most remarkable sentence I think has ever been uttered by anyone purporting to be speaking a version of English. I was buying a forklift truck, and whilst my agent was in nearby Dumfries, the importer was based in Aberdeen. It may be a common occurrence in any nation that has a spread of farming communities, but certainly in England and Scotland, albeit with entirely different accents in their respective countries, the farmers have a similar accent from one side of the country to the other.

In Scotland, there is a dialect evident from Dumfries to the northeast. Sentences such as 'Dinna fash yersel' (don't trouble yourself', or it's not a problem) or 'Y're a sicht fer sair een' (you're a sight for sore eyes) in one way or another can be heard throughout the Scottish farming community. One of the most common words used is 'ken' – which in its most basic translation means 'understand' or 'understood'. Sentences are often finished with 'ken'. You may hear the following conversation:

> Farmer One: 'Fit like?"
> Farmer Two: "Aye. Fit a driech aifterneen."
> Farmer One: "Aye, I ken."
> Which translated goes:
> Farmer One: "How's it going?"
> Farmer Two: "Good. What a miserable afternoon."
> Farmer One: "Yes, isn't it."

You get the drift. Or rather 'ye ken'. Anyway, let's get back to my story

---

1 - 'Home', 'Head', 'Having', and 'Very' – as in 'Hoora windy'.

about the forklift. My agent, James, was getting delivery from the importer, an Aberdonian called Ken. James was trying to explain to me that Ken had his own ways – that he was a bit 'different' – which resulted in the following spectacular sentence:

"Ye'll ken Ken, when ye ken Ken."

The funny thing was I did 'ken' what James was on about. Although admittedly, my brain immediately conjured up images of the French dancers doing the 'Can-Can'. Ken turned out to be as normal as they come. I perhaps should have then confronted James with, "I dinnae ken why I'd ken Ken, when I ken Ken, ye ken?"

It also took me some time to get used to the fact that questions could be answered with 'how' instead of 'why'. This causes my brain issues when 'how' something occurred is very different to 'why' something occurred. For instance, when I hear someone has been rushed to the hospital with the reply being 'How?' my initial thought is to state 'By ambulance'. Or should someone be kicked out of a pub and someone replies 'How?' I am likely to state 'with a boot up the arse'. On another occasion, I was entering a shopping centre in Ayr when two teenagers seemed to be collecting for Gay Dogs:

"Gay Dugs. Collecting for the gay dugs." Each teenager took turns calling out with a yellow collecting bucket in hand.

I had to stop and ponder just what atrocities these poor gay dogs (dugs) were being subjected to. Were other straight dogs picking them out and teasing them? Or was it an issue with being adopted? Were human owners not wanting gay dogs? Whatever was happening, it was enough to send these two lads out into the open with enough care and consideration in their hearts to collect from strangers to help with their affliction and plight. It was only when I got close enough to read their bucket signs that I realised they were, in fact, collecting for 'Guide Dogs', but the 'ui', turning into an 'a' with their regional accent. Ah, the gay dogs are indeed OK, I hope.

A similar mispronunciation created the word 'whisky'. Supposedly, English soldiers stationed in Ireland, and no one knows when exactly, on hearing the locals ask for either a glass of 'Uisge Beatha' (Gaelic for the Water of Life) or just 'Uisge' turned this into the word Whiskey. Why or when different countries started spelling it with or without the 'e' has been lost in time. Most whisky-making countries have dabbled with both spellings, and I'll wager the 'e' was dropped when advertisements were charged by the letter. Canny, ye ken?

For the past 20 or so years having lived in Scotland, the only Gaelic I have ever knowingly learnt and used is the toast Slainte Mhath, which translates to Good Health. This is pronounced 'slanja-var' and is often shortened to just Slainte (slanja). I still prefer Cheers or Bottoms Up when toasting a drink - but to each their own.

Bamse, perhaps the most decorated canine in Europe

The next morning, the weather gods finally stopped quarrelling, and those in charge of sunshine have been awarded the day. There is a cold, northerly wind preventing the discarding of too many layers, but I am not complaining. Heading south out of Montrose, the car climbs up the hill, and I sense that my next distillery must command an impressive view. As I turn left into the car park laid out with empty casks, I am not disappointed. Spread in front of me is Lunan Bay, and the panoramic view is simply magnificent. My desire to be early this time allows me to get a cappuccino and sit in the large visitor centre built with the view in mind. It is seriously impressive. I realise I keep getting blown away by many of these new distilleries, but knowing the costs around the plant, installation, production and maturation, I cannot help but be impressed with the attention to detail.

My guide and I have a one-to-one for this tour, is Gilbert Ionescu - a Romanian ex-chef who has made Scotland his home. He is a 'note-perfect' tour guide retelling every angle, aspect and adjective that can describe Arbikie in one long, engaging monologue. Interruptions are dealt with expertly and expediently, but Gilbert never wavers from the message he wants to get across.

Arbikie Distillery

www.arbikie.com
Open to visitors

This is not Arbikie's best angle

What began as an idea formed on a night out in New York sent brothers Iain, David and John Stirling off into the business of distilling. The Stirling family had farmed the Arbikie estate for several centuries, and, encouraged by their parents to never sit still, the brothers began the process of strategising what would set their distillery apart.

"The area we're in is sometimes called the Sunshine State, which I know is very surreal for Scotland," John states.[1] "But it means we can grow certain crops here more easily than in other parts of Scotland."

Initially, the company began with a gin and a vodka, growing their own juniper berries and using a base spirit distilled from peas, which, unlike traditional crops, require no nitrogen fertiliser.

"We grow all of the botanicals that we use in our spirits, and we also grow the chillies that go into our vodka." John continues. In addition to the peas for the gin,

---

1 - Quotes taken from www.blog.bbr.com

potatoes are grown for the vodka. This allows Arbikie to label itself as a farm-to-bottle distillery.

"It's about going back to the way that whisky used to be done: tapping into that association between land, farm and distillery. As we were looking into the various aspects of making whisky, we realised that rye grain used to be grown in Scotland, but it hadn't been done for nearly two centuries. It took a few years to actually develop the crop, but in the end, we've produced the first Highland rye whisky in Scotland for 190 years."

The original small distillery was moved to a purpose-built 1,000 square-foot location, still on the farm. This allowed the Stirling brothers to incorporate an impressive visitor centre with a shop, café, and restaurant large enough to host themed evenings and live bands. From the car park and front of the building is one of the most spectacular views found at any Scottish mainland distillery – and up there with the best in the world.

The Stirling brothers have added a true destination to the East Coast of Scotland, and drinking in the sun and view on this fine April morning it is easy to admire what has been built. With time the Arbikie whisky will no doubt match the location and view of the distillery.

As pretty as this setup is, this is not Arbikie's best angle either

Gilbert guides me through the distillery, the on-site warehouse and then back into the shop where two glasses of spirit have been laid out for me to nose. I can confidently say that Gilbert is one of the most passionate and informative tour guides I've ever come across. Once again, I am reminded that this industry, and certainly the people it attracts, is not something that is wholly Scottish. That is not meant in any way as a slight against the natives of this fine land; quite the opposite, in fact. You can't build anything worthy without solid foundations. With such a small population spread over the vast majority of the countryside, it is often the migration, the movement of people, that can allow growth (and nurture change). Gilbert is a prime example of this. There is no need to claim any roots, clan heritage or adoption; he embodies the spirit of the country and the product. He is as welcome as anyone else is, and that is how it should be. Arbikie is still a young product and I'm sure Gilbert will have much to be proud of as the years mature and develop the spirit.

This is the best angle of Arbikie

CHAPTER 11

THE GREAT NORTH

"The Highlands of the north are so barren yet so welcoming; you are never that far from solitude or a friend you've yet to meet."

For the first time in this little adventure, I am heading north. Proper north, at least. North in Scotland generally means the A9 – a fairly universally hated road in this part of the world but a crucially important main artery for all those living beyond Perth. That the longest road in Scotland, 273 miles end to end, is not a motorway, or at least a complete dual carriageway, is a bone of contention and a thorny issue politically. All that aside, should you wish to get to Speyside from the central areas of Scotland, you are more often than not heading north on the A9, and you can make up your own mind about the road.

My very first solo jaunt further north than Loch Lomond took me up this road to the small village of Dufftown in 1999. I can't quite remember how or why, but I had befriended Fiona Murdoch, the owner of a relatively new whisky shop. Fiona had initially opened a gallery, but after a continual barrage of visitors asking where they could buy the local whiskies, she decided to change tact. Fiona's shop became a hub for the Speyside Whisky Festival (she also ran a small Autumn festival).[1] I was one year late to attend the first-ever Speyside Whisky Festival but was certainly in attendance at the second, and I am fairly sure I was the youngest guest speaker by a generation or two. Or three.

So 'green' was I that, frankly, I didn't have much to talk about and nothing of any merit to say, but so forgiving are whisky enthusiasts that I was invited back and attended every year for several years. In 2002, when my first book was published, I was asked to stand in as the official 'opener' of the festival when a much older and more established writer had been waylaid.[2] With a small crowd gathered, I tried my hand at a little humour, this being a 'malt' whisky festival:

"In 1881," I began, "George Ballantine brought blended Scotch whisky to England.

---

1 - The shop still exists and is run by a good friend of mine Marc Pendlebury. www.whiskybrother.co.uk
2 - Possibly in a local bar.

I'm here to bring it back."

Stunned silence. I believe for the first and last time in Dufftown, tumbleweed rolled through the streets, and far-off crickets could be heard. Another moment of 'funny in my head but not out loud' – there might be a few more in the book.

Continuing on the A9, although I pass signs for Dewar's 'World of Whisky',[1] Edradour and Blair Athol distilleries in Pitlochry,[2] the first visible distillery I pass is Dalwhinnie. This is the highest distillery in Scotland and is quite distinctive with its copper-topped, twin-pagoda roofs. Affectionately referred to, well at least it used to be, as 'Grandma's malt' on account of its lightness, it is not on my list of places to stop and I continue ever further 'up' the road.

It is almost exactly 100 miles from entering the A9 until arriving at Inverness. Much of the drive is tree-lined with the occasional loch and distant mountain to keep the drive from being dull. I always get a kick out of the sign to 'Killiecrankie', but had you not watched British TV in the 1980s, this might have little meaning. For whisky lovers, the pull is usually to the east with The Malt Whisky Trail and signs for Keith, Dufftown and Elgin but continue on, and before long, you will pass the once mighty Tomatin Distillery on your left.[3] I am too late in the day to call in for a bottle and branded coffee mug as I am keen to catch the light for one of my favourite moments on any Scottish road.

As I said, much of the A9, certainly from about halfway onwards, is tree-lined roads with farmlands and arable countryside. Just as the map begins to show signs of a larger concentration of civilisation, the road climbs, and the trees part, unveiling a quite breath-taking vista of the Moray Firth and the Black Isle. I have driven it numerous times and never cease to feel a reward for the near hundred miles of trucks, tractors, caravans and average speed cameras causing stress on what should otherwise be a pleasant drive. This is the beginning of a stunning journey taking in the Kessock Bridge, which has a fairy-tale view out over the Beauly Firth and beyond the Muir of Ord.

Once over the bridge, you arrive at the Black Isle, or Eilean Dubh, which takes its name from its dark and rocky landscape. It is a peninsula, not an island, and has always felt to me a magical place. At times there is a stillness, a solitude to the land, much like a small island, that adds to the rugged, sea-hugged and wing-shaped stretch of land. I would prefer to drive right around the coast, taking in Fortrose, Cromarty and Cullicudden, but this has been a long trek, and the light is beginning to fade. The Cromarty Bridge takes me across a firth of the same name with views west of Dingwall, where I will head the day after tomorrow.

---

1 - Aberfeldy Distillery.
2 - Pitlochry is south of Blair Atholl but is home to Blair Athol Distillery (the town has two 'L's'). This has caused many needless detours.
3 - Once the largest malt whisky distillery in Scotland.

I am still on the A9, now heading east and into whisky country again. The first sign for a distillery is for Teaninich to the left, a workhorse for the Diageo brands like Johnnie Walker and J&B. Closely followed is Dalmore Distillery on the right – the jewel of the Whyte & Mackay portfolio. A few miles along the road the enormous estate of the Invergordon Distillery comes into view. For those keeping track, it was instrumental in the building of Glengyle Distillery due to the dismantling of the Ben Wyvis malt whisky distillery,[1] once housed within the complex. Heading north again and just before the third bridge on this journey, which takes you off the Easter Ross peninsula, is Glenmorangie Distillery at Tain. And if that wasn't enough for a distillery crawl, signs remind you that one of the hidden gems, Balblair Distillery, is just a short drive further west along the peninsula.

But I am not here for any of these distilleries and continue on and over the Dornoch Firth Bridge. After what has felt like I have stalked the A9 to exhaustion, I finally turn off, heading east to Dornoch and the Castle Hotel, where I shall be staying for the next two nights. Or at least that's what I thought. It turns out, with all of the bookings and travel arrangements I have made over the past couple of months, I neglected to book my room for the first of the two nights and scramble to find an alternative place for my first night. Luckily, although at a price, the Royal Golf Hotel has a spare room just a few hundred yards away. For a not-inconsiderable amount, I get a single bed in a room that looks out over the Royal Dornoch Golf Course.[2]

The hotel is very nice, and I am relieved to get a room at such late notice. I do suffer a small issue, though, with single beds - this is not a criticism of the hotel, which does not have enough time to combine the two beds into a double - but it does result in several moments during the night where I half fall out of the bed.[3] Had I achieved deep sleep, I would have likely fallen out of bed properly, but this is prevented by the central heating system that kicks in and kicks off. A radiator by my door rattles with such ferocity that I think at first a neighbouring room is having a drumming solo contest. This continues throughout the night with enough regularity that I welcome the dawn light that shines through the window at around 4:30 am.

Bleary-eyed and fatigued, I step into the shower. It is more like a half step as the shower can barely contain my frame. I am not a big man - 5 feet 9 inches tall, or 175cm, for those who prefer a way of measuring that makes sense. I am also not very wide – approximately 33 inches round at my fattest point (give or take). And yet I fill this cubicle. I can barely move without that odd sensation of a bare buttock or otherwise touching the cold glass of the door, screen or tile. This is not a major concern for me – in fact, none at all – but it does make me wonder; the golf course is aimed at American tourists (and now a forewarning due to a sweeping generalisation that is on the way). Americans can be on the,

---

1 - Do not fear! There is no quiz at the end of the book.
2 - Clearly, my next book should be a tour of Scottish golf courses. I'll need a generous sponsor to facilitate that...
3 - This always makes me wonder how my Dutch and Danish friends, many being giants, fare when they are forced to take a single bed.

um, well 'larger' side. There are plenty who would not fit in the gap to get into the shower cubicle, never mind under the shower head. There is a separate bath available, but it would have its own issues for someone not overly agile.

While pondering this physical conundrum, I notice that the water gets steadily warmer and then hotter before becoming truly skin-searing. I do my best to squeeze into a corner away from the boiling water, now not minding the cooling glass panel my buttocks are exposed to. I see I can turn a second shower nozzle to the left for cold and right for hot and I turn towards cold as far as the nozzle will go. Incredibly, the water, already hot enough to boil the paint off steel, gets hotter. A single drop on my arm results in a yelp. I quickly turn the shower off and step out of the cubicle in a cloud of steam. Eventually, and not for the first time in my life, I work out that the hotel taps are back to front, and to ensure no repeat, I have a freezing cold shower. At least I am now wide awake.

Despite my four and a half hour drive yesterday, I am still 70 miles, or one and a half hours, away from my next destination, Wolfburn Distillery in Thurso. This drive brings me back, once again, onto the A9. Much of this part of the road hugs the Sutherland and Caithness coast. Looming high on the Ben Bhraggie hill, about 12 miles outside of Dornoch, is the monument to George Granville Leveson-Gower, otherwise known as the Duke of Sutherland. The Earl and his wife, Elizabeth, were central figures in the Highland Clearances. When the Duke died in 1833, a subscription was set up for his memorial, resulting in the statue, known locally as the 'Mannie'. There is another monument to him and his part played during the Clearances: on the wall above the Gentleman's urinals at the Lismore pub in Glasgow. The plaque reads:[1]

This urinal is dedicated to three men who participated in the Sottish Highland Clearances.
PLEASE FEEL FREE TO PAY THEM THE RESPECT THEY ARE DUE

Whilst I am not a statue toppler (and there have been many attempts to try and bring down the impressive Mannie monument), I find it pleasing that the locals prefer to keep the statue as a reminder that history is a lesson to be learned and not forgotten. Although I have no doubt that little by little this statue will slowly find its foundations 'eroded'.

I love this part of Scotland. It is so far removed from the Lowlands and Central belt where most Scots live that it feels like another country – it is similar to a drive across Europe or America. At one point, not too far from Dunrobin Castle, the seat of the Sutherlands, I pass a large stone-built farm and steading that is so picture-perfect I stop to take it in. With views out over the Dornoch Firth and the North Sea, its setting would take some beating. The sun was shining (I have been blessed with the weather once again) through the clouds

---

1 - The three men are: George Granville (Duke of Sutherland), Patrick Sellar and Colonel Fell.

as if wanting to highlight man's ability to sometimes build the perfect house in the most idyllic setting. I set off once again and then abruptly stop due to a 'For Sale' sign hanging at the entrance.

Ah, but you've been keeping up, haven't you? You will remember I've already explained that as tourists, we get caught up in that moment, day or week of sunshine, warmer air, calm waters, longer days, wildlife, blossom and bloom. We forget that there is often half a year of wintry conditions; isolation, boredom, lack of amenities, distance to anything and everything. Still, for that brief moment, that house looked as appealing as anything I'd ever seen.[1]

The road eventually cuts away from the coast at the wonderfully named village of Latheron.[2] I am amused that just before Latheron is the village of Latheronwheel,[3] which makes it sound like a souped-up version - as if part of the original village one day decided they were slightly better or were perhaps the first to discover modes of transport other than horses. Had I continued along the coast on the A99, I would eventually get to Wick, home of the Pulteney Distillery.

Scotland and Temperance

Gie him strong drink until he wink,
That's sinking in despair,
An' liquor guid to fire his bluid,
That's prest wi' grief an' care:
There let him bowse, and deep arouse,
W' bumpers flowing o'er,
Till he forgets his loves or debts,
An' minds his grief no more.
Robert Burns, Scotch Drink. 1785

It is little wonder that a once deeply religious nation might grapple with its national drink - or just with alcohol in general. For each distillery visited, especially the older ones, a church will never be that far away – and often, one of the larger benefactors in the building of churches has been a local distiller. It is also, therefore, little wonder that the UK's Temperance Movement began in Scotland.

Notable early UK successes were Sir Titus Salt, who established a dry village in

---

1 - We both know I looked it up online. It was a touch out of my price range – a lot to be honest.
2 - Gaelic for 'muddy place'.
3 - Gaelic for 'mobile muddy place'. Or, in truth, 'muddy place of the pool'.

West Yorkshire, and several Temperance clubs and societies throughout the UK. Whilst the Kirk or church had long railed against the 'demon drink', it wasn't until the 19th Century that a recognised organisation took on drink and called for abstinence. Most of the efforts were geared towards dissuading the adult drinkers. The Band of Hope organisation, established in 1947, targeted children to get the message in early.

The Scottish Prohibition Party scored a noticeable coup d'état when its leader, Bob Stewart, beat Winston Churchill for the Dundee seat in the 1922 General election. Stewart never achieved prohibition, and Churchill, ever magnanimous, resisted having him arrested during the Second World War as a known Russian sympathiser and open communist. The town of Wick, on the east coast in Caithness, had the most noticeable, or rather successful, temperance movement. Brimming with a heady combination of returning fishing crews and an abundance of licensed premises selling alcohol, the townsfolk (and this was predominantly the women - many of which had received the right to vote in 1918) began to warm to the speeches and public meetings organised by the Temperance Movement. Local funding built two Temperance Halls, and when polling day arrived to determine a ban, 62% of voters revoked all of the licenses to sell alcohol.

This meant that officially, Wick went dry on the 29th May, 1922. Naturally, and just like the more infamous 'speakeasies' of Chicago in the USA, 'Shebeens' began to pop up throughout the town, allowing access only to those who knew the secret knock or password. Illicit stills were hidden in nearby woods and hills supplying the illegal drinking dens. Thurso became the destination of choice for those with a few days off work or at the weekend. Trains would arrive back in Wick with barely a solitary sober passenger. Incredibly, this lasted through four more votes until eventually, and with war imminent, a vote allowed the Wick Burgh Licencing Court to grant table licenses. It wasn't until the end of the war, in May 1947, that full licenses were reinstated. Wick remains, to this day, the only town to have ever gone completely dry in the UK.

The landscape changes dramatically as I head inland. Great barren stretches strewn with the remnants of mighty forests lie all around me. It is as if some horrendous disaster has occurred – incinerating the trees, killing the land, leaving twisted, grey, deadwood everywhere. Perhaps this is the scene of the second Sutherland Clearances as woodland makes way for the gigantic wind turbines that are now scattered as far as the eye can see. To take a phrase from Reeves and Mortimer, 'some are turning, and some are not so turning'. I do wonder if we have possibly robbed Peter to pay Paul in this scenario, but no doubt someone, somewhere, is getting paid handsomely.

I pass the wonderfully named Spital, heading towards the equally superbly-named Scrabster. My turn cuts me off from reaching Scrabster, and upon entering the town of Thurso, I am immediately reminded of Gretna. It's odd that the first and last town on the

Scottish mainland should have such a similar feel. Gretna is more populous but that is hardly surprising as it sits where the main motorway from England meets Scotland. My navigation system once again lets me down as I turn off the main road and through a housing estate to a dead end. Sure enough, I can see the distillery on the map, just over a few fields, and through someone's house, but it cannot be got to from here. Back onto the A9 and I arrive with about five minutes to spare before the tour.

My guide is Wilma Falconer, an ex-police officer (as is the other main guide, Charlie Ross). I remark to Wilma that the whisky industry has employed a good number of ex-police officers. "After all," I reason, "no group of people are better trained at dealing with the mix of people and alcohol." Wilma laughs, acknowledging that she had never thought of it that way. In truth, ex-police officers tend to turn up on time, be presentable and perhaps more importantly, know how to make themselves heard when necessary. I should know - I hired several when I had my own whisky bottling company.

Wolfburn Distillery was clearly not built with tours in mind. There is no café or restaurant, no fancy viewing windows, and even the car park is full with half a dozen vehicles. It is also not near, well, anything. Yet people came and kept coming, and I note that much has changed from my first visit around seven years ago. A new sign proudly reveals the location and a steel wolf sculpture is a dead give-away for anyone missing the sign. The area that had previously been used for dispatching goods is now a small shop, and to the side is an even smaller tasting area. This does mean you start and finish with the stills in front of you – not too many tours can boast that.

A recent boiler breakdown (that is number three on this trip – I hope I don't get barred as some harbinger of bad voodoo or something) means we can see inside the stills, and I take the opportunity to run my hand on the inside of the larger Wash Still. It reappears, covered in a copper-coloured dust, without any hint of spirit smell. It demonstrates how much punishment the stills take when they are regularly heated (and why they often only last about two decades). It also illustrates how important copper is to the process and how much interaction there is between the metal and the spirit. I'll stop there as I'm beginning to get technical. For more information, pull up a chair and ask your friendly tour guide or distillery manager.

Wolfburn Distillery

www.wolfburn.com
Open to visitors

There are a few locations of distilleries in Scotland that, when visited, leave the visitor with an overriding question of 'Why here?' Not to belittle Thurso in any way, but it is one such location for me. It's nice to have that easily relayed quip such as 'highest distillery' or 'largest stills', and Wolfburn Distillery loves to proclaim 'most Northerly mainland' – which it remains to be. That is not reason enough to build a distillery, and as mentioned, anyone making the journey to Thurso will wonder what possessed Harry Taylor and Andrew Thomson to undertake such a remote project.

That is answered only by those who have an affinity for a place. Harry Taylor was originally from the area and the idea to give back to his community was more than enough draw. What started as an idea in 2011 came to fruition with the first distillate running from the stills in 2013 on Robert Burns' birthday, 25th January. Taking its name from a long-lost distillery and the burn that runs adjacent (much of the area's history and names being Norse in origin), the distillery was built with functionality and practicality first. Little provision for visitors was possible, and even today, you won't find a plush visitor centre or café.

The two owners now both live in South Africa but the distillery is set up such that the accomplished team carry on with the production of Wolfburn single malt whisky. The face of the company, Mark Westmorland, joined in 2018 having been asked by a good friend, Charlie Ross, to help with some shows and tastings.

"I am like a kid in a sweet shop," Mark tells me. "Sometimes I don't want to see behind the curtain as I want to be as excited as the next fan about what is coming next. That said, getting to taste our new expressions is amazing. I have seen our spirit maintain its essence and DNA but evolve over the years in various forms of maturation. As traditionalists, our process casts the net wide over the whisky-drinking public."

Mark is a Thurso native, and I doubt you will ever find a more vocal, passionate and prouder advocate of the area, its people and, of course, Wolfburn Distillery. "We employ 18 at the last count and if I remember, when I close a tasting, I name them all. Recognising everyone's part is important - a close-knit team with a common ethos. We store and bottle everything on-site. Space for warehouses is a premium; we have six on-site now. Being in the Far North, logistics can be challenging. Making sure we get deliveries, barley, glass, and labels when promised and making sure our liquid leaves when it should is crucial.

"We could increase our capacity to 160,000 litres from 125,000 without any change or addition of equipment, but more spirit means more warehouse space and building costs are through the roof, pun intended!"

Wolfburn's owner's connection to the military has seen a number of special bottlings for regiments and military anniversaries. The company motto, 'Fortune Favours the Brave', is used by several regiments and is a fitting tribute to the risk and reward facet for anyone building a new distillery.

Mark very much buys into the company ethos and sees his job as getting the public to try Wolfburn whisky and make up their own mind. "Being small, we sometimes fly under the radar – but this keeps us humble. We are not advertising in glossy magazines or on the sides of buses. Instead, we want to evolve organically and naturally. We try to get our product to the lips of consumers, interact with them and grow what we call the 'Wolfpack'. We're not overly concerned with what anyone else is doing and instead focus on what we do."

Wolfburn Distillery's interior

There is little option leaving Wolfburn but to completely retrace my journey back to Dornoch. It is that or continue along the North Coast 500 towards Strathy Point and head south along the more rural and frankly less inviting A897. I am tempted to head this way to see if the 'Borg Broch' looks as interesting as it sounds, but a quick search shows there is not much to see, and I am mindful that I wanted to make a quick stop at Clynelish Distillery on my return journey. Recently rejuvenated, Clynelish Distillery is a firm favourite of many whisky aficionados. A new swish shop and well-stocked bar have replaced the old and outdated shop that used to greet visitors. From the bar a terrace looks over the newly re-equipped Brora Distillery – of which more later. The distillery and bar are quiet and I ponder who the bar is aimed at. The distillery is a 30 minute walk from the tiny village - unless someone is driving you, the array of shiny bottles is just for show.

Annoyingly, Clynelish has discontinued their lovely black matt, ceramic branded coffee mugs and replaced them with a terrible small camping tin version. Ugh. I broke my cherished black one and will not be replacing it with a tin one. I realise this is ridiculously petty to 99.9% of you reading this, but I am gutted.[1] I decided to buy a bottle of 'fill-your-own' Clynelish for a friend. It's a tough decision at £120 for a 12 year old single cask bottle. The shop has one of those vacuum bottle fillers and the very kind server shows me how to fill my bottle. It fills and I instinctively press the button thinking this will stop it, however, the opposite occurs and a second 70cl begins to top off my bottle and flow down my hand over

1 - My wife is delighted as that is one less mug to have to store...

the counter. I'm very glad I didn't tell anyone in the shop that I used to bottle whisky for a living and make a hurried retreat back to Dornoch.

Dornoch is a fairly typical small Scottish town. More modern houses and bungalows are to the west, and to the east is the main draw for many tourists: Royal Dornoch Golf Course. The town appears to have been built around its cathedral, one of just nine in Scotland and the country's smallest. The Castle Hotel is situated adjacent to the cathedral and has more of a baronial house appearance than a castle. Most who visit are not arriving in search of architectural titillation.

I head straight to the offices and shop of the Thompson Brothers and spy Simon, the elder of the two brothers, manning the shop floor. Within seconds of entering, several things have happened; firstly, I have a glass of something wonderful in my hands. Secondly, I have already picked up two bottles to buy, and thirdly, Simon is in full swing about something technical that has intrigued him on a recent visit to a distillery. Although I am older and have over a decade more experience in the industry than the Thompson brothers, I am in awe of both of them. Simon is technically minded. Reading that back, it does not do him justice – he is to whisky distilling what Guthrie Govan is to guitar playing.[1] Whilst Phil is no slouch when it comes to the distilling process, he is also an astute business thinker and strategist. Both are blessed with a heightened sense of what great whisky is. They understand what the passionate whisky aficionados want as they are, first and foremost, whisky geeks.

Dornoch's 'shed' Distillery

1 - I realise this is an obscure reference but I have specifically done so for two reasons. First, it works for me, and second, everyone should know who Guthrie Govan is.

Dornoch Distillery

www.thompsonbrosdistillers.com
Visits by appointment only

There is plenty of serendipity in an industry that relies so much on reactions and metamorphosis. Take, for instance, the two main critical materials required to distil. Copper was available and malleable enough to turn into stills and oak was the preferred wood for coopers making barrels. By some stroke of luck, Copper is quite important in the chemical reactions within the stills and oak is crucial for the maturation process.[1] There are plenty more examples, from the phylloxera aphid[2] to Prohibition in the States, but in the last few decades it has been the addition of pioneering people into the industry that has been the greatest serendipity.

Brothers Phil & Simon Thompson are front and centre of this new breed of exciting and passionate Scotch whisky distillers and bottlers. Having grown up in and around the family business, the Dornoch Castle Hotel, the brothers came to appreciate whisky despite a few youthful sojourns away from the area. The two began concentrating on turning the hotel bar into a whisky drinker's destination. This they achieved with alacrity and in the process, gained a deserved reputation for knowing very good whisky when they came across it.

With two such creative and restless minds at work, a whisky bar was never going to be enough. By crowdfunding their idea of a new distillery, they were able to kit out one of the hotel's outbuildings with some of the smallest distilling equipment available. The first spirit ran from the stills in March 2017, and the brothers haven't looked back since. To supplement much-needed income whilst waiting for the Dornoch spirit to mature into something they were both happy to release, they began the bottling company Thompson Brothers. This had the added bonus of demonstrating to anyone possibly needing it that the two were highly creative when it came to selecting and blending whiskies not of their own making.

In 2020 the first Dornoch single malt Scotch whisky was released and since then demand has dictated that all releases are either available via a ballot system or on

---

1 - Oak barrels or receptacles long predate 'maturing spirits'. It is believed they were first used by the Celts over 3,000 years ago.
2 - A tiny insect that can destroy vineyards. Its desolation of the French wine industry in the late 1800s helped pave the way for consumers to switch to blended Scotch whisky.

allocation. In 2022 Phil & Simon announced their plans to build a new, purpose-built distillery on land bought just a few hundred yards from the hotel. The new distillery will have a capacity of over 400,000 litres of alcohol a year (dwarfing what they can currently produce) using an off-grid power supply.

The Thompsons have created a mecca for whisky enthusiasts in the northeast of Scotland. Their infectious passion for the products they bottle, coupled with a reputation for excellence, has, in a short space of time, elevated themselves and their whiskies to high esteem.

Phil joins Simon and myself and we take a short walk to the small warehouse and bottling hall just a hundred yards from the shop. I'm in luck as the distillery crew, Euan Christie and Jack Lowrie (and with such a small team, they double as bottlers, packers, cleaners and anything else that needs doing), are bottling the next batch of Dornoch Distillery single casks. I get to try a fruit-laden five-year-old matured in an ex-Bourbon quarter cask. Thanks to Simon's insistence on doing the usually absurd in production, this whisky is dripping with apricot jam, Danish pastries and peach cobbler. I break with my usual habit of not entering ballots for whisky and immediately sign up to try and get a bottle.

With the peach cobbler still dancing over my tastebuds, Phil, Simon and I head out to the site where the new distillery will be located. The distillery will have unbroken views over the golf course and the Dornoch Firth. An existing Victorian building will be converted into a visitor's centre. It is ambitious, to say the least, but Simon and Phil are not your normal whisky entrepreneurs. There is nothing normal about how the brothers think, how they make whisky or how they select their bottlings.

Back at the Dornoch Castle Hotel, for the night's stay I did remember to book, I find the bar and restaurant are suitably busy. Guests from Taiwan, the United States, Canada, and even some from England are enjoying browsing the gantry of malts and discussing their charms. It is quite easy to forget how far north Dornoch is at times like this. Had the hotel and bar been situated anywhere near Glasgow or Edinburgh, the task of gaining awareness would have been a much simpler one. However, the business model would look very different, and the two brothers would likely not be planning the distillery they are committed to. In an area with little industry, the new jobs and tourists it will attract will be a very welcome addition. Of all of the planned distilleries, this is one that excites me and fellow whisky geeks the most.

The next morning, I head back down the A9, once again past the Dornoch Firth. This part of the world was once famous for oysters, something I have never managed to stomach, but due to aggressive over-fishing in the 19th century, they all but disappeared.

What was once an abundant reef with slimy bowls of runny snot, sorry, oysters, was left decimated. As with any indigenous species being removed, this had an effect on the entire ecosystem – especially as oysters help to clean the waters they are in. Nearby Glenmorangie Distillery, in conjunction with their new anaerobic digestion plant,[1] is funding the reintroduction of oysters into the firth.[2] The idea is that the new plant will process around 98% of the waste from the distillery, and the oysters will comfortably deal with the remaining 2%. Depending upon what distillery waste is being referred to, perhaps these will be the first oysters I will be able to eat. But probably not. It is a refreshing reversal from an industry that, prior to governing and environment protection bodies such as SEPA, was discharging effluent into rivers and seas.

I head south along the part of the A9 that hugs the northern coastline of the Cromarty Firth, heading towards the town of Dingwall. Dingwall is a picturesque and beautifully maintained town – a great example of what a town can look like when enough of its residents care. Turning north is a narrow climb into hill-sided farmlands. I am on the hunt for GlenWyvis Distillery and it is clear, assuming I am heading in the right direction, that work will be required to ever get this distillery on the tourist routes of even medium-sized minibuses. Once the distillery is open, however, any traveller will be rewarded with one of the most panoramic views.[3]

GlenWyvis Distillery

1 - A process whereby bacteria breaks down organic matter.
2 - www.mcsuk.org
3 - I realise I keep saying the views are incredible. They really are - you'll either have to take my word for it or go see for yourself. Once open to visitors...

GlenWyvis Distillery

www.glenwyvis.com
Not currently open to the public

As settings go, GlenWyvis Distillery's location in the hills above Dingwall is going to take some beating. As you climb north into the Ochil Hills, on perhaps not the easiest of roads to navigate, the small town of Dingwall falls away behind you. There is little inkling of the view until you are parked in front of the distillery. To the east are the Northern Highland mountains. To the southwest are the Western Highland mountains and to the south is a full view of Dingwall, the Cromarty Firth and the Black Isle beyond.

"Sadly, we cannot invite visitors at the moment." Craig MacRitchie, GlenWyvis' Distillery Manager, informs me. "We are working on a solution, but these things take time, and we have other things to deal with."

GlenWyvis is by no means the first distillery in Dingwall's history but it is the first one for nearly 100 years. A germ of an idea from farm owner John McKenzie, of a community-owned distillery with sustainability at its core grew into a fully realised dream when crowdfunding in 2016 brought in over 3,000 investors, raising £2.4 million. Much of which was locally pledged.

"I joined the project in July 2015 as the very first employee - two years before the distillery was built." Craig continues. "It has been great to be involved from the Crowdfund stage through distillery construction to the first casks being filled and ultimately having our first whisky on the market. The distillery is the first 100% community-owned distillery; regardless of investment level, every member gets one vote at the AGM – making the whole process very democratic. The aims of the project were to bring benefit to our Highland community through social investment, which is delivered through our GoodWill Fund."

The distillery build was a relatively simple affair despite the elevated location. "We had to level the site during construction, which required some areas to be dug down several meters and a retaining wall installed behind the distillery. Due to our elevation, we have experienced issues with snow in the winter, so we often have to plan ahead with regards to deliveries of malt and supplies."

GlenWyvis is entirely powered by renewable energy due to a wind turbine, solar arrays and a small hydro-scheme all part of the landlord's farm. A biomass boiler running off locally produced sustainable woodchips provides the heating of the water which is pumped from a borehole behind the distillery. The distillery was finished in mid-2017, and in November, the first distillate ran from the stills. Whilst problems have arisen between McKenzie and the team running the distillery, nothing has held back the progression of the whisky, which was first released in 2023. A small full-time team runs the distillery with much of the background work done voluntarily in keeping with the community spirit and benevolence of the project.

GlenWyvis Stills

Craig is clearly a passionate advocate for Scotch whisky. His father had worked at Glenfiddich and Glenmorangie for most of his life and whilst Craig obtained a Bachelor of Applied Science focused on zoology and animal biology, a job working within a whisky shop allowed him to continue his passion. GlenWyvis is a compact but well-considered distillery. A clear intention is to one day allow visitors, and I have no doubt once certain agreements are in place, it will be open to all. I hope that an area is set aside to take in the incredible panoramic views from their vantage point. Sat with a glass of GlenWyvis whisky with the ever-changing landscape, I would be a happy soul. Assuming I did not have to walk back down the the hill back to Dingwall (or drive it).

Munros

At the end of the 19th century, an eager hillwalker, Sir Hugh Munro, published a list of 545 Scottish mountains measuring over 3,000ft (914m) – a height at which he believed they gained a special significance. Of these summits, he classified 277 as mountains in their own right (since revised to 283), the rest being satellites of lesser consequence (known as 'tops'). Sir Hugh couldn't have realised that his name would one day be used to describe any Scottish mountain over the magical 3,000ft mark. Climbing them is known as 'bagging a Munro'.

Once you've bagged all the Munros, you can move onto the Corbetts, hills over 2,500ft (700m) with a drop of at least 500ft on all sides, and the Donalds, lowland hills over 2,000ft. And for connoisseurs of the diminutive, there are the McPhies, so-called 'eminences in excess of 300ft', on the Isle of Colonsay.

I have bagged Ben Lomond, Ben Nevis, and possibly others without realising. Whilst at a Summer Camp in Loch Lomond, possibly in 1989, our 'dorm' bagged Ben Lomond, and in someone's infinite wisdom, we bivouacked near the top. As any Munro Bagger can attest, weather on a Scottish mountain is fickle and often, what you haven't planned for is what you should expect. Our night near the top of Scotland's 182nd-highest mountain experienced gale-force winds, rain to rival that of the monsoon season and a hail storm just for added effect. I was 13 at the time, but I came down the mountain several years older.

Should you 'bag a Munro' yourself, be sure you add to the wonderful comments that have been submitted to online reviewing platforms. Some of my favourites include summing up Ben Nevis as 'boring and unimaginative' whilst another complained of it being 'very steep and too high'. The latter did at least acknowledge that the 'attraction was free'. As many of the reviews will inform you, mountains, generally, are devoid of facilities. If you're heading up, make sure you've got food and drink (a hipflask of your favourite whisky) and whatever you take up, other than the obvious, should make its way back down with you.

CHAPTER 12

SPEYSIDE: WHISKYOPOLIS

"Whisky is by far the most popular of all remedies that won't cure a cold."
Jerry Vale

The drive south from Dingwall to Inverness is as much a visual treat as it was heading north. I am now heading to the part of Scotland that can boast more distilleries than anywhere else but I am only intending to visit one. In truth, there are three new distilleries since 2000 that could gain entry into the book. I have decided, however, that Chivas Bros' Dalmunach Distillery and Diageo's Roseisle Distillery are not worth inclusion.

Dalmunach, built in 2014 by Pernod Ricard (owner of Chivas Bros), was erected on the site of a previous distillery called Imperial, which ceased production in 1998. Capable of making up to 10 million litres of alcohol a year, it can outproduce most of the distilleries in this book combined. Around 0.1% of its output is currently released as a single malt whisky because its central role is providing fillings for large blends. Whilst an incredibly impressive and modern distillery, it is not open to the public, and it is unlikely that Chivas will ever open its doors for regular tours. Nor will they ever likely give the single malt whisky much promotion as it would compete with some of their more established brands – but never say never.

Roseisle Distillery is Dalmunach's older and slightly larger unrelated rival. Completed several years earlier in 2010, this distillery with its 14 stills can produce 12½ million litres of alcohol a year. Diageo built this colossal distillery to offer several different styles of whisky and fulfil multiple parts required in blends. Without trying to get too technical, blenders want an array of different styles to make up their product. Think of it like soup. The stock or base is often the grain whisky made at huge distilleries - such as Invergordon, North British and Cameronbridge - and the flavourings are the malt whiskies such as Teaninich, Benrinnes or Dailuaine. Each of the malt whiskies fulfils a different flavour profile within the soup or blend. Teaninich might be the onion, Benrinnes the carrots (no offence meant with this analogy).

The idea behind Roseisle was that the ability to change distillation techniques allowed Diageo to replicate parts of the blend recipe that might otherwise be unavailable. For instance, say Mortlach Distillery played a big part in one of the Johnnie Walker brands, but the sales of the malt whisky were such that Mortlach was going to be in short supply, then Roseisle would step in and replicate the style of whisky needed for the blenders. Did it work? The cynic in me desperately wants the project to be an abject failure. Not because of any deep-rooted hatred towards Diageo, but because if Diageo were successful, and any style of whisky can be made anywhere, then any argument of regional variation, or whiskies tasting the way they do because of where they are from, is pure fantasy.

Thankfully, it appears any concerns I may have had are unfounded. Despite their size, Dalmunach and Roseisle have only released a single expression each, and both companies have increased the capacity of sibling distilleries in their portfolios. The industry can still talk about regional variation with confidence that they aren't talking nonsense. If anything, since the creation of Roseisle, there has been more interest in the smaller boutique (craft, if you will) distilleries and not less.

So why are both distilleries excluded from the book? Well, quite simply, I don't classify them as 'Pioneering Spirits'. Instead, they are vast distilleries built by corporate juggernauts. There was no issue with funding; these were not passion projects, the opposite in fact. The two distilleries were not built to highlight a region of Scotland, or as a means to gain meaningful local employment, or really anything other than a mass-produced product for a mass market. I'm generalising, and both Chivas Bros and Diageo have incredible staff and make genuinely excellent products, but the two distilleries are factories of production. There's not much of a story to tell for either – certainly not within the remit of this book.

The Lazarus Distilleries

The first two decades of the 21st century was an extraordinary period for the Scotch whisky industry. Whilst I am only covering most of the new distilleries built since the turn of the millennium, it is worth a look at three distilleries that have risen like phoenixes from their ashes: Brora, Port Ellen and Rosebank. Brora Distillery, situated in the village of the same name north of the Dornoch Firth and Port Ellen Distillery on the Island of Islay, closed in the 1980s due to a downturn in demand (and in Brora's case, being replaced by a more modern distillery in the form of Clynelish). Rosebank, in Falkirk, was closed in 1993 due to requiring complete modernisation and ongoing problems with water supply.

Diageo, who owned all of these distilleries, had little to no interest in the remaining maturing stock, still in casks, and many of these found their way to independent bottlers such as Signatory Vintage and Douglas Laing. From the 1990s onwards, the bottling of these casks garnered a public following and, inevitably, rising values for the whiskies at auction. Enough of a following and, more importantly, demand, caused Diageo to consider rebuilding Port Ellen and Brora and the sale of Rosebank to Ian Macleod Distillers.

Brora was the first to reopen in May 2021, and both Port Ellen and Rosebank began distilling again in 2024. But what made these distilleries, out of the 27 or so that closed between 1983 and 1993, worth resurrection? Well, simply put, because these whiskies were offering incredible returns at auction. There were other distilleries that offered a more straightforward return to distilling, but they weren't causing the buzz to buyers, collectors and investors in the same manner that Brora, Port Ellen and Rosebank were. Herein lies the ultimate question for their future: will the new distilleries, as they are almost entirely rebuilt or, at best, having been much refurbished, be as interesting, as complex and engaging as the whiskies that have built their reputation? Can lightning strike twice..?

...oh, sorry, you were expecting a definitive yes or no reply to that question, weren't you? Well, I can give an opinion, but we are years away from any definitive answer and, more importantly, the public's response. My feelings are that Brora was an absolute enigma of a malt whisky. Rarely dull and sometimes sublime. Can a refurbished distillery be just as enigmatic? I have no idea, but Diageo will almost certainly make a more consistent whisky.[1] Port Ellen? It wasn't generally regarded as the best Islay whisky to begin with, but I have a feeling that the new distillate will exceed what was made before. And Rosebank? In my opinion, it was also never really a stellar whisky, but Ian Macleod doesn't do things by halves – I'm expecting the new owners to produce something exceptional.

I've still not helped you, have I? And I've not really answered many of the questions. The truth is, I'm just one fairly insignificant voice, and I don't have a crystal ball.

Something else occurs to me: as it was the independent bottlers that built the reputation of these distilleries after their closure, will there be any support for them with future stock? I'm going to suppose that unless there is another downturn in demand for Scotch whisky (similar to the one that caused their closure in the 1980s), then probably not. I can't be the only one who thinks this really smacks of 'thanks for all the hard work; we'll take it from here'. We have years and years to wait for any definitive answer to the above, and in the meantime, there are just a few, at least 25, whiskies from new distilleries to explore.

The Speyside region owes much of its heritage and concentration of distilleries to The Glenlivet Distillery and one of Scotch whisky's earliest entrepreneurs, Andrew Usher. In 1823 a certain George Smith opened the first fully licensed distillery in the 'Glenlivet'

---

1 - Perhaps missing part of the appeal of the inconsistent older bottlings.

area, and Andrew Usher, acting as a spirit agent, found a willing market for what he deemed 'The Real Glenlivet whisky'. Usher's success meant that by 1843, he was the sole agent for Smith's Drumin[1] whisky, and such was the success of the brand 'Glenlivet' that the distillery was renamed in 1859 'The Glenlivet'. Andrew's sons, Andrew Jr and John, joined the business and expanded it greatly – primarily due to their brand, Usher's Old Vatted Glenlivet (or OVG).

A quite bitter legal battle followed with the Usher and Smith firms on one side and an alliance of distillers and blenders on the other. The trouble was over the use of the term 'Glenlivet' on labels and in advertising. The Glenlivet area, a large valley that is fed by the River Avon, a tributary of the River Spey, had become widely associated as an area that made quality whisky. The alliance of opposing companies was able to demonstrate that the use of the term 'Glenlivet' preceded the naming of the distillery – even the Ushers had used the term prior to 1859. Ultimately, the battle ended out of court, but the result meant that many distilleries began suffixing their names with Glenlivet.[2] Perhaps now, though, as only The Glenlivet Distillery is associated with the valley, the matter has well and truly been resolved.

Before I leave the A9 and head into the Speyside region, I try my hardest to see the 'Soldiers Head' situated just a few miles south of the signs for Tomatin. The rock formation is strikingly similar to a helmeted German soldier. So much so, that it is known locally as the German Soldier or as Herman the German.[3] Like so many of these 'sights', it is smaller than I expected, which is likely why I'd previously missed it. Fun fact: We both know I had to look this up, but there is a word for naturally forming rock formations that look human: 'Mimetolith'- your QI moment of the book. Thankfully, the rock doesn't resemble Jesus, or there would be a visitor's centre complete with coffee mugs, t-shirts and queues of pilgrims. Would be quite the coffee mug in my collection...

Entering into Speyside, I pass arguably the quirkiest-looking distillery in Scotland - possibly in the world. From the road, Tormore Distillery appears to be an over-designed power station. The site fits in with its surroundings like an ornate fountain in a desert or a thatched cottage in the middle of Birmingham's city centre. The gardens are lawned with manicured hedges and have what can only be described as a large children's paddling pool front and centre. Built by the Seager Evans group in 1960, just the second malt whisky distillery built since the start of the 20th century, the distillery was part of the Long John blend make-up. The more interesting fact about the distillery is that for all its outward personality, it is just a shell, a facade housing a rather large workhorse distillery able to make almost five million litres of alcohol each year. Although not closed or rebuilt, Tormore was recently bought from Pernod Ricard by Elixir Drinks in 2023. Pernod had never given

---

1 - Drumin being the initial name of the distillery.
2 - Such as Longmorn-Glenlivet and Macallan-Glenlivet.
3 - I haven't made that up just for giggles. Please don't write in.

the distillery any attention or importance, and most whisky drinkers eagerly await what the tireless and expert nose of Oliver Chilton, Tormore's Distillery Manager, will be offering in the future.

Just a few miles further along the road sits Ballindalloch Distillery. Like Annandale Distillery, I have watched Ballindalloch's progress from part-way through construction to completion and then production. My first couple of visits were hosted by the endearing Charlie Smith, previously of Diageo, who was brought in to oversee the build. Charlie was one of those exceptional distillery managers, having previously worked at several distilleries including Glenkinchie and Talisker, that was swallowed up in the great machine that is Diageo. Had he worked his tenure during the period of great renaissance that we are witnessing, I am sure he would be one of those names whispered with great reverence at whisky festivals – at least a lot more than it already is.

Ballindalloch Distillery
The restored steadings make for a perfect distillery setting

Ballindalloch Distillery

www.ballindallochdistillery.com
Open to the public

What do you build when you have a derelict steading in the heart of Speyside, a part of Scotland synonymous with malt whisky production? Well, if you own the Ballindalloch Estate, you naturally consider distilling Scotland's national drink and riding the crest of the biggest Scotch whisky wave for several generations.

"There was no blinding flash of light for the idea," Guy McPherson-Grant, Ballindalloch's owner and Managing Director, informs me. "My brother and I had grown up knowing about the family heritage in the whisky industry. A number of elements then came together in 2011 and 2012 to create the plan for the Distillery: I was moving North from London to manage the Ballindalloch Estate; my brother had returned from living abroad and had the time to project-manage the build of the Distillery. The Lagmore Steading was in a desperate state of disrepair, and we were looking for a project for it.

That's when the idea emerged of adding value to our spring barley crop by distilling it." Incredibly, despite the proliferation of distilleries in the area, Ballindalloch was to be the first independently owned, new-build for over a century. And to stand out in an area steeped in distilling history and offerings, Guy knew that the whisky had to be different. "The strategy from the beginning was to come out to the market with a prestige whisky." Guy continues. "With very limited production, it seemed sensible to make sure that we do everything we can to secure the price point necessary for the business model. This included coming out to the market only when we had a fully matured, delicious Scotch whisky.

"Whilst Speyside is a recognised area and some would say 'style', we never set out with that in mind. We did want to adopt a traditional approach to production, however, and that ultimately led us to a style defined by our limited production space and resultant very slow fermentation and distilling processes."

Had someone accidentally raised the steading walls to the ground and allowed the estate owners to build their distillery from scratch, things might have gone smoother and been less costly. The reality was that although several walls existed, with a general footprint of the buildings, everything had to be more or less built or restored - from the earth floor to the missing roofs. The listed status also forced the distillery designers to have to box exceedingly cleverly within the cramped site never intended to house much more than animals.

"We were clear from the start that the historic building itself needed to play a part in the whisky brand, and changing the look substantially would have increased the issues in getting planning permission; and anyway, we did not want something so central to the Estate to look out of keeping with its environment." The result was a distillery with a very limited production capability but whose size fitted perfectly with the amount of spring barley that could be grown on the estate. All tempered by the amount of working capital that the Macpherson-Grant family was prepared to invest.

What Guy and his brother have achieved is to sit a distillery so perfectly in the heart of Speyside as to appear they have been there from the beginning. The attention to detail in the rebuild and sympathetic use of materials and space has allowed for a tourist-friendly destination, and whilst maybe cramped for the workers, gives anyone who visits a true depiction of what estate-distilling would have looked and felt like a century or two ago. Ballindalloch is already one of Speyside's must-visit destinations for aficionados and casual drinkers.

Ballindalloch's stills make excellent heaters during the winter

I am delighted to meet an old friend, Kenny Mackay, on entry to Ballindalloch's small board room. Kenny is an industry veteran, having spent many decades working with the Morrison family and their three distilleries before joining Brian Morrison and establishing the bottling firm Morrison-Mackay. Kenny has also been an instrumental consultant to many of the distilleries within this book. We catch up over a cup of tea, and Kenny explains his current dilemma: trying to get his laptop to talk to a projector. I can profess no technological ability. When it comes to any piece of hardware beginning with the letter 'p', particularly printers and projectors, I often get close to taking a sledgehammer to them when they don't work. I therefore attempt no offer of helpful advice.

My tour of Ballindalloch is with the Distillery Manager Colin Poppy. Colin is also an industry veteran, having worked for several years at the Auchroisk and Knockando distilleries, both in Speyside and owned by Diageo. As we make our way around the cramped distillery, Colin points out several small issues that were either only discovered after work had been completed or have built up over time. One particular thorn in his side is the feeding mechanism of the grist to the mash tun. For anyone who eats muesli or granola, you will note that the larger ingredients will congregate at the top.[1] This is occurring to the grist as the smaller flour parts fall more easily to the bottom, giving an uneven dispersion. Again, I am of no help at all. You can add a lack of engineering know-how to my lack of IT skills.

The still house is incredibly warm, and Colin points out that there will be a considerable task for a future distiller when the stills need replacing. "It is likely the roof will need to come off to allow these stills to be removed or repaired," Colin admits. "More than likely, I'll have retired by then, so it will be someone else's problem." Colin joined Ballindalloch before the distillery's first mash and has been instrumental in every process right up to bottling, which is done on-site. "When the team are not brewing, distilling and cleaning, they are bottling the whisky," Colin says as we pass through a plastic-draped doorway into a small bottling and preparation area. The team are just putting the final labels on the next distillery exclusive before heading back to the multitude of other jobs within the distillery.

Ballindalloch might be one of Speyside's newest distilleries but it stands proudly amongst centuries of establishment and tradition. As has been noted at so many other distilleries already visited, the distillery sits so perfectly within its environment that to anyone not knowing better they would swear it had always been just so. Heading slowly out of the car park I make a mental note to bring my golf clubs next time I visit. The Ballindalloch 18-hole golf course is directly behind the distillery and looks inviting on this lovely, calm Spring day. The eight-year-old within me, however, cannot help but grin at the idea that the name comes from a common occurrence on many golf courses – when you've hit your 'ball in da loch'. Chortle. That appalling 'Dad joke' is very much my signal I have overstayed my welcome.

---

1 - Perhaps the best example of this is chunky peanut butter.

CHAPTER 13

AULD REEKIE - THE CAPITAL

"Edinburgh is a hotbed of genius."
Tobias Smollett 1721-1771

Capital cities often hold a mild fascination for all of the country's inhabitants, or at least for those who do not live in them. There is a modicum of pride and a sense of importance, be it Paris, London, Rome, and so on, but everything is kept at arm's length. Of those I have visited, my favourite capital city is London; I love going, and I love leaving. Capital cities are, for the most part, inaccessible, inhabited by the largest racing rats and almost always congested to the point of near collapse. Edinburgh does not buck that trend, and many Scots refer to it as 'the northernmost English city,' which is not intended as a compliment.

This is harsh, not just on the English, but on those Scots who live and work in Edinburgh and put up with the 55,000 students for at least nine months of the year (10% of the population) and the four million tourists that troop through each year (eight times greater than the population). Also tolerated are the countless number of weirdos, sickos, show-offs, performers, actors, singers, acrobats and wannabees that congregate like moths around a light every summer for the Fringe. When Glasgow always and comfortably wins 'most friendly city' in Scotland (there are no official awards; this is a given), one must remember what the average Edinburgh citizen (or Dunediner - as the old town is known as Dunedin) has to deal with on a near daily basis.[1]

What Edinburgh may lack in friendliness, it makes up for in history. The Holyrood Parliament aside (perhaps one of the ugliest, most out-of-place buildings anywhere in the world), the cobbled streets, leaning houses, alleyways that Jack the Ripper would think twice about entering, and, of course, the Castle, all add to give Edinburgh a sense of history that Glasgow can only dream of. And for those who are wondering why there is so much comparison, well, that's just the way it is in a country with two major cities.

---

1 - Just for a bit of balance, Glasgow is home to more than three times as many students as Edinburgh. Glasgow's weirdos and night performers tend to be more home-grown than migratory.

For my purposes, this is a journey east and along the A702 that crosses from Dalry in Dumfries & Galloway to Edinburgh. I could take the M8, Scotland's busiest Motorway, which is faster but would miss the more scenic route to Edinburgh through the enticingly named Candy Mill and peculiarly named Dolphinton. Disappointingly, this village's name has nothing to do with dolphins – the village is not even twinned with Miami. Just whilst I am on towns and villages being twinned, and as I am having fun with some of the names I am encountering, I think we can all agree that whoever was in charge of the decision to twin the town Dull, in Perthshire, with Boring in Oregon, deserves a blue plaque on their door. Bravo.

As with most, probably all, major cities and capitals, my 63-mile journey is split into two parts: the first 60 miles take an hour to drive, and the remaining three miles take half an hour. Usually, as the councillors of Edinburgh are as determined to make car journeys just as troublesome as public transport, I would take the train. I had even bought a ticket before my hastily re-arranged Isle of Harris trip meant I needed to get to Glasgow Airport on the same day. It is a source of much frustration how difficult it is to get from Edinburgh to Glasgow Airport when time is short. The weather today is lovely, and I am enjoying the drive. Even the moments darting in and out of back roads, as my navigation system is again working hard to get to my destination several seconds earlier than a much safer journey with fewer turns would.

Little of the outside of Edinburgh, certainly from the south-west, gives any indication that this city houses anything worth visiting. Roads lined with 1930s semi-detached houses and interspersed, wherever builders could obtain planning, with uninspiring, functional blocks of flats. There is nothing here to suggest a 'capital city', financial centre, or castles and baronial architecture. If you travel in from the north, there is a greater sense of Edinburgh's 'capital' status with its Georgian terraces and parks, but my route has a similar feel to parts of Surrey or Essex.

Holyrood Distillery, thankfully, has a much more established feel to it, albeit adjacent to a Police Station ("You'd be amazed how many times we have to ask one of the Police officers to move their car or van as it is blocking access to the distillery." I am told by one of the staff later) and with a public right of way almost through the distillery. I'm early, once again, so head off to find a coffee – an easy task in such a student-dense city. On my return, there are signs of life, and before long, Calum Rae is shaking my hand and welcoming me to Holyrood Distillery.

Holyrood Distillery

www.holyrooddistillery.co.uk
Open to visitors

What has always struck me, and I'm not alone, is why someone hasn't built a distillery in Edinburgh earlier. Granted, building anything in this congested city would put anyone into a cold sweat, but the absence of a distillery is odd when you think about it. The 2nd most visited city in the UK and one of the best-known capitals in the world. It is a conundrum to me and my guide, Distillery Manager Calum Rae, that the only option available previously was to be whisked away by bus to Glenkinchie, a half-hour journey south, or Deanston, an hour journey north. For those tourists where time is a premium, and that is most of them, these weren't great options.

"Edinburgh was always in our founder's thinking," Calum tells me. "Rob [Carpenter] and his wife Kelly, along with David Robertson [industry veteran], spent a long time trying to find the right site in the city. Eventually, this old engine hall became available." The old stone building was part of St Leonard's railway station, but there is little indication of that now. Instead, and despite Calum's protestations that the distillery is incredibly constrained due to the building shape ("Everything is built between these two walls." He gestures at one point), it all looks picture-perfect to me. The visitor/shop area is ideally located as the first point for any visitors and, more importantly, those who have already done the tour and just want another bottle or a nip up to the bar to try the latest release.

"There were a number of challenges we encountered during the build." Calum continues, "With the distillery being located in an old engine shed, we had to take the listed nature of the building into consideration. Everything had to be designed so that it would fit within the existing structure but also so that we could squeeze the maximum amount out of the space. Being in a residential area in the heart of Edinburgh meant that we had to deal with narrow, cobbled streets and also be conscious of being good neighbours and making sure to be a positive part of our community.

"This has meant that we have had to constantly refine our production process in terms of working within strict hours and to deal with logistical challenges that come with being inner-city. The distillery was very much designed with visitors in mind so making the distillery as accessible and welcoming as possible was a key factor in many of the decisions." Several extra function rooms can be hired - thoughts of future birthday parties spring to mind - but the distillery does feel akin to a narrow boat at times. Or at least a not-so-narrow boat. For the visitors, everything you'd want to view is, well, on view. The most fascinating part is the ground floor, visible from the courtyard. By viewing the guts of the distillery, you truly get an idea of just how cramped it is for the staff and operations.

"We didn't have room for a mill," Calum states, pointing over to the corner where the mash tun is and where a mill would usually be nearby. "This means that all of our malts come pre-milled as grist, and we must carry each 25kg bag to the mash tun."

Whilst not ideal, and plans are being considered to alter this in the future, "it is what it is" within the site. Holyrood Distillery is just a 15-minute walk from Canongate and the Royal Mile. To have got anything closer would have not just been miraculous but would have also cost considerably more. "We are just close enough to be a tourist attraction and just out of the way enough to get locals who are regulars," Calum says, smiling.

Such is the innovation and experimentation pushed to the fore, that had Willy Wonka been a whisky man – well, you can see where I'm going with this. In one production year, the Holyrood team created no less than 99 different recipes. A neon sign in the tasting room reads "Test. Learn. Improve. Repeat." Coupled with that, the logo for the brand is an hourglass, a nod to the one element no distillery can cheat: time.

"When Holyrood Distillery was originally set up, it had a very clear purpose. Flavour drives everything that we do and we put that before everything - even at the expense of efficiency at times. We have been working with speciality malts and yeasts traditionally used in other parts of the alcohol industry, such as brewing and winemaking, as well as a focus on heritage barley strains. This has allowed us to build a wide range of interesting spirits with varying flavours and textures. The approach enables us to cover a range of styles and tastes, all unified by a focus on high-quality spirit.

"As a result, we will not likely, at least for the foreseeable future, have a 'core' release, but we also won't get bored going through the different casks to see what has changed. It also means our customers continue seeking the next release, knowing it will be completely different from the last. Conversely, if anyone finds a release they like, it could be quite a while before we return to that style of whisky."

What the Carpenters have created in Edinburgh is something quite different to anything else in the new wave movement of distilleries. Whilst Holyrood had no 'Edinburgh' style for comparison, they have nurtured an environment of experimentation, or as the Americans like to say, a 'suck it and see' attitude to distilling. Holyrood will, undoubtedly, make some astonishing whiskies, and they are not afraid to make mistakes, either. With a product that is not easy, quick or cheap to make, this is brave and keeps a keen eye on them from those with such interests. As J K Rowling once wrote, "I expect great things from you, Holyrood." Well, she might have had the Harry Potter books been about distilleries and not wizards.

Calum's own career history has as little to do with whisky as the building we are in that now houses a distillery. A trained musical engineer, he travelled as a roadie before getting into whisky sales and eventually a role with neighbouring distillery, Bonnington's, before becoming distillery manager at Holyrood.

"I joined Holyrood Distillery in 2021. The build was completed in 2019 and was originally on six mashes and six still runs a week. When I joined, my remit was to increase the output of the distillery. We did this by moving at first to ten mashes and ten distillations a week before increasing further to 12 of each. I originally joined the team as a senior distiller before stepping up to assistant distillery manager in 2022 and eventually taking up the distillery manager post in 2023."

Calum directs me to a corner area in the bar with views of Arthur's Seat, possibly named after King Arthur, possibly not, and disappears. He reappears with several bottles. "This is our Carramalt new-make and this is it after two years of maturation."

"That's like toffee popcorn?" I state questioningly. "Had you given me that blind, I would have sworn it was some sort of flavoured liqueur." Calum grins and nods.

"Yeah, we're pretty amazed at how well that has turned out," Calum answers. "But that is the joy of what we do here. From the top down, we encourage experimentation.

Some of it works, and some we have to rethink, but we never rest on any laurels. There are still lots of things we would like to do.

"I will never forget when we first began working with Chevalier, one of the heritage malt varieties we use. It caused a blockage in our draff system that resulted in almost the entirety of our ground floor being covered in spent malt. Myself and Conor, one of the senior distillers, were here till well into the night cleaning up. We were still finding malt in unexpected places weeks later!"

Clutching a couple of Holyrood bottles, including that amazing Carramalt spirit (as it isn't old enough to be labelled as whisky yet), I realise there is enough time to wander into Edinburgh's centre. As it is a day ending in 'y', the Royal Mile and Canongate Road are mobbed with tourists. A slight drizzle has forced some into the many, perhaps too many, tourist shops that line each side of the road. You're in luck if you want anything made out of cashmere, wool, or any item of clothing with a Nessie[1] printed on it. I'm going to put forward Edinburgh as one of the most brand-savvy cities in the world. Every third person you pass is sporting an Edinburgh-branded hoody or cap. It is the most likely place in the world to hear a bagpiper (likely more than several), see someone in full Highland dress with blue paint on their face shouting something about 'freedom' and pass several tourists wearing anything from a bespoke, full Prince Charlie outfit to a wrap-around piece of tartan table cloth, intended as a kilt, held together with a safety pin and kept in place by the wearer's own gravity.

In addition, Edinburgh is also the most likely place in Scotland to hear someone shouting at you about Jesus Christ, see a person in a giant inflatable panda suit, see someone standing still on a plinth for no reason, and, my least favourite, mime artists. The latter should be confined solely to their native habitat, Paris, where they are tolerated along with bad service and expensive food. It is nice to see that no statues have fallen foul or toppled by those offended by history, and Hume's toe, on the Royal Mile, is as golden as ever. David Hume was an Edinburgh native, and whilst arguably not one of the city's greatest proteges, his rejection of miracles and his more atheist, and therefore at the time heretical, views certainly made him notorious. How a man with such non-ethereal views would have felt regarding the superstitious practice of toe-rubbing will forever remain a secret.

The mother, or rather father, of all statues in Edinburgh, and possibly only pipped in the UK by the Albert Memorial in London, is the Scott Monument next to the Waverley station and opposite the Jenners department store.[2] The Scott Monument, built in 1841, cost about one-tenth of the Albert Memorial (1872), possibly because it wasn't covered in gold and, one must assume, London workers charged considerably more. The Scott

---

1 - The Loch Ness Monster.

2 - At the time of writing, it has been just over a year since a fire ripped through the historic building. The Danish billionaire Anders Holch Povlsen owns it and plans to turn it into a hotel. Is Scotland slowly becoming Danish?

monument was made out of 'Binny' sandstone, which led to the stonemasons developing silicosis, a lung disease caused by the fine dust they were inhaling. It was thought at the time that the monument caused the early deaths of half of the masons employed. Tragedy aside, it is a grand and gothic edifice to a great writer. I wonder if J K Rowling will ever be immortalised with something similar.[1]

I have enough time to pop into the only two whisky shops I ever visit when in Edinburgh. The first is Royal Mile Whiskies, which is so named to avoid confusion; it is on the Royal Mile, and it sells whisky. The current manager, Mark Davidson, and I, worked together at my second shop, Wm Cadenhead, just a few minutes walk down the Royal Mile to Canongate. This was over 20 years ago, when there were only two shops selling whisky on the entire street (or two streets, depending upon how you look at it). Now, having left the castle at the top of the Royal Mile, you can visit a whisky shop, starting at the Scotch Whisky Experience, and more or less step into one every third or fourth shop until you arrive at the bottom of Canongate where the Wm Cadenhead shop is.

If you wish to stop for a quiet beer, I recommend the Bow Bar on Victoria Street. It is a proper beer and whisky pub, as it does not play music and has no flashing video games, jukebox or televisions showing a horse race that only the most ardent gambler could possibly know about. It also does not allow children in. This is made clear to a family of tourists who enter with their lad - at most 11 or 12 years of age. The server behind the bar makes it clear that children are not allowed, and the family exits. Seconds later, the father reappears, leaving the wife and child outside, and orders a pint of beer. Slightly selfish, I think to myself. I then watch, dumb-founded, as the man takes his beer to the doorway and beckons his son over to take a drink from his pint. It is a £20,000 fine and possible closure for the supply of alcohol that is then given to minors. This is not lost on the server behind the bar whose shout of 'Stop' jolts all the quiet, contemplative drinkers in the pub out of their meditation. Should your son suddenly need a draught of beer, perhaps it's best to do it out of sight of the bar or shop you've just bought it from. Or question why your child would suddenly need a draught of beer?

Oh, and before I forget, why the term 'Auld Reekie'? This was an unaffectionate nickname for Edinburgh when coal fires left a thick and unrepentant cloud of dark smoke around the crowded streets. Reekie translates to smoky, so roughly translated, Auld Reekie means 'Old Smoky. ' Sadly, it has nothing to do with whisky at all.

---

1 - I sincerely hope so.

CHAPTER 14

THE 'I LOVE ISLAY' STORY

"You might not be a fan of smoky whisky before visiting Islay,
but you'll likely leave as one."

As you may have gathered, my timing for this tour is no accident. The busy season for the distilleries and their staff is from late May onwards. These distilleries sell their brands and products worldwide, and in trying to ensure I can visit and see the right people then, ideally, the period between March and early May is most convenient for those working at the distilleries. In just a few days, the Campbeltown Whisky Festival will begin, and the week after is Fèis Ìle – the Islay Whisky Festival. There is little to no chance of getting time to visit during these periods, not to mention the strains on travel and accommodation.

From experience, I've also timed my tour with some of Scotland's best weather, and today's drive to Tarbert in Argyll proves my case. As I pass Loch Lomond again, the traffic is bumper to bumper, and the Loch is filled with pocket cruisers, water skiers and jet skis. As soon as the weather is nice, water becomes the playground of the well-to-do. The first 150 miles of my journey fly by – mainly, perhaps, as the audiobook I am listening to, "Who Dares Wins", is narrated by its author, Dominic Sandbrook, and his impersonation of Margaret Thatcher is captivating (is that the right word? Mesmerising? Haunting? Something along those lines). Thatcher remains a divisive character to much of the UK and, despite her death in 2013, remains a long-standing reason that the Tories struggle in certain areas (especially in Scotland). Sandbrook's book sits ever-so-slightly on the Baroness's side of the fence. But only just.

Before no time at all, I am making the familiar descent into Tarbert. It is a village I have driven through countless times but never loitered in for more than a few minutes. As we have already learnt from my trip to Harris, Tarbert means 'crossing place', and the town, with its perfect natural harbour and views over Loch Fyne towards Portavadie, is a small strip of land keeping the Kintyre Peninsula attached to the mainland. I'm staying in the Knap Guest House, which offers me an unbroken view over the tranquil marina. Tarbert has around 1,100 inhabitants, and it would appear that there are enough boats that, should the need ever arise, the entire population could set off to sea.

Tomorrow is an early ferry, but I have enough time before retiring for a quick drink at The Corner House, Tarbert's main pub. A few locals, well several, are outside the pub soaking up the sunshine. From the array of empty glasses on their bench it would appear they are enjoying their sixth or seventh round of drinks. The group are having an unreasonably vociferous debate with a nearby seagull who appears to be called 'Phil'. It would appear that 'Phil' is accused of grand theft of the fish-supper variety. I try to avoid getting involved as the complaints appear one-sided and, lacking any evidence of food nearby, without merit. A drink indoors prevents any 'side' from being taken. I believe my non-partisan stance does not go unnoticed by the Union of Seagulls, and they dutifully retire, quietly, around 10 pm, allowing me a few hours of peaceful sleep.

Although I am awake at 04:30, the alarm jolts me up at 05:50. I must have been dozing. Kennacraig, the terminal for the ferry to Islay, is less than 10 minutes away from Tarbert, but the 07:00 sailing means a hurried shower and getaway. It was too early for the complimentary breakfast but also too early for me to want it. The ferry is not busy, with maybe a dozen cars and twice as many vans and trucks. Even so, a delightful little minuet of Britishness is encapsulated. We are famed for our queuing. Usually, but not always, we are polite and orderly but with a bubbling, volcanic anger always tickling the back of our throats should anyone dare not adhere to the correct etiquette. Few things will make a Brit stir out of politeness faster than someone dallying when it is their time to move in a queue; not shuffling forward in the airport for check-in; not having your boarding pass ready when boarding a flight; not knowing what you're going to order in a fast-food restaurant despite having queued for ten minutes with the full menu ahead of you in plain sight... or, as in this case, choosing to get out of your car, and rummage in the boot, when the line of vehicles has started moving. This is a red rag to a Brit. Steering wheels get clenched, teeth grind, and eyes begin to look at the little horn sign in the middle of the steering wheel. The fact that the car has foreign plates means extra 'tutting', louder exhales of breath and a slightly tighter grip on the wheel. Thankfully, the CalMac Ferry operator, who clearly understands that anger is quickly getting to the epic state of car horns being sounded, runs up and waves the oblivious driver back into their car. Disaster averted, and breathing for all those behind returns to normal. Still, I wouldn't want to be that guy when on board, having to deal with a mountainous slice of passive aggressiveness that will be silently and frankly indiscernibly directed towards him.

Those whisky drinkers who appreciate smoky whisky, and even many of those who don't, will have made, or are planning, a pilgrimage to the Isle of Islay. I have spent the morning trying to think of another place that embodies or represents a product more than this small island. Cuba, possibly, with its cigars? But, as that is an entire country, it is hardly a proper comparison. The fact that Islay is an island and its whiskies are so distinguishable (whilst all being different) sets it apart from anywhere else.

When I first began reading about whisky, there were only five working distilleries on the island: Caol Ila, Bunnahabhain, Bowmore, Laphroaig and Lagavulin. Port Ellen had ceased operating in 1983, Bruichladdich in 1994 and Ardbeg in 1996. The poor state of the island's primary industry was due, in no small way, to the overall Scotch whisky industry's thinking or insistence that blended Scotch whisky was the only way to survive. It was ingrained in those with power that peaty, smoky whisky would never sell quantities that could keep an entire distillery in operation. The first major revival and re-think was the purchase of Ardbeg Distillery by The Glenmorangie Company in 1997. Next came Bruichladdich after a private consortium bought the distillery in 2000. Times had changed, and not only was it clear that a distillery on Islay could survive on its own merits, but it could thrive.

Kilchoman was built in 2005 and was the first new distillery on Islay for 124 years. In just seven years, the island of 3,000 inhabitants went from five distilleries to eight, and its whisky, from being considered 'too strong' for the casual drinker, became highly prized worldwide. So, just what is it that makes this island so special? I'm not sure I can distil[1] that down. It's not a tiny island like Barra or Gigha, so its charm is not in its size (it is the fifth largest island). It's not the remoteness either. With two ferry terminals and an airport, it is much easier to get to than Uist or Rum. The landscape cannot rival that of Skye or Orkney. The Illeachs are a friendly and welcoming group, but no more than those on Harris, Raasay or the Peninsulas. And yet, there is something about the island, some Siren's call, or at the very least, something in the whiskies it produces, that captivates drinkers in a way that other regions, areas and countries can only dream of.

As the ferry sails out of the West Tarbert Loch and Gigha comes into sight on the port side, I am reminded of my first time travelling to Islay. The conditions were nearly identical: blue skies, calm waters and a pleasant temperature. The Saltire flag at the stern barely fluttered as the Kintyre peninsula slowly drifted away behind us. I say 'us' as I and two friends embarked upon a five-day slog around as many distilleries in Scotland as possible, all in the name of charity. This trip, particularly the day spent on Islay, cemented my love for the product and instilled a belief that the whisky industry was where my future lay.

Roll on over a quarter of a century, and I am still excited every time I venture out knowing Islay is my destination. When you arrive at Port Ellen, the older part of the distillery glistens with freshly painted walls, plainly spelling out that you have indeed arrived at Port Ellen. Turning left towards Bowmore, I am mindful of the lovely tradition that drivers on Islay wave to each other as they pass. This has evolved into raising two fingers as a salute to keep hands on the wheel. Most small communities, my own included, wave to those they know, even as acquaintances, but on Islay, it is a universal salute, and I appreciate it. By waving at everyone, you don't miss out on anyone – this removes the worrying over a missed wave to someone you know.

---

1 - I hope it has not gone unnoticed how few whisky puns I have allowed to get through the edit.

Much of Islay to the east is flat and ideal not just for peat to occur but also for cutting and collecting. Staying on the main road I pass Laphroaig's Peat Farm, and the machinery is out, although not a soul to be seen, on one of the year's warmest days. This entire section of Islay from Port Ellen to Bowmore is one enormous peat bog. Despite alarmist claims that Islay is running out of peat, there is enough to last the next 2,000 years – by which point I'm sure we'll have found a nearby planet to harvest from.

The Peat Reek

"Why would anyone want to drink something that tastes like that?!"
My wife, every time I hand her a smoky whisky to try.

"General: appearance of a hand-made and hand-sized slab of dense rough-cut organic chocolate cake, with six distinct faces, four of which have clearly been fashioned by a blade. Surprisingly light in weight; a soft, solid brick.
Colour: dull, brown-black with much lighter orange-brown flecks. Fibrous and non-uniform and characterised by darker layers, with some of the strata opening into air-filled elongated cracks and elliptical voids.
Nose: odourless.
Mouthfeel: rough, grainy or slightly gritty. Tasteless. With water, little change – dried peat is hydrophobic, or water-hating.
Finish: disappointing. Short."
Excerpt from the fantastic book, "Peat and Whisky. The Unbreakable Bond" by Mike Billett

"Do you like smoky whisky?" is probably the single most asked question of any Scotch whisky drinker. And perhaps the most oft-repeated nonsense is that Irish whiskey is never smoky and all Scotch whisky is smoky. Some Irish whiskies are peated, and so are some Scottish whiskies but not all in either country. More often than not, it is Laphroaig that we have to thank for this 'Love or Hate' attitude towards smoky whisky. Once someone, often unsuspecting, has tried Laphroaig, then all peaty whisky gets lumped together as a mass of iodine-seaweed-ashtray abominations.[1]

Peat is basically organic matter, consisting mainly of plants that have partially broken down over thousands of years into what appears and feels like mud. When cut into brick-sized segments and dried, it can be used as a fuel, and there is evidence that this practice is at least 3,500 years old in Scotland. Therefore, peat was a natural and readily available fuel for any distiller wanting to dry their steeped grain ready for mashing.

---

1 - I am a huge fan of Laphroaig – just so we're clear...

The burning question all whisky aficionados have is, 'How quickly did the early distillers realise that peat was adding so much flavour to the distillate'? I guess the only plausible answer is immediately. Our ancestors were not diminished in their senses; they would have known that using peat in a fire releases a plethora of smoky and pungent odours. I am postulating here, but I'm reasonably confident the early distillers knew full well that using peat radically affected the spirit.

With the discovery and then widespread use of coal and anthracite, peated whiskies began to phase out, either from distilleries ceasing to use peat or reducing the amount added to their kiln fires. As whiskies began to be matured for longer,[1] this also reduced the smokiness of the finished product, but perhaps the greatest change was the introduction of the Continuous Still.[2] In the first decades of the 18th century, distillers using Continuous Stills could create a more neutral spirit than that made at the Pot Still distilleries. Simply put, these new stills allowed the wash to be fed continuously into one end and a high-strength and fairly neutral spirit to come out the other. This created the lightest spirit possible and, when blended with some of the stronger flavoured pot-still whiskies, resulted in a product that was much more 'crowd friendly'. At least, that was how it was marketed.

Having stills that could run continuously meant there was a constant requirement for raw materials – malted and dried grains in particular – which resulted in the congregation of these larger distilleries around the main industrial hubs of Scotland (Glasgow, Edinburgh and parts of Fife). Peat was not abundant in these locations, but coal was, and therefore, a sweeping change fell over the industry away from heavily smoky whiskies. Some were retained, and areas like Islay and Campbeltown became renowned for their particular 'heaviness' of spirit, allowing blenders to ensure their products had enough oomph to stand out (and still be considered Scotch). But not too much to put the mass-market drinker off.

One remarkable attribute of peated whisky is that it does not require a large amount to fundamentally affect a blend. In other words, a little goes a long way. To demonstrate this, pour a good measure of smoky whisky into a glass and then empty the glass. Without washing it out, pour in something unpeated. You should still smell the remaining peat reek from the previous contents and, more than likely, still taste it. As the requirement for smoky whisky in blends fell, and many distilleries transitioned to less and less peat, using more anthracite, the Scotch whisky landscape changed to where we now categorise whiskies as being 'peated' and 'un-peated'.

In my experience, few products split consumers so vociferously as the enjoyment of peated and non-peated whisky does. The UK market does not have an affinity for

---

1 - As companies used 'Time in Wood' as a point of difference and marketed age as a sign of quality.
2 - Also known as the Patent, Column or Coffey still.

smoky whisky, whereas Scandinavia is infatuated with it. In Scotland, particularly, you will find the majority of drinkers won't touch a smoky whisky. "Like drinking a chain-smoker's cough", was how one of my friends put it. I believe most drinkers can learn to appreciate peated whisky with just a little perseverance. There is such an array of offerings, from those with barely any detectable smokiness to others that leave you wondering if you've just been dunked into a roaring bonfire. Keep an open mind and you might find yourself on the ferry to Islay.

Past the peat farms and the warehouses on the left, Bowmore Church comes into full view like a religious lighthouse shining down onto the villagers below. As with Campbeltown and other parts of Scotland with a long distilling tradition, the Kirk (church) is never far from the Devil Drink. If you mention the Bowmore church, someone, somewhere, will say, 'Built round so the devil had no corner to hide in', and although this is not the reason,[1] it would be rather odd when you consider how many churches are built with perfect corners for a devil to play hide and seek in. The more I think about it, churches are the last place a devil would want to be, never mind be hiding in. Although, if the devil could convert the parishioner, the flock would be easy pickings, I guess. I may have thought about this too much.

A mile before Bruichladdich Distillery, I turn off the main road and head up a single-track lane. I'm going to guess that Kilchoman's location was not chosen for its ease of access. Indeed, as I greet Anthony Wills, Kilchoman's Founder and Managing Director, he confirms that a good water source was foremost in his search for a site.

Kilchoman Distillery

1 - The building's commissioner, Daniel Campbell, had been inspired during a Grand Tour of Europe. Some believe it is Dutch in style; others think it may be French.

Kilchoman Distillery

www.kilchomandistillery.com
Open to the public

"I'm just surprised how long it took someone to build another distillery on the island," Anthony Wills tells me after I had asked about Ardnahoe's recent launch. It's an interesting comment, and only a nuanced and informed response can solve the riddle. In truth, there have been plans for further distilleries on Islay for quite some time, but with everything built on an island, it is never that simple.

Nor was the construction of Kilchoman[1] an easy ride for Anthony and his team. "I knew I could take a single malt to market, but at the time, in the late 1990s and early 2000s, getting premium casks of single malt whisky was becoming a challenge. The idea was for a farm distillery with control from growth to distribution." As this was still the early days of the new wave distillery boom, funding was Anthony's biggest headache.

"It took four years to raise the first million in investment, and I knew it wouldn't be enough. The early response was also sceptical as it wasn't felt more distilleries were needed." Anthony explains. "We were lucky to have some private shareholders come on board who offered considerable support and financial backing. It was a tough ride for them as we constantly had to raise more funds to pay for production."

Once the water source, the Allt Gleann Osamail burn was located amongst some of Islay's most fertile land, next to the Kilchoman Church, the spare steading at Rockside Farm was acquired, and the building work began in 2004. The first distillate ran from the stills in December 2005, making Kilchoman the first independently built distillery in the 21st century. In many ways, Kilchoman was just as crucial to the new wave of distillers as the Isle of Arran had been. Anthony's perseverance and tenacity proved that building an independent and self-sufficient distillery was realisable and feasible.

And why Islay? "We wanted a distinctive whisky." Anthony explains. "Something that would stand out, and Islay had a worldwide reputation for making a certain type of whisky. There also hadn't been a new distillery on Islay for well over a century. I guess no one thought building another distillery on the island was particularly sensible. Looking back now, it is the single best decision we took to locate the distillery here."

---

1 - Pronounced 'kil-ho-man'.

Whilst Arran Distillery released their first whiskies at just three years old against a sea of aged malt whiskies, Kilchoman, coming nearly a decade later, had less of a battle with convincing consumers that young whisky could be good. "Timing is everything," Anthony continues, "and as we launched our non-aged single malt, a number of the well-established distilleries had just launched non-aged expressions. Consumers wanted to explore the labyrinth of single malts from newly established distilleries."

I first visited Kilchoman not long after it began operating in 2006, and whilst I have returned several times, I was unprepared for the changes the last few years have seen. In its infancy, Kilchoman was a farm distillery, growing its barley in the surrounding fields, malting it on a small malting floor and hand bottling on-site everything that left the island. With time and, more importantly, growth, due to the brand's success, the distillery has seen a near tripling in capacity, and that has brought other changes as now approximately 80% of the malt is brought in, and a new semi-automatic bottling machine ensures production keeps up with demand.

Where a small shop used to be is now a deluxe and inviting visitor centre complete with a café, open-fire seating, and rooms for the tour and private tastings. Kilchoman receives around 30,000 visitors a year, and the distillery now employs 45, split across their head office in Edinburgh (where the sales team are based) and the 38 who work at the distillery.

"We produced 640,000 litres of alcohol last year," Anthony informs me. "But we plan to continue with around 500,000 for the foreseeable future. The world, and certainly demand for whisky, is not what it was at the beginning of the decade, and we are comfortable with that amount of spirit being produced."

Hearing those numbers and knowing how little was made when Kilchoman started two decades ago is mind-boggling. Anthony and his team's vision, perseverance and sheer hard work have paid dividends. There is no time for any self-gratitude, however. At some point, the stills will be moved – a mammoth job – each new warehouse now costs close to the amount it was to kit out the original distillery, and as new markets emerge, old markets trail off. But at least their boiler is working... for now.

Whilst Kilchoman is not unique for its smoky whisky, floor maltings, or even being a farm distillery, there is a uniqueness to its whisky. Less coastal than some of its Islay neighbours and less heathery than many of the mainland smoky whiskies, Kilchoman balances a depth of maltiness with a deep, rich, smoky core. It perfectly embodies the coastal farmland where it is made and is a whisky filled with ambition and purpose, a lot like its founder.

Kilchoman is one of the few distilleries still operating a floor malting

The first-class nature of Kilchoman's expansion is a far cry from its start when it very much appeared like a farm distillery. The open space now accommodating the shop, tasting areas, café, and plush seating would not be out of place at a posh garden centre in the Cotswolds. The toilets, as has been my delight to note throughout this tour, are spotless and worthy of such a luxurious environment. I recall my first visit to Kilchoman when the toilets used unfiltered water for filling. A small sign above the latrine read, 'Our water is local and is naturally brown in colour' – or words to that effect. Anyone missing this, and I am guilty of this at least once, would flush the loo, believing the previous occupants had been too hasty in their retreat. Thousands of wasted flushes have now been saved by the water being clear.

Brown-ish water is a feature of the island, and reminds me of my first visit to Bowmore in the Summer of 1998. Along with a couple of friends, we were provided with a guided tour that included a glass of murky-looking water straight from the burn that fed into the Bowmore Distillery. Egged on to drink this dubious-looking bog water by our guide, we were stopped mid-sip by an employee running up shouting, "Don't drink the water! There's a dead sheep lying further up the burn! Did you not see the colour?" In response, all three of us spat out everything we had just sipped, only to be confronted with laughter from the guide and the distillery worker. "Ach, you're fine; there's no dead sheep; the water's always that colour." My fellow travellers and I joined in the laughter before surreptitiously pouring away the rest of the stream water from our glasses.

Leaving Kilchoman's plush visitor centre behind me, I head back down the five-mile single lane towards the main road. As Bruichladdich is just a mile out of my way, I quickly stop to see what they've got in the shop. Considering the title of this book, Pioneering Spirits, it would be completely remiss not to mention the influence and industry-wide changes brought about when Bruichladdich was revived in 2000.

Having been mothballed in 1994 (an industry term for ceasing production) by then owners Whyte & Mackay, the distillery was bought by a consortium of wine and spirits traders, including several locals interested in distilling and, perhaps just as importantly, marketing whisky differently. The new owners' impact on the single malt whisky world was nearly immediate. Whilst the joke was 'each time the ferry returns, Bruichladdich has released a new whisky', the ideas evolving around a single distillery being able to offer a myriad of flavours was ground-breaking and revelatory to the industry and consumers. Gone was the idea that a distillery made a particular style and had to stick to it. Instead, barley types were experimented with, cask types previously not seen (or at the very least not highlighted) and being on Islay, the new owners pushed forward and to the limit the smoky element.

What had been a whisky known only to those on Islay and a few of the wider whisky-drinking public very quickly became the most talked about Scotch whisky around the world. While Arran takes the credit for being the first independent and newly-built distillery to grab people's attention, Bruichladdich and the team behind it played a significant role in demonstrating the business model and potential success possible for a single distillery. I can give no better example of how the Bruichladdich team changed attitudes than the first Fèis Ìle Whisky Festival, in which they participated.

As is customary, each distillery on the island gets its 'day'. On Bruichladdich's day, realising that everyone would be busy dealing with hordes of (thirsty) visitors, the owners asked a group of notable attendees to perform the distillery tours. Rather than give a facts-and-figures tour, as one would expect, the new specially chosen tour guides were informed to 'use their imagination'. My tour guide on the day was the incomparable, and at times, at least to me, abrupt, Richard Joynson.[1] Richard, already renowned for his dislike of industry-speak, particularly marketing spiel, delivered what is still to this day the funniest and most ridiculous distillery tour I, and I'll wager those with me, ever encountered. Not a single fact he provided us with was correct or, at times, relevant. It was brilliant.

It made a statement: we don't take ourselves too seriously, and whilst we care deeply about our products and the quality of what we do, we do it with panache and good humour. Bruichladdich was the first distillery to emphasise its team publicly. At some point during their tenure, each member would get their face emblazoned across a label. They made Bruichladdich a club – filled with, and sought out, by those who 'got' what they were

---

1 - At that time, owner of Loch Fyne Whiskies.

about. Plenty of feathers were ruffled, malicious rumours about 'going broke' circulated and overheard whispers of 'this is not how it is done' reverberated around corridors of larger distilling establishments. The truth was that eyes within and without the industry were widened as to the potential of what a single distillery could do.

Despite protestations from some of the owners, Bruichladdich was eventually sold to Remy Cointreau in 2012 for £58 million - a rumoured ten-times return on initial investment. The legacy of the 'Bruichladdich' effect can be seen in all who have come after them. Arguably, Bruichladdich did more in 12 years to put Islay on the whisky map than the centuries of distilling that came before them. Once at the shop, I quickly peruse the shelves and buy a Renegade bottling and a 50cl bottle of Port Charlotte Valinch edition.[1] I'm not a big fan of 50cl bottles, but the Valinch series has a long tradition of being in smaller bottles, so don't grumble. The shop is busy, and tours are full. The distillery is still drawing in fans despite the change of ownership. It is really nice to see that Remy has not overly changed the philosophy or feel created by those who gave it a new life.

The single-track road that takes you to the Ardnahoe and Bunnahabhain distilleries is not the best road. It was one of the worst I have travelled on this tour, although still a far cry from the ruinous road to Talisker. Mini-humps have the tell-tale signs of metal against the road as cars either too low, too loaded or too fast have bottomed out. From experience, I suggest that you stick to only that which is clearly the road. In other words, treat any vegetation, grass area or verge with all the suspicion you can muster. On one trip, I decided to back up and out of the way for an oncoming vehicle. What looked like a grass border was, in fact, a two-foot drop, and one side of the car plunged in, leaving me, the two other passengers and several boxes of whisky and luggage pressed up against the passenger side of the vehicle. Only by removing everything and gunning the engine were we able to climb back out of the ditch, but the damage was done, and the car required expensive repairs.

This road follows the northern coast of Islay, with views over the Sound of Islay – the channel separating Islay from the Isle of Jura. The 'Paps of Jura', as they are commonly referred to, are not Munro's; the highest, Beinn an Oir, being only 2,576 ft high. The word 'Paps' is from the Nordic for breasts, which is slightly odd as there are three in total:[2] Beinn an Oir, Beinn Shiantaidh and Beinn a' Chaolais.[3] Although not Munros, they are highly visible from large parts of Islay, and the view is genuinely unspoilt from this road. Pulling into the car park of Ardnahoe, it is quite evident that the view was the key to the architectural design of the site.

At first appearance, Ardnahoe Distillery is devoid of any human activity. The café

---

1 - A Valinch is a pipe, often made from copper, with a hole at each end. It allows you to draw liquid out of a cask by placing one end in the cask and putting your thumb over the exposed hole on the other end. It is rudimentary but still widely used.

2 - And the movie "Total Recall" would not hit the cinemas until centuries later.

3 - Translated to Mountain of Gold, Sacred Mountain and Mountain of Sand.

and visitor centre are locked, all the lights are off, and there is little sign of any life save for a rubber hose poking out of a slightly open door.[1] I have no signal on my phone, so I can't call anyone and, therefore, have no choice but to step over the rubber hose and into the distillery. This fills me with dread for several reasons, but mainly because I am forever hearing stories about curious tourists believing they can wander into any part of a distillery and neighbouring buildings as if that was normal at a working factory (and on privately owned land). My jaw drops as soon as I enter the door. Two large, gleaming stills are working away in front of me, and beyond them is a large viewing window offering unspoilt views out over the Sound of Islay and the neighbouring Isle of Jura. If ever a distillery was built with a view in mind, this was it. Realising I am now appearing and acting like a nosy tourist (and as others in the car park have just watched me enter, thereby setting a very bad precedent), I venture deeper into the distillery until finally I find someone who kindly walks me to where Fraser Hughes, the Distillery Manager, has been busy.

"We're building additional warehousing," Fraser says, pointing out in the direction he has just walked. Fraser guides me back into the distillery and turns the lights on for the café. "Coffee?" he asks as he switches on the coffee machine. "You become a master of all the trades working at a distillery," Fraser says, grinning, as he uses the steam wand to heat the milk up. Having had this conversation with Gary Haggarty at Lindores Distillery, I suggest that working at a distillery makes you a 'Jack of all trades and a Master of One'. "Aye," Fraser agrees, grinning again, "I'm just not sure which 'one'?" Thirty seconds into meeting Fraser, I already knew I would like him, and over a very well-made cup of coffee, we chatted about his life, Islay, and whisky people.

Ardnahoe Distillery has incredible views over neighbouring Jura

1 - There was not even the slightest temptation to attempt a similar prank as that performed at Ardnamurchan.

Ardnahoe Distillery

www.ardnahoedistillery.com
Open to visitors

Ardnahoe Distillery was a dream come true for founder Stewart Laing. Born into a whisky family, as his father had established the whisky blending and bottling firm Douglas Laing & Co. in 1948, Stewart began his career in 1963 working at the vast Dumbarton Distillery complex. From there, he was sent to work at the Bruichladdich Distillery on Islay, and an affinity for the island was born.

After several decades of being part of Douglas Laing, Stewart decided to head off on his own and established Hunter Laing & Co. in 2013. This naturally led him towards thoughts of his own distillery, and this meant only one possible location: Islay. Around five different sites were considered. One had already been chosen before the Hunter Laing team; Stewart and his sons, Andrew & Scott, were convinced to look at the 4-acre site adjacent to Loch Ardnahoe. Once they had climbed the hill, taken in the majestic views, and visited the loch, they knew they had the right place.

Island life ensures most builds have their difficulties, and the site chosen for the new distillery proved the same. Hundreds of thousands of tons of rock had to be excavated to create an area so that work could begin on the foundations. Much of the hill where access to the distillery and the car park was to be situated had to be removed. This added to the already challenging issue of getting materials onto the site, and when combined with cold winds causing the concrete mixes to harden before being applied, the overall build took longer than was anticipated.

Helping the team was well-known distiller Jim McEwan. Having spent most of his working life at the Bowmore and Bruichladdich distilleries. Jim had been influential in locating Ardnahoe as the right site and also brought Fraser Hughes to the project. Fraser Hughes has an impressive CV in the whisky industry, having spent time at the Bowmore, Auchentoshan, Glen Garioch and Ardnamurchan distilleries. The chance to return to Islay and see a spirit from creation to release was an easy decision. Joining in 2018, about halfway through the build, Fraser was able to plan the spirit from the start.

"I'd known Jim for a long time since he was the person who gave me my very first start in the whisky industry as a warehouseman at Bowmore Distillery," Fraser tells me. "Jim was the Distillery Manager, taking over the position from my dad in 1985. We kept in touch after Jim left, and eventually, he asked me to become involved in the Ardnahoe project. "It took us about 18 months of distilling before we truly hit our best," admits Fraser.

"It takes time to get the plant working properly, learning as we go and changing where necessary." This involved some tweaks to the Low Wines receiver - something that would likely not occur to anyone without Fraser's experience.

Although not a terrible photo, it barely shows how majestic the view is from the Ardnahoe stills

Like Kilchoman before them, Ardnahoe has centuries of Islay tradition to contend with. No matter how the whisky tasted once bottled, there would be those wanting to compare it, rightly or wrongly, to all of the neighbouring Islay distilleries. "Since this is peated whisky land," Fraser says motioning to all that is around him, "we are producing a peated spirit. It's incredible how water from here enhances the whisky. We've got peated water mixed with peated malted barley, and the softness of the water gives an outstanding smooth balance to our fruit-forward and smoky whisky."

Hunter Laing took the early decision to release their first whisky only when they were completely happy with the maturation of stock. This meant the inaugural release was bottled and labelled as a five year old and in such quantities as to prevent most folk from missing out on tasting it. The response has been nothing short of extraordinary, with whisky drinkers worldwide commenting and reacting positively. What Stewart, his sons, and the Hunter Laing team have achieved with Ardnahoe is beyond admirable. Stewart Laing has secured his place in the annals of whisky folklore as one of the industry's most pioneering spirits.

"My father worked at Tomatin distillery, so I was born and bred in Inverness," Fraser tells me. "When I was 12, my dad moved to Islay to work as the manager at Bowmore Distillery. That was my first time on Islay." I asked whether that was the main draw to coming back. "No, the main draw was that my wife is from Islay. That made the decision to work for Hunter Laing a fairly easy one." Fraser states, once again, flashing that infectious grin. He goes on to tell me that his last job was with Ardnamurchan Distillery, and he has nothing but praise for what they do. As I am so often reminded, the Scotch whisky industry is a very small network of inter-connected people.

"We are looking forward to the first Fèis Ìle with a bottled product." Fraser continues as he shows me around the gleaming distillery. "After five years, it will be amazing to see people react to our first festival bottling." I can sense immense pride in what Fraser has achieved at Ardnahoe. He has a relaxed and considerate manner – attributes that are essential to Island life. Unable to buy a bottle due to the shop being closed[1] on a Monday, I head off back to Bowmore, where I am staying for the night.

I decide to head to a new (at least to me) pizza restaurant a few doors down from my guest house. Called 'Peatzeria'.[2] I order one with mushrooms and then head to The Lochside Hotel for a drink. A group of English gentlemen, not much older than me are sat opposite. I realise that many assumptions have been made in this book based on accents alone. This can get you into a lot of trouble, as I found out at a drinks party not long after moving to the village where I live. Having met someone named something like 'Barnabus Trumpington-Smitherton', I asked, assuming wrongly from the outrageously posh accent, which part of England they hailed from. "I'm from Scotland." He replied. My reply, "But where are you really from?" was received with annoyance by Barnabus. Or maybe his name was Tarquin. He was Scottish but from a class that had long removed the Scots dialect and any trace of an accent. A few of the more recognisably 'local' attendees stifled giggles.

I'm 99% certain the four gentlemen in the restaurant were English, not that it matters. They had all sat with a pint of beer each as they perused the menu. Perfectly normal, as was the round of whiskies that arrived moments later. Before either drink was close to being finished, one of the four fetched a second round of beers. The table was now covered in menus, four whisky glasses and eight pints of beer. Orders for food were then taken, and the removal of the menus alleviated some of the precious space on the crowded table. That was before a bottle of red, and a bottle of white wine were brought over, along with eight wine glasses. There were now 20 glasses on the table. The scene was beginning to look like a wine and spirits trade show – a good one, I'll grant you. This is not meant to sound judgemental; I am incapable of mixing my drinks in this way without suffering a horrible and prolonged gut issue. The abundance of glassware and array of booze reminded

---

1 - Thanks to Hunter Laing's release strategy, adequate supplies of the first release were available, meaning I could buy a bottle at the Whisky West Coast shop in Tarbert on my journey home.
2 - A considerably better whisky pun than any of mine. The pizza was very nice, thank you for asking.

me of how almost every writer and screen depiction of Winston Churchill would have us believe he led his life. I was quite tempted to offer to buy the four gentlemen an additional round of drinks - just to see if we could find out if the table could accommodate them.

After dinner at The Lochside Hotel I decide to take the short walk out to the beach next to Bowmore Distillery to take in the sunset. Again, even a terrible photographer like me cannot fail to get something of the majesty across. The view would have been savoured for a lot longer had there been a breeze strong enough to keep the blasted midges away. Alas, I am forced to return to the hotel and finish the night with a couple of local whiskies. Not the worst ending ever.

Bowmore Beach at sunset
(Midges not in focus)

The Whisky Festival

It is hard to imagine now, but there was a time before whisky festivals existed. And for those of you who are new to whisky, perhaps having picked this book up in a charity shop or been given it by someone who purchased it along with a bottle of whisky (and kept the whisky for themselves), there are hundreds of whisky festivals all over the world. The festivals can take several forms, from a single session one day, say three or more hours, to week-long festivities on Islay or in Speyside. For Americans, the Kentucky Bourbon Festival is one of the largest. For the Irish, there are festivals in Dublin and Cork. There are several in France, Netherlands, Germany, Sweden and so on.

"But you surely can't be just drinking whisky all of the time?"

That is a very sensible question. And frankly, I don't have a sensible answer. The truth is, yes, there is some product sampling. And by 'some', I mean a lot. Quite a lot. More than a lot. You're getting the picture. But the festival is much more than just the continual process of filling glasses and emptying them. Let's not confuse a whisky festival with a beer festival - there is very little singing at a whisky festival, a lot less dancing and the toilets do not become a no-go zone within the first half hour.

The best run festivals are those with few demands of participants other than to behave, be respectful and be responsible. Other than that it is an occasion to seek out whiskies you've never tried, maybe even never heard of. There will often be far too many whiskies to try. So don't try to. Take your time to see what's what, and remember, even if smoky whisky is your 'thing', give your tastes buds a chance before assaulting them with a cask strength Islay whisky or similar. Groove your way in with something lower in strength and perhaps lacking any peat. You can always jump in the deep end later...

The festival is also about meeting the makers and the people behind the brand. It is about old friends and forging new friendships. It is still predominantly a male environment, but this is rapidly changing, and all those who truly care about the product and who make it, market it and enjoy it will do so with anybody and everybody who wants to join in. I firmly believe, from all of the festivals I have attended, that whisky draws in a certain calibre of person. Not necessarily outgoing, not necessarily introverted, but often kind, considerate and open to new tastes, experiences and, most importantly, the desire to share the drinking experience. Clubs, festivals and tastings are the very best way to begin this journey of discovery.[1]

---

1 - The most complete list of whisky festivals can be found at www.whiskyglass.com/whisky-events-calendar

An off-centre picture of Bowmore Church to get the moon in

CHAPTER 15

THE FINAL LEG

"This is not the end. It is not even the beginning of the end.
But it is perhaps, the end of the beginning."
Winston Churchill

You all hate me now, don't you? Galivanting around Scotland in a comfortable car, having fun, meeting amazing people and going to cool places - I've certainly not been roughing it. Perhaps I should stress that no one paid me to do this – will that ease some of the envy that some readers may be feeling? No sponsors, no publishing advance and no contracts with any companies. I'm not looking for any sympathy here. Frankly, I've loved almost every second of this mini-adventure and would happily do it again – although next time, not on my own.

I had several agendas behind the idea of the book, but first and foremost, I wanted to meet the many owners and operators of these new-wave distilleries. I wanted to talk with them in situ, see their surroundings, and understand their vision. I realise that many whisky fans are not able to visit all of these distilleries, so I wanted to drip-feed enough of the journey and places to at least plant a seed. Never before have so many distilleries been so accessible. Nor has there been a greater choice of whiskies to choose from. In no way have I tried to sway you to favour one whisky over another; that would be against my nature, but I have perhaps tempted you to visit some of the distilleries in this book and seek out the whiskies of those you cannot.

My bias for this industry is plain for all to read throughout this tour. I don't try to hide it. Instead, I have attempted to do what whisky does best: bring a little joy to the consumer. I could have approached the trip with a complete day-to-day diary, but frankly, I am not that interesting. I could also have made this a travelogue with guides to hotels, bars, restaurants and modes of transport, but that would bore me and most likely be out of date the moment the book was available. What I have attempted is to mix a little Bill Bryson with a little Iain Banks and stir in a dollop of my life and career in Scotland.

Hopefully, you've enjoyed this little jaunt. And I hope I've inspired you to check flights, trains, buses, taxis, ferries, hotels and anything else you'll need to get out and tour. Perhaps I've inspired you to try a whisky you'd previously never heard of or attend a local whisky festival. Maybe you will also try and join a whisky club or start your own – they don't have to be big. My village club started with just six friends around a table. Good times.

What I will take away from this happy little hop from distillery to distillery is that this is still the greatest industry in the world, filled with the greatest people, making one of the greatest products. Many of the places I have visited hold a place in my heart; some I have lived in, whilst others were a first visit. Many of the locations I have sworn to return to and everyone I shared my time with will hopefully be at a whisky festival or event for me to say hi to.

One other overriding takeaway from this trip and the 20-plus years I have lived north of Hadrian's Wall is that the Scots are a friendly bunch. That is not to suggest that they hold a monopoly on kindness of spirit or a unique possession of an amiable nature - most of us, everywhere, are individually lovely. However, with so much of Scotland being a 'destination,' there is a prerequisite that visitors and immigrants are welcomed and made to feel at home. It is this attribute that has spread throughout the world and made Scotland a must-visit, or bucket-list, destination. Let's be honest; it cannot claim the most spectacular mountain ranges nor the largest lakes, waterfalls, forests or vistas. Scotland cannot compete with England (or Ireland) for stately homes, museums or galleries. Nor can it boast more visitor attractions and is not high up the list when it comes to areas of outstanding beauty. Yet, it welcomes almost as many visitors each year as there are inhabitants. People may come from all over the world for the beaches at Harris, the ruggedness of Skye, to island-hop or to delve into the history of the Picts and Celts, but more often than not, they return due to the embrace from the locals and inhabitants.

Scotch whisky is a seamless addition to this embrace. It is a drink made for sharing – so much so that Scottish weddings traditionally pass around a sharing cup, known as a Quaich, filled with whisky. The recognition of this sharing element has resulted in the highest honour for anyone within the trade to be made a 'Keeper of the Quaich'. The society could just as easily have been named the 'Scotch Whisky Club', but it was imperative that the broadcasting, ambassadorial and sharing role of the drink and its people was first and foremost.

One of my favourite movies, despite Kevin Costner being the star, is 'Field of Dreams'. Beyond the dreariness of Baseball as a game and the notion that there is something out there in the afterlife, it is the movie's simple message of 'Build it, and they will come' that captivates me. Considering what has possessed the founders of the distilleries in this book to irrevocably alter their lives, plough their own corn fields (to continue the analogy with the movie) and build something with no guarantees of success nor acceptance it is likely that it would bring a tear to Archie 'Moonlight' Graham's eye (I apologise if this reference is meaningless). How do you convince someone that a project costing millions to build, millions to fund and several years before any sign of a viable product is anything but insanity? How do you persevere when locations become difficult, costs spiral, economies struggle, habits change, and the world begins to elbow each other at borders?

Much like those great gardeners or planners of estates and parks who plant seedlings and foliage, this new wave of pioneering spirits will have to wait a considerable amount of time to truly see the fruits of their labour. To build a distillery is to imprint a new identity on a location. Raasay is no longer just a small island off of Skye. It is now the home of the Raasay Distillery. Harris will now be known not just for its tranquillity and beaches but also for its gin and whisky. Hawick can now boast of its manufacturing and textile heritage as much as it can now promote its new distillery. And so on the list goes. Each new addition, if done with passion, pride and a realisation that this is a long-term project (one as much for the location it is situated in as for the founders and owners), has added that additional raison d'etre to an area. Each distillery has been built so people will come. Whether they be new staff, side industries, casual tourists or dyed-in-the-wool whisky aficionados, they will come.

As I mentioned somewhere along this journey, I have tried, whenever possible, not to date this book. This is not a whisky book, per se. As Roy states in his Introduction, there are plenty of those. It is, instead, a cheerful romp around Scotland to meet those buccaneering, hurdle-leaping, barrier-breaking entrepreneurs. The book has been my excuse to mix with the Pioneering Spirits that make the whisky industry what it is: an engaging, thought-provoking, stereotype-challenging, all-welcoming space. The fact that the products they make are drunk and enjoyed worldwide is just an added bonus.

I now have a bank of memories to add to each and every dram I buy and try from these distilleries. I can now put a face, name, team and event on every purchase. These are not multi-national, share-holder-pleasing conglomerates. Each purchase is helping to keep someone local and someone important in a job. There is nothing faceless about these products, and it adds immensely to my enjoyment to know my purchases are helping provide a career in parts of this wonderful country that perhaps otherwise there might not be. And I hope that these careers are not just for this generation but for several to come. The industry is 400 years old, give or take. With the efforts of these Pioneering Spirits, let's hope the next 400 is one long journey of delicious drams and amazing memories.

Oh, and if it's your turn to buy or share a dram, well, I have an affinity for Glen Garioch single malt Scotch whisky – but that's a whole other story for another book.

Bottoms up!

Acknowledgements

Whilst whisky is Scotland's 2nd largest export, the industry that makes and promotes it is an incredibly close network of individuals. Without the help and support of so many, this book would never have been possible.

First and foremost, I must thank my wife, Dawn, for her encouragement and continued holding of the fort whilst I trekked all over Scotland, sending picture after picture of incredible locations. This has also put me well behind in my dog-walking duties...

Thanks to all of the distilleries and staff that accommodated me:

Joe Webster, Ben Callow @ Annandale Distillery. John Stirling, Gilbert Ionescu @ Arbikie Distillery. Fraser Hughes, Paul Main @ Ardnahoe Distillery. Alex Bruce, Connal Mackenzie, Graeme Mackay, Jenny Karlsson @ Ardnamurchan Distillery. Guy Macpherson-Grant, Kenny Mackay, Colin Poppy @ Ballindalloch Distillery. John Fordyce @ The Borders Distillery. Becky Marshall, Alistair McDonald, Andrew Morrison, Tim Morrison @ The Clydeside Distillery. Francis Cuthbert @ Daftmill Distillery. Phil Thompson, Simon Thompson @ Dornoch Distillery. Euan Kinninmonth @ Eden Mill Distillery. Sebastian Bunford-Jones, Alex Foulis, Libby Barmby, Michael Hayward @ Glasgow Distillery. Meeghan Murdoch, Craig MacRitchie @ GlenWyvis Distillery. Melanie Stanger, David Allen @ Glengyle Distillery. Blair Sterrick, Cat Mackay, Shona Macleod, Simon Erlanger @ Isle of Harris Distillery. Elliot Rogerson, Calum Rae @ Holyrood Distillery. Ian Palmer @ Inchdairnie Distillery. Anthony Wills, Catherine MacMilan @ Kilchoman Distillery. James Evans, Douglas Clement @ Kingsbarns Distillery. Graham Omand, Fred Baumgärtner @ Lagg Distillery. Matthew Hastie, Drew Mckenzie-Smith, Gary Haggart, John Dorrian @ Lindores Abbey Distillery. Sarah Snedden, Darren McCormick, John Campbell @ Lochlea Distillery. Annabel Thomas, Quinten Fyfe @ Nc'nean Distillery. Alasdair Day, William Dobbie @ Isle of Raasay Distillery. Bruce Perry, Stewart Dick, Ann O'lone @ Torabhaig Distillery. Wilma Falconer, Mark Westmorland @ Wolfburn Distillery.

Thanks also to Mike Billett and Thijs Klijverstijn for their help and Roy Duff for his introduction and input.